USB Mass Storage

Designing and Programming
Devices and Embedded Hosts

Jan Axelson

Lakeview Research LLC
Madison, WI

USB Mass Storage: Designing and Programming Devices and Embedded Hosts
by Jan Axelson

Published by Lakeview Research LLC, 5310 Chinook Ln., Madison WI 53704

janaxelson.com

Distributed by Independent Publishers Group (ipgbook.com).

14 13 12 11 10 9 8 7 6 5

Printed and bound in the United States of America

ISBN 978-1-931448-04-8 (paper)
ISBN 978-1-931448-23-9 (epub)
ISBN 978-1-931448-19-2 (Kindle)
ISBN 978-1-931448-05-5 (pdf)

Contents

Contents

4 Accessing Flash Memory Cards 79

5 MultiMediaCard Protocol 93

6 SCSI Commands 131

Contents

Contents

11 Embedded Hosts 259

Inside an Embedded Host 259

Host Options 266

Acknowledgements

Many people helped in the development and writing of this book.

My technical reviewers helped to keep me on track, pointed out errors, suggested additions to improve the book, and answered many questions. (With that said, any errors that remain are my fault alone.) Thanks to Paul E. Berg of MCCI and USB-IF Device Working Group Chair for encouragement and help in finding reviewers. Thanks also to John Hyde of *USB Design by Example,* to Pat LaVarre, to Hiromichi Oribe of Hagiwara Sys-Com Co., Ltd., to Rawin Rojvanit and Gurinder Singh of Microchip Technology, Inc., and to Alan Stern of the Rowland Institute at Harvard.

For their help in obtaining products used in the writing of the book, thanks to Laurent Guinnard of Ellisys, Gus Issa of GHI Electronics, and Alan Lowne of Saelig Co. Inc.

Introduction

A mass-storage device can provide access to data for just about any purpose. Every time you load an application or save a file on a PC, you're using a mass-storage device. A computer's hard drive is a mass-storage device, as are flash, CD, and DVD drives. Devices with dedicated functions—data loggers, robots, and other embedded systems—can use mass storage as well. Every mass-storage device contains a microcontroller, microprocessor, or other intelligent hardware that knows how to access the contents of the storage media.

A USB device controller enables a mass-storage device to share its data with other computers. For example, a data logger can collect data in the field and then connect to a PC, where an application reads the data from the logger's storage media. Or a robot can attach to a PC to receive a file containing configuration data to use in robotic tasks.

Flash-memory cards provide convenient storage for many small systems. Other systems function as USB hosts that can access files in off-the-shelf USB flash drives and hard drives.

If you're involved with designing or programming devices that incorporate a USB mass-storage device or host interface, this book will help you get your projects up and running. You'll also find the book useful if you're designing or programming devices that use flash-memory cards for data storage, whether or not the devices have USB interfaces.

Interfaces, Protocols, and Technologies

Designing and programming a USB mass-storage device or embedded USB host involves a variety of interfaces, protocols, and structures.

Every USB mass-storage device must support two interfaces:

- A USB device interface to enable the device to communicate with a PC or other USB host.
- An interface between the device's microcontroller or other CPU and the storage media. Flash-memory cards typically use the Serial Peripheral Interface (SPI), MultiMediaCard bus, SD-Card bus, or a bus derived from the ATA interface or PC-Card bus. Hard drives typically use the ATA parallel interface.

A USB mass-storage device must implement these protocols and structures:

- Generic USB protocol. Every USB device must respond to requests sent by the USB host and other events on the bus.
- USB mass-storage protocol. Every USB mass-storage device must detect and respond to requests that are specific to the USB mass-storage class.
- SCSI commands. USB hosts access mass-storage devices via commands originally developed for devices that use the Small Computer Systems Interface (SCSI).
- Media-specific protocol. The storage media's controller typically supports a command set for accessing the media's contents. Many flash-memory cards use the MultiMediaCard protocol or the SD Card protocol. Hard drives use the ATA protocol.

Reading and writing data to a mass-storage device also involves understanding logical structures in the media:

- Media structure. Program code accesses the storage area in drives as a series of logical blocks, or sectors. Dedicated areas in the media store information about the logical blocks and other logical structures in the media.

• File system. If the device firmware reads or writes to files on its own, rather than via a USB host, the device must implement a file system such as FAT16 or FAT32.

This book shows how to put all of these interfaces, protocols, and structures to work in a USB mass-storage device. The book assumes you have a basic familiarity with microcontroller programming and interfacing. For more about USB, I recommend my book, *USB Complete: Everything You Need to Develop Custom USB Peripherals*.

About the Code

This book include code examples written for the Microchip PIC18F4550 microcontroller using Microchip's MPLAB® C18 C compiler. On my website (janaxelson.com) you can find links to complete mass-storage firmware for this chip and example mass-storage firmware for other microcontrollers.

For More Information

In addition to example code, janaxelson.com has links to specification documents, white papers, corrections and additions to this book, and other information to help you design and program USB mass-storage devices.

I hope you find the book useful!

Jan Axelson
jan@janaxelson.com

Mass Storage Basics

A mass-storage device is electronic hardware that stores information and supports a protocol for sending and retrieving the information over a hardware interface. The information can be anything that can be stored electronically: executable programs, source code, documents, images, spreadsheet numbers, database entries, data logger output, configuration data, or other text or numeric data. Mass-storage devices typically store information in files. A file system defines how the files are organized in the storage media.

In Windows computers, mass-storage devices appear as drives in My Computer. From Windows Explorer, users can copy, move, and delete files in the devices. Program code can access files using file-system APIs or .NET's File class.

When to Use a Storage Device

Implementing a mass-storage function is a solution for systems that need to read or write moderate to large amounts of data.

If the device has a Universal Serial Bus (USB) interface, any PC or other USB host can access the storage media. Generic USB mass-storage devices include the hard drives, flash drives, CD drives, and DVD drives available from any computer-hardware store. Table 1-1 lists popular device types. These devices have just one function: to provide storage space for the systems they connect to.

Another type of USB mass-storage device (or storage device for short) is the special-purpose device with storage capabilities. For example, a camera can capture images and store the images in files. A data logger can collect and store sensor readings in files. A robotic device can receive files containing configuration parameters. With the addition of a USB mass-storage interface, any of these devices can use USB to exchange files with PCs and other USB hosts.

Generic storage devices are readily available and inexpensive. Unless you're employed by a storage-device manufacturer, there isn't much point in designing and programming your own generic devices. But special-purpose USB storage devices are useful in many embedded systems, including one-of-a-kind projects and products manufactured in small quantities.

Another option for some systems is to add USB host-controller hardware and mass-storage firmware. The embedded system can then store and read files in off-the-shelf USB storage devices.

Benefits

Adding storage-device capabilities to a system has several benefits:

- With a USB device controller, a system can make the contents of its storage media available to any PC or other USB host computer.

- File systems provide a standard way to store and access data. A PC or other USB host can format the media in a USB storage device to use the FAT16 or FAT32 file system. When the device is connected to a PC, the operating system enables reading and writing to files. Users can access the files without having to install and learn a vendor-specific application.

- Storage media is readily available. Flash-memory cards are convenient and have enough capacity for many applications. Some cards require only a few port pins to access. Devices that need large amounts of storage can interface to hard drives.

Table 1-1: Common USB mass storage devices use a variety of storage media.

Device	Storage Media	Local CPU Interface to Media	Removable Media?
Hard drive	Hard disk	ATA	No
CD drive	CD	ATA + ATAPI	Yes
DVD drive	DVD	ATA + ATAPI	Yes
Flash drive	Flash memory	Local CPU data bus	No
Flash-memory-card reader/writer	Flash memory	SPI, MultiMediaCard bus, SD-Card bus	Yes

Other Considerations

A storage device isn't the solution for every application, however.

- Mass-storage firmware is complex. A USB mass-storage device must support the USB protocols required for all USB devices as well as class-specific mass-storage protocols. If the device firmware needs to create, read, or write to files and directories on its own (not via the USB interface), the firmware must also support a file system. For some applications, a different USB class or a vendor-specific protocol would require less time and expense to implement.

- USB mass-storage devices transfer data using bulk transfers. These provide the fastest transfers on an otherwise idle bus but have no guaranteed timing or bus bandwidth. If your device needs precise timing in transferring data, the mass-storage class isn't appropriate.

- A storage device should have one mass-storage master at a time. The master, or mass-storage host, is the computer that reads and writes to the storage media. Special-purpose mass-storage devices can function as masters on their own and can also permit a PC or other USB host to function as the master. If one master adds, deletes, or changes a file and the other master isn't aware of the changes, confusion or worse problems can result. Devices that support two masters can have a manual or electronic switch to enable one master at a time, or a device can use firmware protocols to inform the host when the media's contents have changed. For some designs, another approach without this added complexity makes more sense.

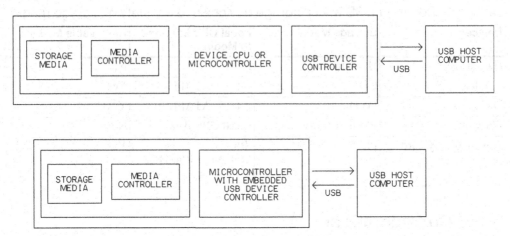

Figure 1-1: A USB mass-storage device contains storage media, a media controller, a device CPU or microcontroller, and a USB device controller, which can be on a separate chip or embedded in a microcontroller.

Alternate approaches for USB devices that transfer generic or vendor-specific data include the human-interface device class, a device accessed via a virtual COM port, or a generic or vendor-specific driver.

Requirements

Adding storage capabilities and a USB interface to an embedded system requires hardware and firmware to support accessing the storage media and communicating over the USB interface.

Devices

An embedded system that functions as a USB mass-storage device requires the following hardware (Figure 1-1):

- A microcontroller or other CPU or intelligent hardware to manage the embedded system's operation.
- A USB device controller, which can be embedded in a microcontroller chip or on a separate chip that interfaces to a CPU or microcontroller.
- A generic hard drive, flash drive, or other media that interfaces to the device's CPU.

In a USB mass-storage device, the hardware or firmware must perform the following functions:

- Detect and respond to generic USB requests and other events on the bus.
- Detect and respond to USB mass-storage requests for information or actions from the device.
- Detect and respond to SCSI commands received in USB transfers. These industry-standard commands read and write blocks of data in the storage media, request status information, and control device operation.

In addition, devices that create, read, or write to files and directories on their own (not via a USB host) must implement a file system. A file is a named collection of data. A directory structure provides an index to the files. Popular file systems for embedded systems include FAT16 and FAT32.

Two popular types of storage media for embedded systems are flash-memory cards and hard drives. A flash-memory card contains flash-memory chips to provide storage, a controller that manages reading and writing to the memory, and an interface to the outside world. Common types of flash-memory cards includes the MultimediaCard (MMC), Secure Digital (SD) Card, and CompactFlash® (CF®) card. A hard drive contains a hard disk that provides storage, drive components to perform functions such as spinning the disk and positioning the heads, a drive controller, and an interface to the outside world. An embedded system that accesses flash-memory cards or hard drives must have a microcontroller or other CPU or intelligent hardware to manage communications with the cards or drives.

This book focuses on block storage devices, where data is transferred in blocks of defined sizes. USB hard drives and flash drives are block storage devices. Other devices are stream devices, where each data transfer is a sequence, or stream, of data that can be any length. An example of a stream device is a modem that carries voice communications.

Embedded Hosts

An embedded system that functions as a USB host for flash or hard drives requires the following hardware (Figure 1-2):

- A microcontroller or other CPU or intelligent hardware to manage the embedded system's operation.

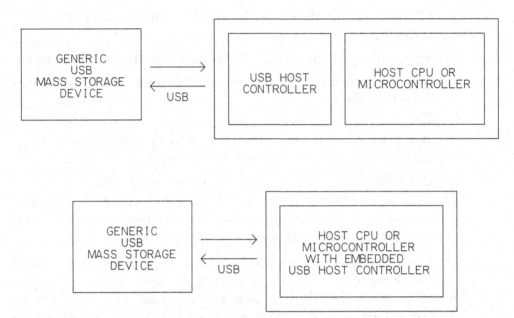

Figure 1-2: To access generic USB mass-storage devices, an embedded system must contain a USB host controller, which can be on a separate chip or embedded in a microcontroller.

- A USB host controller, which can be embedded in a microcontroller chip or on a separate chip that interfaces to the CPU, microcontroller, or other intelligent hardware.
- A generic hard drive, flash drive, or other media connected to a USB port on the host.

The hardware or firmware in an embedded USB mass-storage host must provide the following functions:

- Issue USB requests and initiate other events on the bus to identify attached devices and manage traffic and power on the bus.
- Issue USB mass-storage requests that ask for status information or specify actions for the device to perform.
- Issue SCSI commands in USB transfers. The commands read and write blocks of data in the storage media, request status information, and control the device operation.
- Support a file system to access files in the media.

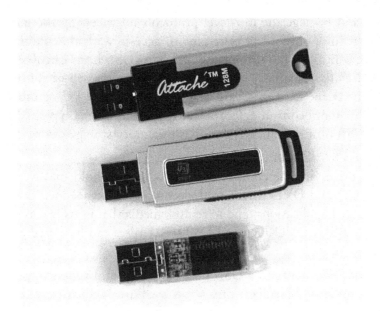

Figure 1-3: USB flash drives provide convenient storage that PCs and other USB hosts can access.

Selecting a Media Type

The storage media is the physical entity that holds a device's data. In embedded systems, a storage device's media is typically separate from the system's program memory, which stores the code executed by the system's CPU. Over time, various storage technologies and form factors have come and gone in popularity. Currently popular technologies include hard drives, CD/DVD drives, flash-memory cards, and USB flash drives (Figure 1-3). Other names for a USB flash drive (UFD) include USB key, pen drive, ThumbDrive®, DiskOnKey®, and JumpDrive®.

The different media types vary in the hardware and circuits required to access the media, the ability to erase and rewrite, methods of write protection, whether the media is removable from its drive, and interface options for external CPUs.

For many devices, flash memory is a good choice for storage media. Flash-memory cards are physically small, can store moderate amounts of data, and manage the low-level protocols for accessing the memory. Some cards require only a few port pins to access. With the addition of a USB device controller and supporting firmware, USB hosts can access the data in a device's flash-memory card. Users can also remove a card from the device and insert the card in a card reader attached to a PC or other computer. Flash memory consumes less power than other media types. When attached to a USB host or hub, a typical flash-memory storage device can receive all of its power from the bus.

Hard drives are the cheapest per byte and can hold massive quantities of data. CD and DVD drives are less common in embedded systems because embedded applications tend to require media that is easily erased and rewritten. CD-RW, DVD-RW, and DVD+RW discs can be erased and rewritten, but not as easily as magnetic media.

A device that contains a USB host controller and supporting firmware can access ordinary USB flash drives and hard drives. Because a USB host must manage the bus, USB host programming is more complex than USB device programming. But for some applications, the ability to store data in generic drives makes the increased complexity worthwhile.

Drive Mechanisms

Hard disks require a drive mechanism to spin the disks and position the read and write heads (Figure 1-4). A hard drive contains a stack of platters. Each platter has magnetic storage media arranged in concentric circles, called tracks, on both sides. Each surface of a platter has a head positioned above the platter's surface. The head can read or write to the bit of data directly opposite the head.

An area on a drive can be identified by cylinder, head, and sector. A cylinder is a stack of tracks of the same diameter. Each surface has a head, so the head identifies a surface on a platter. A sector is a portion of a track and contains the smallest addressable quantity of data in the media. All sectors in a drive have the same capacity, typically 512 bytes.

The drive mechanism spins the disks and moves the heads to requested tracks. When a requested sector on a spinning disk passes under the head,

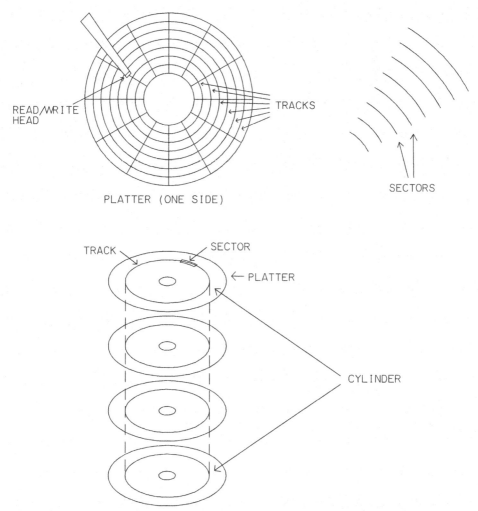

Figure 1-4: A hard drive contains multiple platters. Each side on a platter has circular tracks containing magnetic media and a read/write head. A cylinder consists of all of the tracks with the same diameter on all of the platters.

the head performs the read or write operation on the media. The head reads and writes a minimum of a sector's data in each read or write operation.

Flash memory resides in chips. Accessing flash memory requires no moving parts. USB storage devices with flash memory don't have mechanical drives, but the term *flash drive* for these devices has stuck.

Addressing Methods

All USB drives and other drives of recent vintage support logical block addressing (LBA). With LBA, blocks of storage capability are numbered sequentially beginning at zero. All blocks have the same size, again typically 512 bytes. The logical block address is often referred to as a sector address because the block size equals the capacity of a sector in a hard drive. To access the media, software specifies the logical block address to read or write to. For hard drives, the drive's controller translates each LBA to a cylinder, head, and sector on the drive. For flash drives, the drive's controller translates each LBA to a block, page, and column in the memory array. The sequence of logical block addresses doesn't have to correspond to the physical locations of the sectors in a drive or the memory in a chip. All that matters is that the media's controller knows what area of storage corresponds to each address.

In older systems, software accessed storage media using CHS addressing, where the software specifies a cylinder, head, and sector number to read or write to. A storage device can support both CHS addressing and LBA.

Compared to CHS addressing, LBA is simpler, more flexible, and supports larger capacities. File-system drivers in embedded systems are unlikely to need to use CHS addressing.

Reading and Writing Considerations

Storage media varies in the available methods of write-protecting the contents, support for erasing, and copy-protection technologies.

Write Protection

The storage media, drive mechanism, circuits, or a manual switch can permit or forbid writing to the media. For example, a flash-memory controller can forbid writing to all or a portion of the memory. Or a manual switch on a flash-memory card can inform the host that the media shouldn't be erased or overwritten. Higher-level software in the mass-storage master can also control access to data on a storage device.

Erasing

The media in a hard drive can be erased and rewritten virtually endlessly, while flash memory can survive 10,000 or more erase cycles, depending on the technology. Some memory cards contain programmed ROM chips, which can't be erased and rewritten.

The flash memory used in storage devices must be read and written in pages and erased in blocks. The page size for read and programming (write) operations is typically either 528 bytes (small block) or 2112 bytes (large block). A 528-byte page can hold one 512-byte sector and 16 additional bytes for error-correcting codes (ECC), address-mapping information for use in wear leveling, and other information. A 2112-byte page holds four 512-byte sectors with 16 additional bytes per sector. Newer memory chips tend to use large blocks.

The block size for erase operations is much larger than the page size for reading and writing. In the past, blocks of 16 KB and 32 KB were common, while current flash memory has erase blocks of 128 KB or 256 KB. Before writing to previously programmed memory, the area to be written must be erased. So to write even a single byte to a previously programmed area, the memory controller must erase an entire erase block and then program a page's contents back into the memory.

The controllers in flash-memory cards manage the erase operations and enable device firmware to work with 512-byte blocks. To write a byte to a flash-memory card, device firmware typically reads 512 bytes into a buffer, changes the byte to be written, and writes the buffer back to the memory card. The card's controller handles the erase and write operations.

The controllers in flash-memory cards use wear-leveling techniques that help extend the useful life of the memory array by spreading erase/write cycles evenly among all of the memory cells. A file-system driver that accesses raw flash-memory chips can implement wear leveling as well.

Security

Some media types have built-in copy-protection capabilities. For example, an SD Card can be configured to require authentication before allowing access to the card's contents, and a card can restrict the number of allowed copies.

Removable Media and Devices

A device can have removable media, and an entire device can be removable from the computer that communicates with the device.

Removable Media

In a drive with removable media, users can easily insert and remove media in the drive. CD and DVD drives have removable media because you can easily swap discs. A memory-card reader with a card slot has removable media. Hard drives and flash drives have non-removable media because you can't easily remove the hard disk from its drive or the flash memory from its circuit board. A device reports whether it has removable media in the response to a SCSI INQUIRY command. Some flash drives with non-removable media report that they have removable media. Chapter 6 has more about the INQUIRY command.

Removable Devices

An entire storage device can also be removable or non-removable from the computer that accesses the drive. USB drives are removable. An internal drive is considered non-removable because removing the drive requires more work than detaching a cable.

Managing Removal

A user can detach a USB device or remove a flash-memory card at any time. If a device or card is removed while the host is writing to the media, the device and host should detect the removal and handle it as gracefully as possible.

Hardware Interfaces

A storage device can support one or more interfaces to its storage media. In most cases, the device's CPU doesn't access the media directly. Instead, the CPU communicates with an intelligent controller embedded in a drive or flash-memory card. In devices that support USB, the CPU also interfaces to a USB device controller.

Hard Drives

When you need a lot of storage, a hard drive is the most economical choice. At this writing, a megabyte of hard-drive storage is 50 to 100 times cheaper than a megabyte in a flash-memory card. Prices for both media continue to fall, and the price differential may change over time, but for the near future, hard drives are likely to continue to be the favored solution for storing very large amounts of data.

Technology

Because they use mechanical drive components, hard drives tend to be more fragile than completely electronic media such as flash memory. Modern drives are much more rugged than in the past, however. For embedded systems that need to fit in a small space, tiny hard drives are available in the USB key-drive form factor and in Type II CompactFlash cards.

Interfaces

The most common interface between a hard drive and its CPU is the Parallel AT Attachment (ATA) interface, also known as the Integrated Drive Electronics (IDE) interface. A drive that uses ATA must have an intelligent controller embedded in the unit. The ATA specification defines the cables and connectors, signals, and registers and commands for communicating with the drive's controller. ATA devices must support logical block addressing. A single ATA interface on a host computer can connect to up to two storage devices. The host computer communicates by reading and writing to registers in the device.

ATA with Packet Interface (ATAPI) is an extension to ATA that defines a protocol for sending SCSI and other commands to an ATA device in structures called command packets. CD and DVD drives use the ATAPI protocol. More information about ATA/ATAPI and links to the standard documents are at www.ncits.org.

Flash Memory

Flash memory is non-volatile, electrically erasable storage available as chips and in cards that incorporate memory chips and a controller.

Technology

Both flash memory and EEPROM provide non-volatile, electrically erasable storage. Compared to EEPROM, flash-memory cells are physically smaller, can withstand more erase/write cycles, and are cheaper to manufacture. The main disadvantage of flash memory is that unlike EEPROM, flash memory is erasable only in blocks, not by individual byte. Even so, for most storage devices, flash memory is the more practical choice, while EEPROM is useful for storing infrequently changed configuration settings.

Two flash-memory technologies in popular use are NOR and NAND.

NOR flash is suited for storing program code, where the CPU wants fast read access but rarely writes to the memory. NOR flash has fast read times but slow erase and write times. NOR flash has low density, so large amounts of storage may require multiple chips. To access NOR flash, a CPU uses the same data and address lines used to access other parallel memory chips.

Storage devices use NAND flash, which has fast erase and write times. NAND flash also has lower power consumption and is much cheaper than NOR flash. A CPU accesses NAND flash chips via data lines and command and address registers. NAND flash has high density, so large amounts of memory can fit in a small package. The advantages of NAND flash are so attractive that some devices use NAND flash for program memory along with a RAM cache to improve performance.

Three varieties of NAND flash are Old Single-level Cell (SLC), New SLC, and Multi-level Cell (MLC). MLC memory stores multiple bits in each cell and is popular because it's cheaper to manufacture. However, compared to SLC memory, MLC memory supports fewer erase cycles, has slower write times, and consumes more power. These are the typical number of erase cycles supported by each memory type: Old SLC: 1,000,000, New SLC: 100,000, MLC: 10,000.

Wear Leveling

Wear-leveling techniques can extend the useful life of flash memory by writing to different physical locations in each erase/write cycle. A typical write operation accesses only a portion of the memory in a flash-memory card. Writing to different locations with each write operation helps to spread the erase/write operations evenly to all areas of the memory and extends the life of the memory as a whole. A card that uses chips rated for 10,000 erase cycles can thus withstand a much greater number of erase operations if each operation erases a portion of the memory. Wear leveling is especially important if the chip stores files or structures such as file allocation tables (FATs) that are rewritten frequently.

To accomplish wear leveling, firmware can map each logical address to a physical address that changes with each write operation. Higher-level firmware writes to the logical addresses, and the wear-leveling firmware translates the addresses to physical locations in the memory. For example, write operations can be mapped to the physical addresses in sequence, starting over at the beginning after reaching the end.

Error Correcting

Error correcting code (ECC) bytes enable a controller to verify data in read operations. The controller generates and stores an ECC when writing to a block and can use the code to verify the data after reading the block.

Manufacturers of flash-memory cards may implement additional protocols to help ensure data reliability. For example, under margin conditions, the controller in a Sandisk MultiMediaCard reads data back after writing to verify the write operation. If a bit is bad, the controller replaces the bit with a spare bit. The controller can also replace an entire bad block with another block. Higher-level protocols can also support error correcting via checksums sent with data.

Options for Flash Memory

Using flash-memory cards rather than raw flash chips has two advantages. The controller in the card greatly simplifies accessing the memory. And cards are easily removable and replaceable, so you can store data in multiple cards and replace cards that fail or wear out.

Things to consider when selecting a type of flash-memory card include physical size, capacities, interfacing options, data-transfer speed, power-supply voltage, and cost. Cost includes the price for the memory cards and connectors as well as any charges for specification documents, licensing, and royalties. If protecting the media's contents from writing or copying is important, some cards have this capability built in.

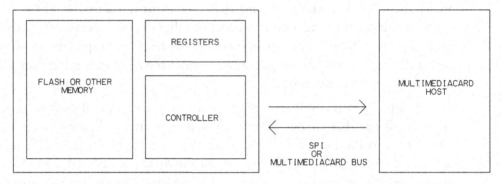

Figure 1-5: Each MultiMediaCard contains memory, registers, and an intelligent controller.

For many embedded systems, a MultiMediaCard host is a good choice because the cards are small, many microcontrollers can interface to them, and MultiMediaCard hosts have no licensing fees. A MultiMediaCard host can also communicate with SD Cards if the connector accepts the slightly thicker SD cards. Other options are an SD-Card host or CompactFlash host.

MultiMediaCard

A MultiMediaCard contains these elements (Figure 1-5):

- Memory for data storage. The memory is typically flash memory but ROM-based MultiMediaCards are also available.
- Five registers that can store configuration and status information such as valid power-supply voltages and whether the card has completed its power-up procedure.
- An interface that supports communicating via the MultiMediaCard bus and SPI.
- A controller that executes MultiMediaCard commands.

There are three classes of MultiMediaCards. The Read/Write (RW) class encompasses cards that can read and write to storage media, typically flash memory. Read-only Memory (ROM) cards support reading but not writing to the storage media. I/O cards perform additional functions beyond data storage.

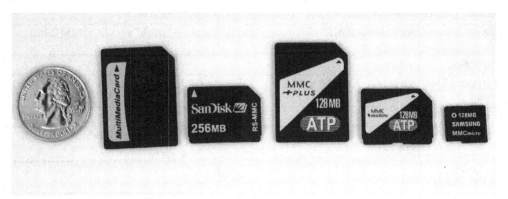

Figure 1-6: From left to right: MultiMediaCard, RS-MultiMediaCard, MMCplus, MMCmobile, and MMCmicro.

The MultiMediaCard specifications are a product of the MultiMediaCard Association (MMCA) (www.mmca.org). The MMCA board consists of over a dozen semiconductor and technology companies. The organization is dedicated to open, royalty-free standards.

The MultiMediaCard specifications are the ultimate authority on the physical interface and command set. Data sheets for specific MultiMediaCards are another helpful source of information about the interface, protocols, and card-specific information.

Packages

Table 1-2 compares the five MultiMediaCard variants. The cards are available in three form factors and with interfaces of 7, 10, and 13 pins (Figure 1-6). The original MultiMediaCard has a 7-pin interface and is about 1.25 x 1 inch in size. The RS-MultiMediaCard is functionally identical and about half the size. The MMCplus™ and MMCmobile™ add 13-pin interfaces in both form factors. The MMCmicro™ has 10 pins and is about half an inch square.

Interfacing

A MultiMediaCard can use either of two synchronous serial interfaces: the MultiMediaCard bus or SPI. Just about any microcontroller can implement either bus. The MMCplus, MMCmobile, and MMCmicro can also use a

Table 1-2: MultiMediaCards are available in several formats.

Card	MultiMediaCard	RS-MultiMediaCard	MMCplus	MMCmobile	MMCmicro
Sponsor	mmca.org				
Physical Size (mm)	32 x 24 x 1.4	18 x 24 x 1.4	32 x 24 x 1.4	18 x 24x 1.4	14 x 12 x 1.1
Pins	7		13		10
Interface	MultiMediaCard bus (serial), SPI		MultiMediaCard bus (serial or parallel), SPI		
Data Bus Width (bits)	1		1, 4, 8		1, 4
Maximum Data Transfer Rate (Mbits/sec.)	20		416		208
Maximum Clock Speed (Mbits/sec.)	20		52		52
Power Supply (V)	3/3.3/1.8				
Security	SecureMMC interface supports digital rights management				
Specification Cost	$500 or MMCA member @$2500/year		$1000 or MMCA member @$2500/year (includes all MultiMediaCard variants)		
Licensing Fees and Royalties	none				

4-bit parallel MultiMediaCard bus. The MMCplus and MMCmobile can use an 8-bit parallel MultiMediaCard bus.

An SPI host must have a clock output (SCLK), a data output (DataIn on the card), and a data input (DataOut on the card). The host must also control a unique chip-select output (CS) for each device the host communicates with.

A MultiMediaCard-bus host must have a clock output (CLK), a bidirectional pin for commands (CMD), and a bidirectional pin for data (DAT). The master uses commands to assign addresses and select cards, so the MultiMediaCard bus doesn't need a chip-select line for each card.

On power-up, a MultiMediaCard must be clocked at 400 kHz or less. When the initialization procedure is complete, the host can increase the clock frequency.

These are advantages to using SPI:

- Many microcontrollers include hardware support for SPI. The hardware support simplifies programming.
- All SPI signals are unidirectional so the host doesn't need to have bidirectional port pins.
- A variety of chips and modules in addition to MultiMediaCards have SPI interfaces. The options include EEPROMs, analog-to-digital converters, and other I/O functions. A microcontroller can thus use one bus to access multiple components.
- For interfaces that don't require error checking, an SPI host can instruct a card to ignore error checking. Error checking is mandatory with the MultiMediaCard bus.

These are advantages to using the MultiMediaCard bus:

- The host doesn't require a chip-select line for each card. Instead, addresses are assigned via firmware.
- The host can broadcast commands to multiple cards.
- The host can perform stream reads and writes, where the data isn't in defined blocks and the card or host transmits continuously until the host issues a STOP_TRANSMISSION command. SPI hosts can perform block reads and writes only.
- MMCplus, MMCmobile, and MMCmicro cards can use a parallel data bus for faster transfers.

A host selects the MultiMediaCard bus or SPI by controlling the CS pin on the card when sending the GO_IDLE_STATE command to the card. To use SPI, the host brings CS low while sending the command. To use the MultiMediaCard bus, CS remains high. All communications that follow use the selected bus.

The MultiMediaCard specification doesn't mandate power-consumption limits. A typical MultiMediaCard consumes 50 mA during read operations and 60 mA during write operations. Cards can support a low-power sleep mode when the card isn't being accessed.

Protocols

The MultiMediaCard specification defines a set of MultiMediaCard commands. The host uses the commands to retrieve information about a card and its status, to send control information to a card, and to read and write data in the storage media. An SPI host can use most of the MultiMediaCard commands. Chapter 4 and Chapter 5 have more about MultiMediaCard programming.

Fees

MultiMediaCard hosts have no licensing fees, but the MMCA charges to download the specifications. At this writing, the cost is $500 for version 3.1 of the specification and $1000 for version 4.1, which adds the MMCmobile and MMCplus variants. Those who join the MMCA at $2500/year get the specifications for no additional charge plus other benefits.

SD Memory Card

Secure Digital (SD) Memory Cards, or SD Cards for short, are similar in capability, size, and pinout to MultiMediaCards. An SD-Card host can communicate with both MultiMediaCards and SD Cards.

Compared to MultiMediaCards, SD Cards have these differences:

- In the original form factors, SD Cards are thicker than MultiMediaCards (2.1 mm versus 1.4 mm). Card connectors that accommodate both types are available. With adapters, you can use any form factor of either card type in a full-size SD-card connector.
- Some SD Cards have a manual write-protect switch.
- SD cards have additional registers with configuration and status information.
- SD Cards support additional commands, including a command that enables the host to specify a power-supply voltage.
- Unlike MultiMediaCards, SD Cards don't need to be clocked at 400 kHz or less until the card is initialized (but doing so causes no harm).

The SD-Card technology was developed by Matsushita Electric Industrial Co., Ltd., SanDisk Corporation, and Toshiba Corporation.

Packages

Table 1-4 compares the SD-Card variants. SD Cards are available in three form factors: original SD Card, miniSD™ Card, and microSD™ Card (Fig-

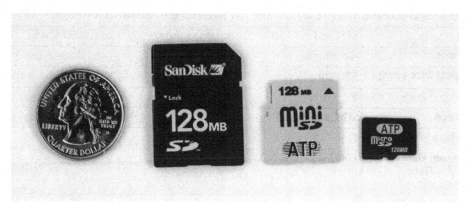

Figure 1-7: SD Cards are available in three form factors. From left to right: original SD Card, miniSD Card, and microSD Card.

ure 1-7). The form factors are similar to the options available for MultiMediaCards. A card that performs I/O functions such as modem, GPS device, or network interface is called an SDIO Card.

The optional write-protect switch is a sliding tab on the side of the card. If the tab is in the lock position, the host must write-protect the contents. The switch by itself doesn't offer protection. The firmware accessing the card is responsible for reading the state of the switch and protecting the contents when appropriate. SD-Card connectors include a pin that enables reading the switch state. The miniSD and microSD Cards don't have write-protect switches but can be inserted in an SD-Card adapter that contains a switch.

Interfacing

An SD Card can use SPI or the SD-Card bus. The SD-Card bus can use a bus width of one or four bits. The SD-Card bus can have shorter timeout values and doesn't require a clock frequency of 400 kHz or less on power up. A typical SD Card uses 65 mA to read and 75 mA to write and has a low-power sleep mode when the card isn't being accessed.

Protocols

SD Cards use the same commands and protocols defined by the MultiMediaCard specification. SD Cards also support a series of commands that are specific to SD Cards. These commands support security functions and

Table 1-3: Secure Digital (SD) Cards are available in several formats.

Card	SD Card	miniSD Card	microSD Card
Sponsor	sdcard.org		
Physical Size (mm)	32 x 24 x 2.1	20 x 21.5 x 1.4	11 x 15 x 1
Pins	9	11	8
Interface	SD Card bus, SPI		
Data Bus Width (bits)	1, 4		
Maximum Data Transfer Rate (Mb/sec.)	100 (SD Card bus); 25 (SPI)		
Maximum Clock Speed (Mbits/sec.)	25		
Power Supply (V)	2.7-3.6 or 1.6-3.6(LV)		
Security	support for digital rights management		
Write Protect Switch	optional	no	no
Specification Cost	Membership @ $1000/year		
Licensing Fees and Royalties	Host/ancillary product license for $1000/year, available to members only		

enable reading additional status information and controlling a pull-up on the Card Detect pin.

Fees

Implementing an SD-Card host isn't practical for developers of inexpensive products that sell in modest quantities. Every device that contains an SD-Card host must be licensed. At this writing, it costs $1000/year to join the SD Card Association and another $1000/year for a member to license a host. Membership includes access to the SD Card specifications.

If you don't need the additional capabilities of SD Cards, a MultiMediaCard host is a less expensive option. If you use a connector wide enough to accept SD Cards, the host can communicate with both MultiMediaCards and SD Cards operated as MultiMediaCard-compatible devices.

CompactFlash

Another option for flash memory is the CompactFlash card (Figure 1-8). Like MultiMediaCards and SD Cards, CompactFlash cards contain memory, registers, and an intelligent controller. CompactFlash was introduced by SanDisk Corporation. These cards are a solution if you need to store a lot of data in a small package or need very fast transfers.

Packages

Table 1-4 compares the two CompactFlash variants. Both are 1.7 in. wide and 1.4 in. or greater in length. A Type II CompactFlash card is thick enough (about 0.2 in.) to hold a tiny hard drive. A CF+™ card is any card that has the CompactFlash form factor and contains storage media other than flash memory or performs I/O functions other than storage.

Interfacing

CompactFlash cards can use an 8- or 16-bit parallel data bus. Storage devices can use either of two modes. PCMCIA mode is based on the PC Card (PCMCIA) interface and uses an 11-bit address bus. True IDE Mode is based on the ATA-4 specification, is compatible with the IDE disk drive interface, and uses a 3-bit address bus to select registers.

A CompactFlash card can draw up to 75 mA at 3.3V or 100 mA at 5V. A CF+ card can use either of two power levels. The limits for Power Level 0 are the same as for CompactFlash, while Power Level 1 allows drawing up to 500mA at 3.3V or 5V. All currents specified are average RMS currents.

Figure 1-8: A CompactFlash card is another option for flash-memory storage.

Table 1-4: CompactFlash cards are available in several formats.

Card	CompactFlash	CompactFlash II
Sponsor	compactflash.org	
Physical Size (mm)	36.4 or greater x 42.8 x 3.3	36.4 or greater x 42.8 x 5
Pins	50	
Interface	PC Card/True IDE Mode	
Data Bus Width (bits)	8 or 16	
Maximum Data Transfer Rate (Mbits/sec.)	528	
Power Supply (V)	3.3/5	
Security	Security Mode password protection, recommended for use only in non-removable devices	
Specification Cost	none	
Licensing Fees and Royalties	Membership @$2500/year enables using the logo and trademarks	

Protocols

CompactFlash and CF+ cards with storage media are accessed much like other ATA hard drives. A series of registers store status and control information and data being transferred. The CompactFlash specification defines a CF-ATA command set for communicating with cards.

Fees

The CF+ and CompactFlash specification is available at no charge. Use of the CompactFlash logo and trademarks on products requires membership in the CompactFlash association at $2500 per year.

2

Supporting USB

Many mass-storage devices store files that PCs or other computers must access. To make files available to any PC or other USB host, a device can use either of these approaches:

- Include a USB device controller and support for USB's mass-storage class. The files can be stored in any media. To access the files from a USB host, attach the device to a USB port on the host.
- Include a USB host controller and a mass-storage driver. The device can then store files on the same USB drives that PCs and other USB hosts can access. To access the files from another USB host, remove the drive from the device and attach the drive to the other host.

An additional option that doesn't require USB support on the device is to store files in flash-memory cards. To access a card's contents from a PC, insert the card in a card reader/writer device either built into the PC or attached via USB. (You can also use flash-memory cards as the storage media in a device that has a USB interface.)

A USB device interface is a popular choice for mass-storage devices because it's inexpensive to implement and convenient to use. Every recent PC has

USB 2.0 ports that support the bus speeds used by mass-storage devices: 12 megabits/sec and 480 megabits/sec. Windows and other operating systems support USB's mass-storage class. A USB host interface is a good solution if you need a host controller to communicate with other devices or if you want to use off-the-shelf USB storage devices.

This chapter introduces the USB interface and USB's mass storage class.

The Interface in Brief

The Universal Serial Bus is an interface and protocol that enable a single host computer to communicate with a variety of peripheral devices. USB is appropriate for just about any kind of mass-storage device, including hard drives, CD and DVD drives, and flash drives.

The USB specifications are available from the USB Implementers Forum (USB-IF) (www.usb.org). The USB-IF is the non-profit corporation founded by companies involved with developing the USB specification. The USB-IF also sponsors a developers Web forum, provides software and hardware to help in developing and testing products, and develops compliance tests for devices, hosts, and related hardware.

The USB 2.0 specification is the main document that defines the interface.

Hosts and Devices

Every USB communication is between a host and a device. The host is in charge of the bus. Devices communicate only when requested to do so by the host. The only exception is the remote-wakeup feature, which enables a device in the low-power Suspend state to request communications with the host.

A USB host is a computer that contains USB host-controller hardware, a root hub with one or more USB ports, and program code to manage communications and events on the bus. The host-controller hardware formats data for transmitting on the bus and converts received data to a format that host software can understand. The host controller also performs functions related to managing communications on the bus. The root hub has one or more connectors for attaching devices. The root hub, in combination with the host controller, detects newly attached and removed devices, carries out requests received from the host, and passes data between devices and the host controller.

A USB host can be a desktop or notebook computer, a handheld, or any embedded system that contains host-controller hardware and software. To communicate with mass-storage devices, the host must have a driver that supports the protocols defined for USB's mass-storage class.

A USB device contains USB device-controller hardware and a microcontroller, CPU, or other intelligent hardware. As Chapter 1 explained, some devices contain a microcontroller with an on-chip USB device controller, while other devices use a microcontroller or CPU that interfaces to a USB controller on a separate chip. The hardware that implements the low-level USB protocols in the device controller is called the serial interface engine (SIE). Program code in a USB device is typically firmware stored in non-volatile memory. Some devices manage USB communications entirely in hardware and require no programming for the USB communications.

A USB device can connect to a host's root hub or to an external hub. The device can have a standard USB series-B or mini-B receptacle, a vendor-specific connector, or a permanently attached USB cable. The upstream (toward the host) end of the device's cable has a series-A plug that attaches to a host or hub or a mini-A plug that attaches to an On-The-Go device. Figure 2-1 shows the different plug types.

An On-The-Go (OTG) device is a special kind of USB device that can function as a limited-capability host or as a device. An On-The-Go device has a mini-AB receptacle that can accept a mini-A plug or a mini-B plug. An example of a USB On-The-Go device is a camera that can function as a mass-storage device that stores images that PCs can access via USB and as a host that sends images to a USB printer.

Host Responsibilities

A USB host manages power and communications on the bus. The USB host has these responsibilities:

Figure 2-1: USB cable plugs from left to right: series-A, series B, mini-A, and mini-B.

Detect Devices

On power-up, hubs make the host aware of all attached USB devices. In a process called enumeration, the host assigns an address and requests a series of data structures called descriptors from each device. After power-up, whenever a device is removed or attached, the host learns of the event and enumerates any newly attached device or removes any detached device from the record of available devices.

Provide Power

The host provides power to all devices on power-up or attachment and works with the devices to conserve power when possible. Some devices draw all of the power they need from the bus, while others have their own power supplies to supplement or replace the bus power.

Manage Traffic on the Bus

The host manages the flow of data on the bus. Multiple peripherals may want to transfer data at the same time. The host controller divides the available time into segments called frames (on a full-speed host) or microframes (on a high-speed host). The host gives each transmission a portion of a frame or microframe. A frame is 1 millisecond; a microframe is 125 microseconds.

Handle Error Checking

When transmitting data, the host adds error-checking bits. When receiving data, the host uses received error-checking bits to detect errors.

Exchange Data with Peripherals

All of the above tasks support the host's main job, which is to exchange data with peripherals. On a PC, users can access mass-storage devices via file-system functions supported by the operating system.

Device Responsibilities

In many ways, a device's responsibilities mirror the host's, but devices also have unique duties.

The most important thing to remember in writing USB device firmware is this: the device should assume nothing about what the host will do next. For the most part, the host isn't obligated to perform communications or initiate events on the bus in any particular order. Different hosts might do things differently, and the same host might do things differently at different times. A device should concentrate on responding properly to each received communication or other event on the bus. The device should not assume that any particular sequence of communications or events will occur.

A USB device has these responsibilities:

Detect the Bus Voltage

A device must be able to detect voltage on the bus's power-supply line and on detecting the voltage, switch in a pull-up resistor to announce the device's presence to the host.

Manage Power

In normal operation, a device must limit the bus current consumed to either 100 milliamperes or a higher amount, up to 500 mA, approved by the host during enumeration. A device must also detect the presence of the host's periodic timing markers and enter the low-power Suspend state when the markers are absent. While in the Suspend state, the device must monitor the bus and exit the Suspend state when bus activity resumes.

In the mass-storage class, most hard drives provide their own power supplies to replace or supplement the current available from the bus, while most flash drives use bus power only.

Respond to Standard Requests

On power-up or on attachment to a powered host, a device must respond to standard requests sent by the host during enumeration. The host may also send requests any time after enumeration completes. The requests query the capabilities and status of the device or request the device to take other action.

Handle Error Checking

When transmitting data, the device adds error-checking bits. When receiving data, the device uses received error-checking bits to detect errors.

Exchange Data with the Host

All of the above tasks support the main job of the device's USB port, which is to exchange data with the host.

Each device on the bus has an address and every transaction between a host and a device contains a device address. On detecting a matching address, a device must return requested data or status information. A device may store received data and trigger an interrupt to notify device firmware that a communication has occurred.

Implement the Device's Function

Of course, a device must also do anything required to implement its function. For some mass-storage devices, the device's only task is to store blocks of data received from the host and send blocks of data requested by the host.

Other mass-storage devices have additional duties such as operating as a camera, data logger, or other special-function device.

Bus Speeds

The USB 2.0 specification defines three bus speeds: high speed at 480 megabits/sec., full speed at 12 megabits/sec., and low speed at 1.5 megabits/sec. A USB mass-storage device must support full speed, high speed, or both. Almost all high-speed devices also support full speed because adding support for full speed is rarely difficult and enables the device to work when attached to full-speed hosts. USB hosts in recent PCs support all three speeds. An On-The-Go host or an embedded host with mass-storage support can support full speed, high speed, or both.

The bus speeds describe the rate that information travels on the bus. In addition to data, the bus must carry status, control, and error-checking signals. Plus, all peripherals must share the bus. So the data throughput for a device is always less than the bit rate on the bus.

In theory, on an otherwise idle bus, a full-speed device can transfer just over 1.2 megabytes/sec., and a high-speed device can transfer more than 53 megabytes/sec. Some full-speed hosts can achieve the maximum speed or close to it. At this writing, some high-speed hosts can transfer close to 40 megabytes/sec. The actual rate of data transfer varies depending on the efficiency of the host's and device's programming, how busy the bus is, and hardware capabilities of the host and drive.

Endpoints

All bus traffic is to or from device endpoints. An endpoint serves as a buffer for received data or data waiting to transmit. Typically an endpoint is a block of data memory or a register in the device controller.

Every device must have endpoint zero, which is the default endpoint used for control transfers. Endpoint zero is bidirectional.

A device can have up to 30 additional endpoint addresses. Each of these endpoint addresses has a number (1 to 15) and direction (IN or OUT). The direction is defined from the host's perspective: an IN endpoint provides data to send to the host and an OUT endpoint stores data received from the host. Device hardware or firmware configures each endpoint address for a specific USB transfer type. The number of available endpoints and supported transfer types vary with the device controller. A mass-storage device must have one IN endpoint and one OUT endpoint in addition to endpoint zero.

Transfer Types

One reason why USB is suitable for a wide range of devices is its support for four types of data transfers.

Control transfers enable the host to learn about a device, set a device's address, and select configurations and other settings. Control transfers can also send vendor-specific requests that transfer data for any purpose. All USB devices must support control transfers. A control transfer has two or three stages. In the Setup stage, the host sends a request. In the Data stage, the host or device sends data. Some requests don't have a Data stage. In the Status stage, the receiver of data in the Data stage returns status information. If there is no Data stage, the device returns the status information.

The other transfer types don't have stages. A class specification or vendor-specific protocol determines the length of a transfer. Bulk transfers are intended for situations where the rate of transfer isn't critical. If the bus is very busy, bulk transfers are delayed, but if the bus is otherwise idle, bulk transfers are the fastest. Mass-storage devices use bulk transfers. Interrupt transfers are for devices that must receive or send data periodically. Mass-storage devices rarely use interrupt transfers except for some full-speed floppy drives, which use interrupt transfers to report the status of a received command. Isochronous transfers have guaranteed delivery time but no error correcting. Mass-storage devices don't use isochronous transfers.

Transactions

Each transfer consists of one or more transactions. Each transaction contains a token packet, a data packet, and a handshake packet. (The handshake packet isn't present in isochronous transfers.) Each packet begins with a packet ID (PID). The function of the PID varies with the packet type.

The token packet contains the device address and the endpoint number the transaction is directed to. The token packet's PID identifies the packet as one of these types: SETUP (first packet in a control transfer), OUT (other host-to-device packet), IN (device-to-host packet), or SOF (start-of-frame marker).

The data packet contains any data the host or device is sending in the transaction. For control transfers, the transfer stage and the request determine who sends the data. For other transfers, the endpoint's direction determines who sends the data. The PID contains the data-toggle value, as explained below.

The handshake packet is sent by the receiver of the data packet. The PID contains a code to indicate whether the data was received without error. A code of ACK means success, NAK means busy, and STALL means either that the device doesn't support a received request in a control transfer or that the endpoint's Halt feature is set. High-speed bulk OUT endpoints can also return a NYET handshake code, which means that the endpoint accepted the data in the current transaction but isn't yet ready for more data.

The Data Toggle

The data toggle is a data-sequencing value that guards against lost or duplicated data. If you're debugging a device where it appears that the proper data is transmitting on the bus but the receiver is discarding the data, chances are good that the device isn't sending or expecting the correct data toggle.

Each endpoint maintains its own data-toggle value, which alternates between DATA0 and DATA1. Devices typically store the value in a register bit. When the host configures a device on power up or attachment, the host and device each set their data toggles to DATA0. On detecting an incoming data packet, the host or device compares the state of its data toggle with the data toggle in the received data packet. If the values match, the data packet's receiver toggles its value for the next transaction and returns an ACK. On receiving the ACK, the data packet's sender toggles its value for the next transaction.

The next received packet should contain a data toggle of DATA1, and again the receiver toggles its bit and returns an ACK. In additional transactions, the data toggle continues to alternate between DATA0 and DATA1. An exception is control transfers, where the Status stage always uses DATA1.

If the receiver is busy and returns a NAK, or if the receiver detects corrupted data and returns no response, the sender doesn't toggle its bit and tries again with the same data and data toggle.

Control transfers always use DATA0 in the Setup stage, use DATA1 in the first transaction of the Data stage, toggle the value in any additional Data-stage transactions, and use DATA1 in the Status stage. Bulk endpoints toggle the value in every transaction, resetting the data toggle only after a bus reset or completing a Set Configuration, Set Interface, or Clear Feature(ENDPOINT HALT) request.

Descriptors

During enumeration, the host computer uses control transfers to request the device's descriptors, which are data structures that contain information about a device's capabilities and requirements. The descriptors enable the host computer to select an appropriate driver for the device. The descriptors also provide information the driver needs to communicate with the device. Table 2-1 shows a set of descriptors for a mass-storage device. Every USB device must have descriptors and the ability to send the descriptors to the host on request. The USB specifications define the descriptors.

A device that can operate at both full and high speeds must support two sets of descriptors. For a mass-storage device, the values in each set can be identical except that the bulk endpoints in the high-speed descriptors have a wMaxPacketSize of 512 instead of 64. Chapter 3 has more about descriptors.

Mass Storage Requirements

In addition to what's required for any USB device, a USB mass-storage device must have all of the following:

- An interface descriptor with the class code = 08h (mass storage).
- A bulk IN endpoint and a bulk OUT endpoint that belong to the mass-storage interface.
- A serial number stored in a string descriptor.
- Storage media.
- The ability to access the storage media's contents using logical block addressing.

Table 2-1: Example descriptors for a full-speed mass-storage device (Sheet 1 of 2).

Device Descriptor	
0x12	Descriptor size in bytes (18)
0x01	Descriptor type (DEVICE)
0x0200	USB specification release (BCD) (2.00)
0x00	Class (specified at interface level)
0x00	Subclass (specified at interface level)
0x00	Protocol (specified at interface level)
0x40	Maximum packet size for endpoint zero (64)
0x04D8	Vendor ID (Microchip Technology; assigned by USB-IF)
0x0009	Product ID (assigned by vendor)
0x0100	Device release number (BCD, assigned by vendor) (1.00)
0x01	Manufacturer string index
0x02	Product string index
0x03	Serial number string index
0x01	Number of possible configurations
Configuration Descriptor	
0x09	Descriptor size in bytes (9)
0x02	Descriptor type (CONFIGURATION)
0x0020	Total length of this and subordinate descriptors
0x01	Number of interfaces in this configuration
0x01	Identifier for this configuration
0x00	Configuration string index (no string defined)
0xC0	Attributes: self powered, no remote wakeup
0x32	Maximum power consumption (100 mA)
Interface Descriptor	
0x09	Descriptor size in bytes (9)
0x04	Descriptor type (INTERFACE)
0x00	Interface Number
0x00	Alternate Setting Number
0x02	Number of endpoints in this interface
0x08	Class code (mass storage)
0x06	Subclass code (SCSI transparent command set)
0x50	Protocol code (bulk-only transport)

Table 2-1: Example descriptors for a full-speed mass-storage device (Sheet 2 of 2).

0x00	Interface string index (no string defined)
Endpoint Descriptor	
0x07	Descriptor size in bytes (7)
0x05	Descriptor type (ENDPOINT)
0x81	Endpoint number and direction (1 IN)
0x02	Transfer type (bulk)
0x0040	Maximum packet size (64)
0x00	Maximum latency (doesn't apply to full-speed bulk endpoints)
Endpoint Descriptor	
0x07	Descriptor size in bytes (7)
0x05	Descriptor type (ENDPOINT)
0x01	Endpoint number and direction (1 OUT)
0x02	Transfer type (bulk)
0x0040	Maximum packet size (64)
0x00	Maximum latency/high-speed OUT NAK rate (doesn't apply to full-speed bulk endpoints)
String Descriptor 0 (Language ID)	
0x04	Descriptor size in bytes (4)
0x03	Descriptor type (STRING)
0x0409	Language ID (U.S. English)
String Descriptor 1 (Manufacturer String)	
0x34	Descriptor size in bytes (52)
0x03	Descriptor type (STRING)
"Microchip Technology Inc."	String contents, Unicode, 2 bytes per character
String Descriptor 2 (Product String)	
0x3A	Descriptor size in bytes (58)
0x03	Descriptor type (STRING)
"Microchip Mass Storage Drive"	String contents, Unicode, 2 bytes per character
String Descriptor 3 (Serial Number)	
0x1A	Descriptor size in bytes (26)
0x03	Descriptor type (STRING)
"123456789ABC"	String contents, Unicode, 2 bytes per character

- The ability to detect and respond to the class-specific Bulk Only Mass Storage Reset and Get Max LUN requests. (A device with a single logical unit can stall the Get Max LUN request.)
- Support for the USB mass-storage class's protocol for receiving and responding to commands required for the mass-storage interface's subclass and peripheral device type.

The device firmware doesn't have to support a file system. The USB transfers just read and write blocks of data at logical block addresses in the storage media. The device doesn't have to know or care about the contents of the data blocks. The host software translates requests to read and write files and directories into requests to read and write to blocks at specific LBAs.

Choosing a Device Controller

A mass-storage device can use just about any full- or high-speed device controller chip. Low-speed chips aren't an option because they aren't allowed to do bulk transfers. Some device controllers are designed specifically for use in mass-storage devices. These controllers provide dedicated interfaces and other support for accessing popular media types, including flash memory and hard drives.

Controllers with Support for Flash Memory

Standard Microsystems Corporation (SMSC) has the USB2228 flash media controller with support for communicating with MultiMediaCards, SD Cards, CompactFlash, and other flash-memory card types. The chip can also access raw flash-memory chips via a generic memory and I/O interface. The chip includes an 8051-compatible microcontroller and 15 general-purpose I/O pins. The USB interface supports the control endpoint and two bulk endpoints required for a mass-storage device. Internal FETs can switch power to memory cards. There is hardware support for ECC error correction and SD-Card security commands.

The microcontroller can run code from ROM or from external memory. If running code from ROM, an external EEPROM can provide product-specific and chip-specific information such as a serial number and configuration data.

Prolific Technology is another source for USB controllers with support for flash memory.

Controllers with support for ATA/ATAPI

For controlling hard drives and CD/DVDs, SMSC has the USB97C202 ATA/ATAPI controller. Like the USB2228, the chip contains an 8051 microcontroller, but with support for ATA/ATAPI instead of flash memory. The chip includes support for accessing hard drives that use the Compact-Flash II form factor.

These device controllers also have ATA/ATAPI interfaces:

Cypress Semiconductor CY7C68300B EZUSB AT2LP high-speed USB-to-ATA/ATAPI bridge.

Philips Semiconductor ISP1583 Hi-Speed Universal Serial Bus peripheral controller.

Texas Instruments TUSB6250 USB 2.0 to ATA/TAPI Bridge Controller.

Firmware Options

Additional sources offer USB mass-storage firmware for use with a variety of embedded-system architectures and operating systems.

Accelerated Technology has the Nucleus real-time operating system with optional USB "middleware" that supports mass storage.

Jungo Ltd. has a USB device stack that consists of a device-controller driver, USB core driver, and class drivers, including a mass-storage driver. The device stack is compatible with a variety of embedded-system operating systems and CPU architectures.

MCCI's USB DataPump firmware package supports mass storage, several real-time operating systems, and many device controllers.

Micro Digital's smxUSBD USB device stack supports device controllers from Philips and has a class emulator for mass storage.

An embedded Linux system with a USB device controller can use the file-backed USB storage gadget (FSG) driver. When attached to a USB host, the system enumerates as a mass-storage device. The FSG driver is in Linux/drivers/usb/gadget/file_storage.c.

Microchip PIC18F4550

Microchip Technology's PICmicro® microcontrollers are popular because of their low cost, wide availability, speed, capabilities, and low power consumption. The PIC18F4550 is a PICmicro microcontroller with an embedded USB device controller that can communicate at low and full speeds. The chip doesn't have specific support for mass storage but is suitable for mass-storage applications that need to store and transfer moderate quantities of data at moderate speeds. The example firmware in this book is written for the PIC18F4550 and Microchip's C18 C compiler.

Architecture

The PIC18F4550 is a member of Microchip's high-performance, low-cost PIC18 series. Program memory is flash memory. The chip also has 256 bytes of EEPROM. A bootloader routine can upgrade firmware via the USB port.

The chip has 34 I/O pins that include a 10-bit analog-to-digital converter, a USART, a synchronous serial port that can be configured to use the I²C bus or SPI, enhanced PWM capabilities, and two analog comparators.

The USB module and CPU can use separate clock sources, enabling the CPU to use a slower, power-saving clock even when using the USB port.

Firmware Support

Microchip provides USB Firmware Framework code for the Microchip compiler and example applications for USB communications. The Framework code is structured to make it as easy as possible to develop firmware for devices in different classes and vendor-specific devices. This book includes excerpts from Microchip's mass-storage firmware, which uses the Framework.

The USB Controller

The microcontroller's USB controller supports all four transfer types and up to 30 endpoint addresses plus the default control endpoint. The endpoints share 1 KB of buffer memory. Endpoints can use double buffering for more efficient transfers. For isochronous transfers, USB data can transfer directly to and from a streaming parallel port (SPP).

For each enabled endpoint address, firmware must reserve memory for a buffer and a buffer descriptor. The microcontroller's CPU (in other words, the device firmware) and the USB controller's SIE share access to the buffers and buffer descriptors. The UOWN bit in the buffer descriptor's status register determines whether the CPU or SIE owns the resources. The SIE has ownership when data is ready to transmit and when waiting to receive data on the bus. When the SIE has ownership, device firmware shouldn't attempt to access the buffer or buffer descriptor except to read the UOWN bit. When readying an endpoint to perform a transfer, the last operation the firmware should perform is updating the status register to set UOWN to pass ownership to the SIE. When a transaction completes, the SIE clears the UOWN bit, passing ownership back to the CPU.

The buffer descriptor consists of four registers. The buffer descriptor status register contains status information and the two highest bits of the endpoint's byte count. The functions of the status bits change depending on who owns the buffer descriptor: the CPU (Table 2-2) or the SIE (Table 2-3). The byte-count register's eight bits plus the two bits in the status register contain the number of bytes to be transmitted or sent in an IN transaction or the number of bytes expected or received in an OUT transaction. The address-low and address-high registers contain the 16-bit starting address for the endpoint's buffer in RAM.

In firmware, each endpoint buffer descriptor has a name that uses this format:

ep<#>B<d>

where # is the endpoint number and d is the direction, with i = IN and o = OUT. In the code below, MSD_BD_IN is the buffer descriptor for endpoint 1 IN and MSD_BD_OUT is the buffer descriptor for endpoint 1 OUT:

```
#define MSD_BD_IN        ep1Bi
#define MSD_BD_OUT       ep1Bo
```

Table 2-2: Bit functions for an endpoint's buffer descriptor status register when the CPU owns the buffer descriptor.

Bit	Name	Description
7	UOWN	0 = the CPU owns the buffer descriptor and its buffer.
6	DTS	Data toggle synchronization: 0 = DATA0, 1 = DATA1.
5	KEN	Buffer descriptor keep enable: 0 = the SIE gives up ownership after processing a packet. 1 = the SIE keeps ownership when UOWN = 0 (use for SPP configuration).
4	INCDIS	Address increment disable: 0 = address increment enabled. 1 = address increment disabled (use for SPP configuration).
3	DTSEN	Data toggle synchronization enable: 0 = accept packets with incorrect data toggle. 1 = ignore packets with incorrect data toggle.
2	BSTALL	Buffer stall enable: 0 = don't return STALL handshake. 1 = return STALL handshake.
1	BC9	Byte count, bit 9.
0	BC8	Byte count, bit 8.

A BDT union can store the contents of the buffer descriptor's four registers:

```
typedef union _BDT
{
    struct
    {
        BD_STAT Stat;        // status
        byte Cnt;            // byte count
        byte ADRL;           // buffer address, low byte
        byte ADRH;           // buffer sddress, high byte
    };

    struct
    {
        unsigned :8;
        unsigned :8;
        byte* ADR;           // buffer address
    };
} BDT;
```

41

Table 2-3: Bit functions for an endpoint's buffer descriptor status register when the SIE owns the buffer descriptor.

Bit	Name	Description
7	UOWN	1 = the SIE owns the buffer descriptor and its buffer.
6	reserved	Not written by the SIE.
5..2	PID3:PID0	Packet identifier. The PID of the last received IN, OUT, or Setup packet.
1	BC9	Byte count, bit 9.
0	BC8	Byte count, bit 8.

The BD_STAT structure enables access to the status register's eight bits:

```
typedef struct
{
    unsigned BC8:1;      // byte count, bit 8
    unsigned BC9:1;      // byte count, bit 9
    unsigned BSTALL:1;   // return STALL handshake: 1 = true; 0 = false
    unsigned DTSEN:1;    // ignore packets with incorrect data toggle:
                         // 1 = true; 0 = false
    unsigned INCDIS:1;   // disable address increment: 1 = true; 0 = false
                         // (normally false, set true to use SPP)
    unsigned KEN:1;      // SIE keeps control of endpoint's buffer after UOWN is set:
                         // 1 = true; 0 = false
                         // (normally false, set true to use SPP)
    unsigned DTS:1;      // Data Toggle: 1 = DATA1; 0 = DATA0
    unsigned UOWN:1;     // ownership of the endpoint's buffer and buffer descriptor:
                         // 0 = CPU; 1 = SIE
} BD_STAT;
```

Two macros determine who currently owns an endpoint's buffer descriptor by reading the UOWN bit in the status register. The macros return true if the SIE has ownership and false if the CPU has ownership.

The mMSDTxIsBusy macro is for the bulk IN (device to host) endpoint:

```
#define mMSDTxIsBusy()        MSD_BD_IN.Stat.UOWN
```

The mMSDRxIsBusy macro is for the bulk OUT (host to device) endpoint:

```
#define mMSDRxIsBusy()        MSD_BD_OUT.Stat.UOWN
```

The mUSBBufferReady macro gives ownership of an endpoint's buffer descriptor and buffer to the SIE. Firmware calls the macro when a bulk IN endpoint buffer has data ready to send and after reading received data from a bulk OUT endpoint. The macro accepts the name of a buffer descriptor, such as ep1Bi or ep1Bo.

```
#define _DTSEN          0x08   // data-toggle synchronization bit
#define _DTSMASK        0x40   // data-toggle bit
#define _USIE           0x80   // SIE owns the endpoint's buffer descriptor
#define _UCPU           0x00   // CPU owns the endpoint's buffer descriptor

#define mUSBBufferReady(buffer_dsc)
{
    buffer_dsc.Stat._byte &= _DTSMASK;          // Get the data toggle state
    buffer_dsc.Stat.DTS = !buffer_dsc.Stat.DTS; // Toggle the data toggle
    buffer_dsc.Stat._byte |= _USIE | _DTSEN;    // Give ownership to the SIE
}
```

Each bulk endpoint can transfer up to 64 bytes in each USB transaction:

```
#define MSD_OUT_EP_SIZE  64
#define MSD_IN_EP_SIZE   64
```

Each endpoint number also has a control register that can enable a control endpoint, an IN endpoint, an OUT endpoint, or a pair of IN and OUT endpoints with the same endpoint number. Other bits in the register can stall the endpoint and disable handshaking (for isochronous transactions). Additional registers provide general USB capabilities such as storing the device's address on the bus and storing status and control information for USB communications and interrupts. The chip's data sheet has more details about these registers.

3

The USB Mass Storage Class

This chapter describes USB's mass storage class and presents device firmware that demonstrates how mass-storage devices exchange data with USB hosts.

Requirements

In addition to complying with the USB 2.0 specification, a mass-storage device must meet the requirements of the mass-storage class. The requirements include hardware capabilities and support for software protocols.

Specifications

The mass-storage class specification encompasses several documents. The Specification Overview and Bulk-Only Transport documents are relevant to almost all devices. The Bootability document applies to devices that systems can boot from. Two additional documents, Control/Bulk/Interrupt (CBI)

Transport and UFI Command Specification, are relevant only to some floppy drives.

Devices must also support one or more industry-standard command-block sets to exchange data, control devices, and read status information. Chapter 6 has more about these command blocks.

Logical Block Addressing

A USB mass-storage host specifies locations to read and write to in the storage media using the logical block addressing (LBA) method described in Chapter 1. Every USB mass-storage device must support accessing its media via LBA.

Mass Storage Requests

The bulk-only transport protocol has two defined control requests. Bulk Only Mass Storage Reset requests the device to become ready to receive a new mass-storage command block. Get Max LUN requests the highest logical-unit number supported by the device. In Windows, each logical unit, or volume, is represented by a drive letter. A device with a single logical unit can return zero or stall the request. A device with LUN 0 and LUN 1 returns 1. The maximum is 15. All other mass-storage data travels in bulk transfers.

The control/bulk/interrupt (CBI) protocol has one defined control request: Accept Device-Specific Command (ADSC). The Data stage of the request carries the command. A device can use an interrupt transfer to indicate that the device has completed a command's requested action.

A mass-storage host can also use control transfers to clear halt conditions on bulk endpoints. To do so, the host sends the standard USB request Clear Feature with the feature specified as ENDPOINT_HALT.

Descriptors

As Chapter 2 explained, every USB device has a series of descriptors that provide information about the device's capabilities. Every mass-storage device has a device descriptor, a configuration descriptor, an interface descriptor, at least two endpoint descriptors, and at least one string descriptor in addition to string descriptor zero.

In the descriptors, multi-byte numeric values transmit in little-endian format, with the least-significant-byte (LSB) first. For example, if a device's Product ID is 1234h, byte 10 in the device descriptor contains 34h and byte 11 contains 12h.

Device Descriptor

The device descriptor contains information about the device, its configurations, and any classes the device belongs to as a whole. Table 3-1 shows the fields in the device descriptor. Here are more details about the fields and how they're used in a mass-storage device:

bLength. The length in bytes of the descriptor. Always 12h.

bDescriptorType. The constant DEVICE (01h).

bcdUSB. The USB specification version that the device and its descriptors comply with in BCD (binary-coded decimal) format. If you think of the version's value as a decimal number, the upper byte represents the integer, the next four bits are tenths, and the final four bits are hundredths. Version 2.0 is 0200h. A 2.0 device does not have to be high speed. Any new full-speed mass-storage device should comply with the latest version of the specification.

bDeviceClass. For devices whose function is defined at the device level, this field specifies the device's class. Many devices, including mass-storage devices, specify their class in the interface descriptor and set the bDeviceClass field in the device descriptor to 00h.

bDeviceSubclass. A subclass within bDeviceClass. In mass-storage devices, this field is 00h.

bDeviceProtocol. A protocol defined by a class or subclass. In mass-storage devices, this field is 00h.

bMaxPacketSize0. The maximum packet size for endpoint zero. Full-speed devices may use 08h, 10h, 20h, or 40h. High-speed devices must use 40h.

Table 3-1: The device descriptor is 18 bytes.

Byte	Field	Description
0	bLength	Descriptor size in bytes (12h)
1	bDescriptorType	The constant DEVICE (01h)
2	bcdUSB	USB specification release number (BCD). For USB 2.0, byte 2 = 00h and byte 3 = 02h.
4	bDeviceClass	Class code. For mass storage, set to 00h (the class is specified in the interface descriptor).
5	bDeviceSubclass	Subclass code. For mass storage, set to 00h.
6	bDeviceProtocol	Protocol Code. For mass storage, set to 00h.
7	bMaxPacketSize0	Maximum packet size for endpoint zero.
8	idVendor	Vendor ID. Obtained from USB-IF.
10	idProduct	Product ID. Assigned by the product vendor.
12	bcdDevice	Device release number (BCD). Assigned by the product vendor.
14	iManufacturer	Index of string descriptor for the manufacturer. Set to 00h if there is no string descriptor.
15	iProduct	Index of string descriptor for the product. Set to 00h if there is no string descriptor.
16	iSerialNumber	Index of string descriptor containing the serial number. Must be > 00h for mass-storage devices.
17	bNumConfigurations	Number of possible configurations. Typically 01h.

idVendor. Members of the USB-IF and others who pay an administrative fee receive the rights to use a unique Vendor ID. Every device descriptor must have an assigned Vendor ID in this field.

idProduct. The owner of the Vendor ID assigns a Product ID to identify the device. Each Product ID is specific to a Vendor ID, so multiple vendors can use the same Product ID without conflict.

bcdDevice. The device's release number in BCD format. The owner of the Vendor ID assigns this value.

iManufacturer. Index to a string descriptor that contains a string describing the manufacturer. This value is zero if there is no manufacturer string descriptor.

iProduct. Index to a string descriptor that contains a string describing the product. This value is zero if there is no product string descriptor.

iSerialNumber. An index that points to a string containing the device's serial number. Virtually every mass-storage device must have a serial number whose final 12 characters differ from the final 12 characters in the serial number of any other device with the same Vendor ID and Product ID. The only exception is devices that use the CBI protocol, which don't require serial numbers.

bNumConfigurations. The number of configurations the device supports. This value is almost always 01h.

Configuration Descriptor

Each device has at least one configuration that defines the device's features and abilities. Multiple configurations are allowed but rare. The configuration descriptor contains information about the device's use of power and the number of interfaces supported. Table 3-2 shows the fields in the configuration descriptor. Here are more details about the fields and how they're used in a mass-storage device:

bLength. The length in bytes of the descriptor. Always 09h.

bDescriptorType. The constant CONFIGURATION (02h).

wTotalLength. The number of bytes in the configuration descriptor and all of its subordinate descriptors. The subordinate descriptors include interface and endpoint descriptors but do not include string descriptors.

bNumInterfaces. The number of interfaces in the configuration. The minimum is 1. A device with multiple interfaces can perform multiple functions, such as mass storage and human-interface device.

bConfigurationValue. Identifies the configuration in Get Configuration and Set Configuration requests. Set to 01h for the first (or only) configuration.

Table 3-2: The configuration descriptor has information about the device's power requirements.

Byte	Field	Description
0	bLength	Descriptor size in bytes. Always 09h.
1	bDescriptorType	The constant CONFIGURATION (02h).
2	wTotalLength	The number of bytes in the configuration descriptor and all of its subordinate descriptors.
4	bNumInterfaces	The number of interfaces in the configuration.
5	bConfigurationValue	Identifier for Set Configuration and Get Configuration requests. Use 01h for the first configuration.
6	iConfiguration	Index of string descriptor for the configuration. Set to 00h if there is no string descriptor.
7	bmAttributes	Self/bus power and remote wakeup settings.
8	bMaxPower	The amount of bus power the device requires, expressed as (maximum milliamperes / 2).

iConfiguration. Index to a string descriptor that contains a string describing the configuration. This value is zero if there is no configuration string descriptor.

bmAttributes. Bit 6 = 1 if the device is self-powered or zero if bus-powered. Bit 5 = 1 if the device supports the remote wakeup feature, which enables a suspended USB device to tell its host that the device wants to communicate. A USB device must enter the Suspend state if there has been no bus activity, including Start-of_Frame markers, for 3 milliseconds. If a suspended device requires action from the host, a device with remote wakeup enabled can request the host to resume communications. Mass-storage devices typically don't support remote wakeup. Bits 0..4 must equal 0. Bit 7 must equal 1.

bMaxPower. Specifies how much bus current a device requires. The bMaxPower value equals one half the number of milliamperes requested. If a device requires 200 milliamperes, bMaxPower = 100. The maximum current a device can request is 500 milliamperes. If the requested current isn't available, the host can refuse to configure the device. Some battery-powered hosts and all bus-powered hubs supply only 100 milliamperes per port. To enable a device to operate entirely from bus power when attached to these hosts and hubs, bMaxPower must equal 32h or less.

Interface Descriptor

The interface descriptor is where a device specifies the mass-storage function. A configuration can have multiple interfaces that are active at the same time. Each interface has its own interface descriptor and subordinate descriptors. Table 3-3 shows the fields in the interface descriptor. Here are more details about the fields and how they're used in a mass-storage device:

bLength. The number of bytes in the descriptor. Always 09h.

bDescriptorType. The constant INTERFACE (04h).

bInterfaceNumber. Identifies the interface. Each interface must have a descriptor with a unique value in this field.

bAlternateSetting. A single interface number can have alternate settings. Each setting has its own interface descriptor with the same value in bInterfaceNumber and a unique value in bAlternateSetting. Each setting also has its own endpoint descriptors. Only one setting is active at a time. The default interface setting (bAlternateSetting = 00h) is active immediately after the host has enumerated the device and selected a configuration. Mass-storage host drivers typically support only the default setting.

bNumEndpoints. The number of endpoints an interface supports in addition to endpoint zero. Set to 02h for a bulk-only mass-storage device.

bInterfaceClass. Set to 08h to specify the mass-storage class.

bInterfaceSubClass. In mass-storage devices, the bInterfaceSubClass field specifies either an industry-standard command-block set or the SCSI transparent command set (06h). Each device also specifies a peripheral device type (PDT) in response to a SCSI INQUIRY command. Each PDT corresponds to a document that specifies a command set. Virtually all new mass-storage designs should set bInterfaceSubClass = 06h. The device then declares its command set in a single location, in the PDT value in the response to an INQUIRY command. Devices that use other values for bInterfaceSubClass should be sure that the value is compatible with the PDT returned in the INQUIRY response. Chapter 6 has more about the INQUIRY command.

The mass-storage overview specification is somewhat confusing when it says that the contents of bInterfaceSubclass specify "transport protocols and

Table 3-3: The interface descriptor specifies the mass-storage function.

Byte	Field	Description
0	bLength	Descriptor size in bytes (09h).
1	bDescriptorType	The constant INTERFACE (04h).
2	bInterfaceNumber	Number identifying this interface.
3	bAlternateSetting	Set to 00h for the default setting.
4	bNumEndpoints	Number of endpoints supported, not counting endpoint zero. Set to 02h for a bulk-only mass-storage device.
5	bInterfaceClass	Class code. Mass storage = 08h.
6	bInterfaceSubclass	Subclass code. Mass-storage values: 01h: Reduced Block Commands (RBC). 02h: SFF-8020i, MMC-2 (ATAPI) (CD/DVD drives) 03h: QIC-157 (tape drives). 04h: USB Floppy Interface (UFI). 05h: SFF-8070i (ATAPI removable rewritable media devices). 06h: SCSI transparent command set. Use the SCSI INQUIRY command to determine the peripheral device type. Recommended value for most devices.
7	bInterfaceProtocol	Protocol code. Mass storage values: 00h: CBI with command completion interrupt transfers 01h: CBI without command completion interrupt transfer 50h: bulk only. Recommended value for most devices.
8	iInterface	Index of string descriptor for the interface.

command code systems transported by the interface." In reality, bInterfaceSubclass names the command-code system, or command blocks, that a device uses (either explicitly or by leaving the issue to the INQUIRY command), and the bInterfaceProtocol field (described below) names the transport protocol.

bInterfaceProtocol. In mass-storage devices, the bInterfaceProtocol field specifies a mass-storage transport protocol. The transport protocol defines structures and specifies USB transfer types for carrying mass-storage commands, data, and status information on the bus. A device may use either of two protocols: bulk-only transport (BOT, sometimes called BBB because all three phases use bulk transfers) or control/bulk/interrupt (CBI). The mass-storage specification recommends using the bulk-only transport protocol (50h) for all new devices. CBI is approved for use only with full-speed floppy drives.

iInterface. Index to a string descriptor that contains a string describing the interface. This value is zero if there is no interface string descriptor.

Endpoint Descriptors

Each endpoint specified in an interface descriptor has an endpoint descriptor. Endpoint zero never has a descriptor because every device must support endpoint zero, the device descriptor contains the maximum packet size, and the USB specification defines everything else about the endpoint.

Table 3-4 shows the fields in the descriptors. Here are more details about the fields and how they're used in a mass-storage device:

bLength. The number of bytes in the descriptor. Always 07h.

bDescriptorType. The constant ENDPOINT (05h).

bEndpointAddress. The endpoint number and direction. Bits 0..3 are the endpoint number, which can be any value from 1 to 15 supported by the device's hardware. Bit 7 is the direction: Out = 0, In = 1 Bits 6..4 are unused and must be zero. For example, an interface could use endpoint 1 OUT (01h) and endpoint 1 IN (81h), or endpoint 2 OUT (02h) and endpoint 3 in (83h).

bmAttributes. Bits 1..0 specify the type of transfer the endpoint supports. Bits 7..2 are zero. For bulk transfers, set to 02h.

wMaxPacketSize. The value in bits 10..0 is the maximum number of data bytes the endpoint can transfer in a transaction. The allowed values vary with the device speed and type of transfer. A full-speed bulk endpoint can have a maximum packet size of 08h, 10h, 20h, or 40h bytes. For best performance, use 40h. If a full-speed bulk endpoint's wMaxPacketSize is less than 40h, some host controllers schedule no more than one transaction per frame. For high speed, the maximum packet size must be 200h. Bits 15..11 are zero for bulk endpoints.

bInterval. The host ignores this value for full-speed bulk endpoints and high-speed bulk IN endpoints. For high-speed bulk OUT endpoints, the

Table 3-4: A bulk-only mass storage device must have two endpoint descriptors.

Byte	Field	Description
0	bLength	Descriptor size in bytes (07h).
1	bDescriptorType	The constant Endpoint (05h).
2	bEndpointAddress	Endpoint number and direction.
3	bmAttributes	Transfer type supported. Bulk = 02h.
4	wMaxPacketSize	Maximum packet size supported.
6	bInterval	Maximum NAK rate for high-speed bulk OUT endpoints. Otherwise ignored for bulk endpoints.

value indicates the endpoint's maximum NAK rate. This value is relevant when the device has received data and has returned ACK, and the host has more data to send. By returning ACK, the device is saying that it expects to be able to accept the next transaction's data. (Otherwise the device would return NYET.) If the next data packet arrives and for some reason the device can't accept the packet, the endpoint returns NAK. The bInterval value says that the endpoint expects to return NAK no more than once in each period specified by bInterval. The value can range from 0 to 255 microframes. A value of zero means the endpoint doesn't ever expect to return NAK immediately after an ACK.

String Descriptors

A string descriptor contains descriptive text. Support for most string descriptors is optional, but every mass-storage device that uses the bulk-only transport protocol must have a string descriptor that contains a serial number. The serial number must have at least 12 characters and must contain only characters in the range 0–9 (0030h–0039h) and A–F (0041h–0046h). Note that lower-case text, hyphens, and many other characters are not allowed. The last 12 characters must be different from the last 12 characters of the serial number of any device with the same values in the idVendor and idProduct fields in the device descriptor. The serial number enables a host to retain properties such as the drive letter and access policies after a user moves a device to another port or attaches multiple devices with the same Vendor ID and Product ID.

The device descriptor's iSerialNumber field contains an index to the string descriptor containing the serial number.

Table 3-5 shows the fields in a string descriptor. Here are more details about the fields and how they're used in a mass-storage device:

bLength. The number of bytes in the descriptor.

bDescriptorType. The constant STRING (03h).

wLANGID[0...n] or **bString**. When a host requests a String descriptor, the low byte of the wValue field in the Setup stage is an index value. If the index value is zero, the host is requesting language IDs. If the index value is greater than zero, the host is requesting the string descriptor with that index.

String descriptor zero contains one or more 16-bit language ID codes that indicate the languages that the strings are available in. The code for U.S. English is 0409h. This is likely to be the only code supported by an operating system. The wLANGID value must be valid for any of the other strings to be valid. Devices that return no string descriptors must not return an array of language IDs. The USB-IF's web site has a list of defined USB language IDs.

For index values of 1 and higher, the bString field contains a Unicode string. With a few exceptions, ANSI character codes 00h through 7Fh correspond to Unicode values 0000h through 007Fh. For example, a product string for a product called "Gizmo" would contain five 16-bit Unicode values that represent the characters in the product name:

0047 0069 007A 006D 006F

In the string descriptor, each Unicode character transmits LSB first:

47 00 69 00 7A 00 6D 00 6F 00

The strings are not null-terminated. The bLength field for a string descriptor that contains a string equals (2 * number of characters in string) + 2.

Responding to Commands

In mass-storage communications that use SCSI commands, the USB host sends a command block, the host or device may send data, and the device

Table 3-5: A string descriptor has three or more fields.

Byte	Field	Size (bytes)	Description
0	bLength	1	Descriptor size in bytes
1	bDescriptorType	1	The constant String (03h)
2	bSTRING or wLANGID	varies	For string descriptor zero, an array of 1 or more Language Identifier codes. For other string descriptors, a Unicode string.

returns status. When reading or writing blocks of data, the host identifies the locations to read or write to by specifying a logical block address. The USB communications don't have to know or care anything about files, directories, or data clusters in the media.

In the bulk-only transport protocol, a successful communication has two or three phases: command transport, data transport (not used for some commands), and status transport. (Don't confuse these phases with the phases of a USB transaction or the stages of a USB control transfer.) In the command-transport phase, the host sends a command block in a structure called a command block wrapper (CBW). In the data-transport phase, the host or device sends data. Some commands don't have a data-transport phase. In the status-transport phase, the device sends status information in a structure called a command status wrapper (CSW).

The mass-storage and SCSI specifications don't define how long a host should wait for a device to return requested data or accept received data before giving up. The drivers in Windows and other operating systems typically wait 20–30 seconds.

The Command Block Wrapper

The host sends the CBW to the device's bulk OUT endpoint. The CBW contains a command block and other information about the command (Table 3-6). The CBW is 31 bytes.

Table 3-6: The CBW contains a command descriptor block and other information about the command.

Name	Bits	Description
dCBWSignature	32	The value 43425355h, which identifies the structure as a CBW. The LSB (55h) transmits first on the bus.
dCBWTag	32	A value that associates this CBW with the CSW the device will send in response.
dCBWDataTransferLength	32	If bit 7 of bmCBWFlags = 0, the number of bytes the host will send in the data-transport phase. If bit 7 of bmCBWFlags = 1, the number of bytes the host expects to receive in the data-transport phase.
bmCBWFlags	8	Specifies the direction of the data-transport phase. Bit 7 = 0 for an OUT (host-to-device) transfer. Bit 7 = 1 for an IN (device-to-host) transfer. If there is no data-transport phase, bit 7 is ignored. All other bits are zero.
Reserved	4	Zero.
bCBWLUN	4	For devices with multiple LUNs, specifies the LUN the command block is directed to. Otherwise the value is zero.
Reserved	3	Zero.
bCBWCBLength	5	The length of the command descriptor block in the CBWCB field in bytes. Valid values are 1–16. Currently defined command descriptor blocks are all at least 6 bytes.
CBWCB	128	The command block for the device to execute.

The _USB_MSD_CBW structure can hold a CBW:

```
#define MSD_CBW_SIZE 0x1F

typedef struct _USB_MSD_CBW
{
    dword dCBWSignature;
    dword dCBWTag;
    dword dCBWDataTransferLength;
    byte bCBWFlags;
    byte bCBWLUN;
    byte bCBWCBLength;
    byte CBWCB[16];
} USB_MSD_CBW;
```

The CBWCB field of a CBW contains a command descriptor block (CDB), or command block for short. The CDB is a structure that contains a command and supplementary information that varies with the command. The CBWCB field is always 16 bytes, but many CDBs are shorter than 16 bytes. Any remaining bytes in the CDB are pad bytes of zero.

In most cases, the bCBWCBLength field indicates the length of the CDB within the CBWCB field excluding pad bytes. For devices with bInterface-SubClass = 04h (UFI), the host must pad CDBs shorter than 12 bytes with zeroes and set bCBWCBLength to 12. For CBWs carrying the 6-byte SCSI REQUEST SENSE command block, the Windows mass-storage driver incorrectly sets bCBWCBLength = 12 even for non-UFI devices.

The bmCBWFlags field indicates the direction of the data-transport phase. The dCBWDataTransferLength field indicates how many bytes the host will send or how many bytes the host expects to receive.

On receiving a CBW, a device should check that the structure is valid and has meaningful content. A CBW is valid if all of the following are true:

• The CBW is received after a CSW or reset.
• The CBW is 31 bytes.
• The dCBWSignature field has the correct value.

The contents are considered meaningful if all of the following are true:

• All of the reserved bits are zero.
• The bCBWLUN field contains a supported LUN value.

- The bCBWCBLength and CBWCB fields are valid for the interface's subclass.

The IsValidCBW function checks a CBW's size and signature. The function uses the MSD_BD_OUT identifier defined in Chapter 2 for the bulk OUT endpoint buffer descriptor.

```
byte              gblCBWLength;
USB_MSD_CBW  gblCBW;

gblCBWLength = MSD_BD_OUT.Cnt;

byte IsValidCBW()
{
    // A valid CBW is 31 bytes and
    // its dCBWSignature field contains 0x43425355.

    if ((gblCBWLength != MSD_CBW_SIZE) ||
        (gblCBW.dCBWSignature != 0x43425355))

        return FALSE;

    else

        return TRUE;
}
```

The IsMeaningfulCBW function checks for bCBWLUN less than or equal to 0Fh, bCBWCBLength of 01h to 10h bytes, and bCBWFlags equal to 00h or 80h. Note that a meaningful CBW must have a LUN value that is valid for the specific device. (Few devices have 16 LUNs.)

```
byte IsMeaningfulCBW()
{
    if ((gblCBW.bCBWLUN <= 0x0f) &&
        (gblCBW.bCBWCBLength <= 0x10) &&
        (gblCBW.bCBWCBLength >= 0x01) &&
        (gblCBW.bCBWFlags == 0x00 | gblCBW.bCBWFlags == 0x80))

        return TRUE;

    else
        return FALSE;
}
```

After receiving a CBW, depending on the command, the device must prepare to receive data from the host on the bulk OUT endpoint or prepare to send data or a CSW to the host on the bulk IN endpoint.

The Command Status Wrapper

Table 3-7 shows the fields in the CSW, which is 13 bytes. The _USB_MSD_CSW structure can contain a CSW:

```
#define MSD_CSW_SIZE 0x0d

typedef struct _USB_MSD_CSW
{
    dword dCSWSignature;
    dword dCSWTag;
    dword dCSWDataResidue;
    byte bCSWStatus;
} USB_MSD_CSW;
```

On receiving a CSW, a host should check that the structure is valid and has meaningful content. A CSW is valid if all of the following are true:

- The CSW is 13 bytes.
- The dCSWSignature field has the correct value.
- The value of dCSWTag equals the value in the dCBWTag field of a previously sent CBW.

The contents are considered meaningful if *either* of the following is true:

- The bCSWStatus field equals 02h.
- The bCSWStatus field equals 00h or 01h *and* dCSWDataResidue is less than or equal to dCBWDataTransferLength.

In the dCSWDataResidue field in the CSW, a device indicates whether it has received and processed all of the data the host promised to send in the CBW or whether the device has sent all of the data requested by the CBW.

In a command where the host sends data in the data-transport phase, dCSWDataResidue contains the difference between dCBWDataTransferLength in the command's CBW and the amount of data the device has processed. If the device processes dCBWDataTransferLength bytes, dCSWDataResidue is zero.

Table 3-7: The CSW contains status and related information about a command.

Name	Bits	Description
dCSWSignature	32	The value 53425355h, which identifies the structure as a CSW. The LSB (55h) transmits first on the bus.
dCSWTag	32	The value of the dCBWTag in a CBW received from the host.
dCSWDataResidue	32	For transfers where the host sends data to the device in the data-transport phase, the difference between dCBWDataTransferLength and the number of bytes the device processed. For transfers where the device sends data to the host in the data-transport phase, the difference between dCBWDataTransferLength and the number of valid bytes the device has sent, excluding any pad bytes.
bCSWStatus	8	00h = command passed. 01h = command failed. 02h = phase error. Host should perform a reset recovery.

In a command where the device sends data in the data-transport phase, dCSWDataResidue contains the difference between dCBWDataTransfer-Length in the command's CBW and the amount of valid data the device sent, excluding any pad bytes. If the device has sent dCBWDataTransfer-Length bytes, dCSWDataResidue is zero.

The bCSWStatus field indicates whether the command completed without error. A value of 00h means success. A value of 01h means the command failed and the host should immediately issue a SCSI REQUEST SENSE command to get status information. The protocol that causes the host to send REQUEST SENSE on receiving a response code of 01h is sometimes called auto sense because the host's USB driver, rather than higher-level code, requests the status information. The handling of the error and sense data is thus "automatic" to higher-level software. Chapter 6 has more about the REQUEST SENSE command.

A value of 02h means that the host should perform a reset recovery on the device. A reset recovery consists of the following control transfers in order:

1. Bulk-only Mass Storage Reset. On completion of the request, the device is ready to receive a new CBW. The reset should not change the states of data-toggle bits and endpoint STALL conditions. This is a

class-specific request for the mass-storage class.

2. Clear Feature(ENDPOINT_HALT) request for the bulk IN endpoint. The device resets the endpoint's data toggle to DATA0. The endpoint resumes normal communications if possible. This request is a standard USB request.

3. Clear Feature(ENDPOINT_HALT) request for the bulk OUT endpoint. The device resets the endpoint's data toggle to DATA0. The endpoint resumes normal communications if possible. This request is a standard USB request.

As an alternative to a reset recovery, a host might issue a Set Port Feature (PORT_RESET) request to the device's hub port. The host must then re-enumerate the device. This option isn't ideal for composite devices, which have multiple active interfaces, because the port reset will affect all of the device's interfaces. But a port reset can be necessary when communicating with a device that crashes when the host attempts a reset recovery. (Such devices exist.) The Windows mass-storage driver favors the port reset over the reset recovery.

The PrepareCSWData function sets the CSWTag and CSWSignature fields in the CSW. The other fields in the CSW are set in other functions later in this chapter.

```
volatile far USB_MSD_CSW msd_csw;

void PrepareCSWData()
{
    // Set dCSWTag to match dCBWTag in the command's CBW.

    msd_csw.dCSWTag = gblCBW.dCBWTag;
    msd_csw.dCSWSignature = 0x53425355;
}
```

Managing Communications on the Bulk Endpoints

One way to manage communications on the bulk endpoints is to set a variable that specifies whether the device is waiting for a CBW, ready to send data or a CSW to the host, or ready to receive data from the host.

Firmware can call a function repeatedly to check the value of the variable and take any needed action:

```
#define MSD_WAIT        0   // Waiting for a CBW.
#define MSD_DATA_IN     2   // IN Data State (device to host).
#define MSD_DATA_OUT    3   // OUT Data State (host to device).

byte MSD_State;             // Holds the current state of the device.
```

The msd_buffer array holds a 512-byte block of data:

```
volatile far char msd_buffer[512];
```

The mMin macro returns the lower of two values (A or B):

```
#define mMin(A, B) (A < B) ? A:B
```

The code that follows uses these macros from Chapter 2: MSD_BD_IN, MSD_BD_OUT, MSD_IN_EP_SIZE, MSD_OUT_EP_SIZE, mUSB-BufferReady, and mMSDTxIsBusy. The code also calls the USBDriverService function included in Microchip's Framework firmware. USBDriverService handles interrupts related to USB communications.

Sending Data

The SendData function accepts a pointer to data to send (dataAddr) and the number of bytes to send (dataSize). The function stores the passed address in the buffer descriptor's address registers, stores the number of bytes to send in the byte-count register, and gives ownership of the buffer descriptor to the SIE. The device sends the data in the next IN transaction on the endpoint.

```
void SendData(byte* dataAddr, byte dataSize)
{
    // Wait for the SIE to give up ownership of the bulk IN endpoint.

    while (mMSDTxIsBusy())
    {
        // Service USB interrupts. See Microchip Framework firmware for details.

        USBDriverService();
    }
    // Set the address in the buffer descriptor to the passed address.

    MSD_BD_IN.ADR = dataAddr;
```

```
// Set the buffer descriptor's count to the passed data size.

MSD_BD_IN.Cnt = dataSize;

// Give ownership of the buffer descriptor to the SIE.

mUSBBufferReady(MSD_BD_IN);

// Service USB interrupts.

USBDriverService();
}
```

Preparing to Send Data to the USB Host

The MSDDataIn function manages sending data in the data-transport phase of a command. The function sets fields in the CSW to indicate how many bytes in the transfer have been received and how many additional bytes the device expects to receive.

```
byte *ptrNextData; // must be set to the location of the first byte to send

void MSDDataIn(void)
{
    byte    i;
    dword   size;

    // Does bCSWStatus = no error AND is the total data to be sent >= the endpoint's size?

    if ((msd_csw.bCSWStatus == 0x00) &&
        (msd_csw.dCSWDataResidue >= MSD_IN_EP_SIZE))
        {
        // Send MSD_IN_EP_SIZE bytes of data on the bulk IN endpoint.
        // The data begins at ptrNextData.

        SendData (ptrNextData, MSD_IN_EP_SIZE),

        // Subtract the sent bytes from dCBWDataTransferLength in the CBW.

        gblCBW.dCBWDataTransferLength -= MSD_IN_EP_SIZE;

        // Subtract the sent bytes from dCSWDataResidue in the CSW.

        msd_csw.dCSWDataResidue -= MSD_IN_EP_SIZE;
```

```
    // Increment the pointer to the next data to send.

    ptrNextData += MSD_IN_EP_SIZE;

} else
  {
  if (msd_csw.bCSWStatus != 0x0)
    {
    // bCSWStatus indicates an error.
    // Set size to the lower of the endpoint size or dCBWDataTransferLength.

    size = mMin (MSD_IN_EP_SIZE, gblCBW.dCBWDataTransferLength);

    // Reset msd_buffer's contents to zeroes to send pad data.

    for (i = 0; i < size; i++) msd_buffer[i] = 0;

    if (gblCBW.dCBWDataTransferLength > MSD_IN_EP_SIZE)
      {
      // There was an error (bCSWStatus != 0x0)
      // and dCBWDataTransferLength is greater than the endpoint size.
      // Send MSD_IN_EP_SIZE bytes from msd_buffer.

      SendData((byte*)&msd_buffer[0], MSD_IN_EP_SIZE);

      // Subtract the sent bytes from dCBWDataTransferLength in the CBW.

      gblCBW.dCBWDataTransferLength -= MSD_IN_EP_SIZE;

      // Subtract the sent bytes from dCSWDataResidue in the CSW.

      msd_csw.dCSWDataResidue -= MSD_IN_EP_SIZE;
```

```
        } else
          {
          // There was an error (bCSWStatus != 0x0)
          // and dCBWDataTransferLength is <= the endpoint size.
          // Send dCBWDataTransferLength bytes from msd_buffer.

          SendData((byte*)&msd_buffer[0], gblCBW.dCBWDataTransferLength);

          // Set dCBWDataTransferLength = 0 to cause the CSW to be sent.

          gblCBW.dCBWDataTransferLength = 0;

          //  Decrement dCSWDataResidue by the number of bytes sent.

          msd_csw.dCSWDataResidue -= gblCBW.dCBWDataTransferLength;
          }
      } else
          {
          // There is no error and the data to be sent is <= the endpoint size.
          // Send dCSWDataResidue bytes beginning at ptrNextData.

          SendData(ptrNextData, msd_csw.dCSWDataResidue);

          // Subtract the sent bytes from dCBWDataTransferLength.

          gblCBW.dCBWDataTransferLength -= msd_csw.dCSWDataResidue ;

          // Set dCSWDataResidue equal to dCBWDataTransferLength.

          msd_csw.dCSWDataResidue = gblCBW.dCBWDataTransferLength;

          // If the host expected more bytes than were sent,
          // dCBWDataTransferLength is greater than zero.
          // Set dCBWDataTransferLength = 0 to cause the CSW to be sent.

          gblCBW.dCBWDataTransferLength = 0;
          }
        }
      }
    }
```

Receiving Data from the USB Host

If the data-transport phase is host-to-device, firmware calls the MSD-DataOut function to get data received from the host.

```
void MSDDataOut(void)
{
    // To enable receiving data, give ownership of the endpoint's buffer to the SIE.

    mUSBBufferReady(MSD_BD_OUT);

    // Service USB interrupts. (See Microchip's Framework firmware for details.)

    USBDriverService();

    // Wait until the SIE has returned ownership of the endpoint buffer to the CPU,
    // indicating that data was received.

    while (mMSDRxIsBusy())
    {
        USBDriverService();
    }
    // Subtract the number of received bytes from dCBWDataTransferLength in the CBW.

    gblCBW.dCBWDataTransferLength -= MSD_BD_OUT.Cnt;

    // Subtract the number of received bytes from dCSWDataResidue in the CSW.

    msd_csw.dCSWDataResidue -= MSD_BD_OUT.Cnt;

    // For the next transaction, set the OUT endpoint's count to the endpoint size.

    MSD_BD_OUT.Cnt = MSD_OUT_EP_SIZE;

    // Increment the OUT endpoint's address by endpoint-size bytes
    // in case there is more data to receive.

    MSD_BD_OUT.ADR += MSD_OUT_EP_SIZE;
}
```

Sending the CSW

Firmware calls the SendCSW function after completing the command-transport and data-transport (if required) phases of a command. The function places the CSW in the IN endpoint's buffer and transfers ownership of the buffer descriptor to the SIE.

```c
void SendCSW(void)
{
    // Wait until the CPU has ownership of the endpoint's buffer descriptor.

    while (mMSDTxIsBusy())
    {
        // Service USB interrupts. See Microchip's Framework firmware for details.

        USBDriverService();
    }
    // Set the IN endpoint's address registers to the CSW's address.

    MSD_BD_IN.ADR = (byte*)&msd_csw;

    // Set the IN endpoint's count to the CSW's size.

    MSD_BD_IN.Cnt = MSD_CSW_SIZE;

    // To enable sending the CSW, give ownership of the endpoint descriptor to the SIE.

    mUSBBufferReady(MSD_BD_IN);

    // Service USB interrupts.

    USBDriverService();

    // Prepare to receive another CBW.
    // Set the OUT endpoint's count to the size of a CBW.

    MSD_BD_OUT.Cnt = sizeof(msd_cbw);

    // Set the OUT endpoint's buffer descriptor's address to the location that will store
    // the received CBW.

    MSD_BD_OUT.ADR = (byte*)&msd_cbw;

    // The next bulk OUT data from the host should be a CBW.

    MSD_State = MSD_WAIT;
}
```

Managing Transfers

The ProcessIO function manages transfers on the bulk endpoints. The function implements a state machine that determines what to do depending on the value of MSD_State. The function calls the MSDCommandHandler function in Chapter 6 to decode and respond to command blocks in the CBW.

```
void ProcessIO(void)
{
    byte    i;
    dword   size;

    // Is the bulk IN endpoint sending data to the host?

    if (MSD_State == MSD_DATA_IN) {

        // Has all of the data been sent?

        if (gblCBW.dCBWDataTransferLength == 0)
        {
            // Prepare to send the CSW.

            SendCSW();
        }
        else
        {
            // Prepare to send data.

            MSDDataIn();
        }
        return;
    } // End: sending data to host.
```

```
// Is the bulk OUT endpoint receiving data from the host?

if (MSD_State == MSD_DATA_OUT) {

    // Has all of the data been received?

    if (gblCBW.dCBWDataTransferLength == 0) {

        // If dCSWDataResidue isn't zero, the quantity of received data
        // doesn't match the quantity expected.

        if ((msd_csw.bCSWStatus == 0x00) && (msd_csw.dCSWDataResidue != 0))

            // Set bCSWStatus to phase error (02h).

            msd_csw.bCSWStatus = 0x02;

        // Prepare to send the CSW.

        SendCSW();
    }
    return;

} // End: receiving data from the host

// If the CPU owns the OUT endpoint's buffer descriptor,
// was the device waiting for a CBW?

if ((MSD_BD_OUT.Stat.UOWN == _UCPU) && (MSD_State == MSD_WAIT))
{
    // Copy the received CBW into the gblCBW structure.

    gblCBW.dCBWSignature =          msd_cbw.dCBWSignature;
    gblCBW.dCBWTag =                msd_cbw.dCBWTag;
    gblCBW.dCBWDataTransferLength = msd_cbw.dCBWDataTransferLength;
    gblCBW.bCBWFlags =              msd_cbw.bCBWFlags;
    gblCBW.bCBWLUN =                msd_cbw.bCBWLUN;
    gblCBW.bCBWCBLength =           msd_cbw.bCBWCBLength;
    for (i = 0; i < msd_cbw.bCBWCBLength; i++)
        gblCBW.CBWCB[i] =          msd_cbw.CBWCB[i];
```

```
// Save the size of the CBW.

gblCBWLength = MSD_BD_OUT.Cnt;

if (IsValidCBW()) {
    if (IsMeaningfulCBW()) {

        // The CBW is valid and meaningful.
        // Set fields in the CSW.

        PrepareCSWData();

        // Is the data-transport phase device to host?

        if (gblCBW.bCBWFlags == 0x80)

            // Prepare to send data.

            MSD_State=MSD_DATA_IN;

        // Is the data-transport phase host to device?

        else if (gblCBW.bCBWFlags == 0x00) {

            // Prepare to read received data in msd_buffer.

            MSD_BD_OUT.Cnt = MSD_OUT_EP_SIZE;
            MSD_BD_OUT.ADR = (byte*)&msd_buffer[0];
            MSD_State = MSD_DATA_OUT;
        }
        // Decode and process the received command block.

        MSDCommandHandler();
    }
}
// To enable receiving data,
// give ownership of the endpoint's buffer descriptor to the SIE.

mUSBBufferReady(MSD_BD_OUT);
```

```
    // Service USB interrupts. (See Microchip's Framework firmware for details.)

    USBDriverService();

  } // End received CBW.
}
```

More about STALL

The mass-storage class is unique in its use of the STALL handshake to end bulk transfers. In other USB classes, a sender can indicate the end of a transfer by transmitting a short packet, which is a data packet that contains zero data bytes or any quantity fewer than wMaxPacketSize. In contrast, mass-storage devices use STALL for this purpose and to respond to other error conditions.

After a bulk endpoint returns STALL, the endpoint is in the halt condition. To resume communications with the endpoint, the host must issue a Clear Feature(ENDPOINT_HALT) control request with the endpoint's address in the Setup transaction's wIndex field.

(Endpoint zero can also use the STALL handshake. On receiving a Get Max LUN request, a device with a single LUN may return a STALL to indicate that the device doesn't support the command. The endpoint resumes normal operation on receiving a new Setup transaction.)

A mass-storage device *must* stall one or both bulk endpoints in these situations:

If a device sends less than the requested amount of data in the data-transport phase, the device must stall the bulk IN endpoint.

If a received CBW isn't valid, the device must stall the bulk IN endpoint and must either stall the bulk OUT endpoint or accept and discard any received data on the endpoint.

On experiencing an internal error that requires a reset, a device must either stall the endpoint being used in any data transfer in progress and set bCSWStatus = 02h or stall the bulk IN and bulk OUT endpoints until a reset recovery.

A mass-storage device *may* stall a bulk endpoint in these situations:

If a device expects to send more data than the host specified in the CBW, after sending the requested quantity of data, the device may stall the bulk IN endpoint.

If a device expects to receive a different quantity of data than the host specified in the CBW, the device may stall the bulk OUT endpoint.

If a device determinines that it can't complete a command during the data-transport phase, the device may stall the bulk IN or bulk OUT endpoint as appropriate.

The thirteen cases described below have more about the use of STALL with mass-storage commands.

Thirteen Cases for Any Situation

The mass-storage bulk-only transport specification spells out how the host and device should behave after the host sends a command in each of thirteen cases. Cases 1, 6, and 12 (in bold) are the normal cases, where the host and device each expect the same quantity and direction of data transfer in the data-transport phase. The other cases are situations where the host and device have differing expectations.

1. **The host expects no data-transport phase.**
   The device expects no data-transport phase.

2. The host expects no data-transport phase.
   The device expects to send data.

3. The host expects no data-transport phase.
   The device expects to receive data.

4. The host expects to receive data.
   The device expects no data-transport phase.

5. The host expects to receive data.
   The device expects to send less data than the host intends to receive.

6. **The host expects to receive data.**
   The device expects to send the exact amount of data the host
   intends to receive.

7. The host expects to receive data.
   The device intends to send more data than the host expects to receive.

8. The host expects to receive data.
    The device expects to receive data.

9. The host expects to send data.
    The device expects no data-transport phase.

10. The host expects to send data.
    The device expects to send data.

11. The host expects to send data.
    The device expects to receive less data than the host intends to send.

12. The host expects to send data.
    The device expects to receive the exact amount of data the host
    intends to send.

13. The host expects to send data.
    The device expects to receive more data than the host intends to send.

The following sections summarize the device's behavior in each of the 13 cases.

The Host Expects No Data Transfer

When dCBWDataTransferLength is zero, the host expects the command to have no data-transport phase.

In the most common situation (case 1), the device agrees that there is no data-transport phase. The device sets bCSWStatus to 00h or 01h and sets dCSWDataResidue to zero.

If the device expects to send (case 2) or receive (case 3) data in the data-transport phase when the host expects no data, the devices sets bCSW-Status to 02h and may stall the bulk IN endpoint. On receiving bCSWSta-tus = 02h, the host ignores dCSWDataResidue and performs a reset recovery or resets the device's port.

The Host Expects to Receive Data

When dCBWDataTransferLength is greater than zero and the Direction bit in bmCBWFlags = 1, the host expects to receive data in the data-transport phase.

In the most common situation (case 6), the device intends to send dCBW-DataTransferLength bytes. The device sets bCSWStatus to 00h or 01h and sets dCSWDataResidue to zero.

If the device expects to send no data (case 4) or less than dCBWDataTransferLength bytes (case 5), the device may pad the data up to the requested length, or the device may send no data or less data. A device that sends less than the requested amount of data must stall the bulk IN endpoint. In either case, the device sets bCSWStatus to 00h or 01h and sets dCSWDataResidue to the difference between dCBWDataTransferLength and the amount of data sent, excluding any pad bytes.

If the device expects to send more than dCBWDataTransferLength bytes (case 7) or expects to receive data from the host (case 8), the device may send up to dCBWDataTransferLength bytes. On sending less than dCBWDataTransferLength bytes, the device must stall the bulk IN endpoint and set bCSWStatus to 02h. On sending dCBWDataTransferLength bytes, the device may stall the bulk IN endpoint and must set bCSWStatus to 02h. On receiving bCSWStatus = 02h, the host ignores dCSWDataResidue and performs a reset recovery or resets the device's port.

The Host Expects to Send Data

When dCBWDataTransferLength is greater than zero and the Direction bit in bmCBWFlags = 0, the host expects to send data in the data-transport phase.

In the most common situation (case 12), the device expects and receives dCBWDataTransferLength bytes. The device sets bCSWStatus to 00h or 01h and sets dCSWDataResidue to zero.

If the device expects to receive less than dCBWDataTransferLength bytes (case 11) or no data (case 9), the device may accept dCBWDataTransferLength bytes (recommended) or the device may end the transfer early by stalling the bulk OUT endpoint. In either case, the device sets bCSWStatus to 00h or 01h and sets dCSWDataResidue to the difference between dCBWDataTransferLength and the amount of data processed. The amount of data processed by the device can be less than or equal to the amount of data received and accepted by the device. Stalling the bulk OUT endpoint in these cases can cause problems under Windows, so most devices accept dCBWDataTransferLength bytes and set dCSWDataResidue to the appropriate value.

If the device expects to receive more than dCBWDataTransferLength bytes (case 13) or expects to send data to the host (case 10), the device may accept up to dCBWDataTransferLength bytes or may end the transfer early by stalling the bulk OUT endpoint. In either case, the device sets bCSWStatus to 02h. If bCSWStatus = 02h, the device may stall the bulk IN endpoint as well. On receiving bCSWStatus = 02h, the host ignores dCSWDataResidue and performs a reset recovery or resets the device's port.

PC Support

Major operating systems include drivers to support communications with mass-storage devices

Windows

Windows 2000 and later include a driver that supports USB devices that use the bulk-only transport protocol and CBI. When a device's descriptors identify the device as mass-storage class with a supported bInterfaceSubClass, the operating system loads the USB storage port driver (usbstor.sys). This driver manages communications between the lower-level USB drivers and Windows' storage-class drivers. The operating system assigns a drive letter to the device's volume or volumes, which appear in My Computer. Mass-storage devices don't need a vendor-specific INF file to specify a driver. The Windows file usbstor.inf causes Windows to load the mass-storage drivers for any mass-storage device in a supported bInterfaceSubClass.

The mass-storage driver in Windows XP supports bInterfaceSubClass codes 02h, 05h, and 06h. Support for drives with multiple LUNs was added in Windows 2000 SP3.

Users with administrator access rights can run applications that send SCSI commands to devices using the IOCTL_SCSI_PASS_THROUGH function. To open a device for sending SCSI pass-through requests, the application must call CreateFile with the dwDesiredAccess parameter requesting both GENERIC_READ and GENERIC_WRITE access.

One point of confusion relating to the mass-storage support under Windows is Windows' support for Autoplay (previously called Autorun). Autoplay enables the operating system to run a program, play a movie, or perform other actions when a disk or other removable media is inserted. To support Autoplay, a USB flash drive must contain a startup application and an autorun.inf file that identifies the application. For operating systems previous to Windows XP SP2, the drive must report that it has non-removable media in the response to a SCSI INQUIRY command. Chapter 6 has more about the INQUIRY command.

Flash drives that incorporate U3 smart drive technology can hold a self-contained application that runs on a Windows PC without having to install the application on a hard drive, make registry changes, or reserve other system resources. Running an application from a U3 drive copies temporary files to the host computer,. The temporary files run the application and disappear when the application closes. U3 is an open standard developed by SanDisk and M-Systems. More information and development kits are at www.u3.com. A similar technology is available in the Ceedo portable operating system from Ceedo Technologies.

Linux

Linux has two drivers that support communications with USB mass-storage devices. The usb-storage driver in Linux/drivers/usb/storage supports a wide range of devices and has fast performance. The ub driver in Linux/drivers/block/ub.c focuses on reliable operation but is slower and doesn't support as many devices. The ub driver supports only the bulk-only transport protocol and PDT = 00h, doesn't try to accommodate non-compliant devices, uses its own SCSI stack, and waits for each USB request block (URB) to complete before submitting the next one.

4

Accessing Flash Memory Cards

For many embedded systems, a good choice for storage is a a MultiMediaCard accessed via SPI. This chapter shows what's involved in implementing SPI communications with MultiMediaCards. SD-Card hosts can use the same interface and firmware.

The Interface

The Serial Peripheral Interface (SPI) originated at Motorola (now Freescale Semiconductor). Many microcontrollers from Motorola/Freescale and others have hardware support for SPI. In systems without hardware support, the communications can be controlled entirely in firmware.

Every SPI communication is between a host, or master, and a MultiMediaCard or other slave device. The host controls the interface's clock and chip-select lines.

Signals and Power

SPI has no official specification document other than the data sheets for the components that support the interface. As a result, different implementations use different names for the signals (Table 4-1). Note that the MultiMediaCard signal names are from the perspective of the MultiMediaCard card: DataIn is an input on the card, while DataOut is an output on the card.

Data and Clock Lines

Table 4-2 shows the pin functions for a MultiMediaCard in SPI mode.

SCLK (also called SCK) is the card's clock input. The clock provides transitions that determine when to write and read data on the data lines. The SPI host generates the clock pulses.

DataIn (also called MOSI, or Master Out Slave In, or SDI) is the card's data input. The host uses the DataIn line to send commands and to send data to the storage media.

DataOut (also called MISO, or Master In, Slave Out, or SDO) is the card's data output. The card uses the DataOut line to send responses to commands, other status information, and data requested from the storage media.

CS (also called /SS, or Slave Select) is the device's chip-select input. The host must control a unique chip-select output for each card on the bus. The host selects a card by bringing the card's CS input low.

Power

Each card also has a power-supply pin (VDD) and two ground pins (VSS and VSS2). A high-voltage MultiMediaCard requires a supply voltage of 3.3V. A low-voltage MultiMediaCard can be powered at either 3.3V or 1.8V.

Example Circuit

An SPI host can be a microcontroller with hardware SPI support or any generic microcontroller or other intelligent hardware with available port pins and the ability to implement communications entirely in firmware.

Table 4-1: Because there is no signal specification document for SPI, the signal names used by different sources vary.

MultiMediaCard Signal Name	Freescale Signal Name	Microchip Signal Name	Direction	Function
SCLK	SCK		host to card	clock
DataIn	MOSI	SDI	host to card	data
DataOut	MISO	SDO	card to host	data
CS	/SS		host to card	chip select

Microchip's PIC18F4550 microcontroller has an SPI port and can serve as a MultiMediaCard host. Chapter 2 discussed using this chip for USB mass-storage communications.

Figure 4-1 shows connections between a PIC18F4550 and a MultiMediaCard/SD-Card connector. The circuit is similar to the circuits on Microchip's PICtail® board for SD Cards and MultiMediaCard cards. The PICtail board attaches to a header on Microchip's PICDEM® Full Speed USB demonstration board. A spring-loaded latch holds the card in place. The microcontroller is powered at +5V to enable clocking the chip faster than 16 Mhz (up to 48 Mhz). The MultiMediaCard operates at +3.3V. Pull-up resistors and buffers perform the voltage translations.

On the MultiMediaCard connector, pins 1–7 connect to the MultiMediaCard's pins. The CD pin connects to a card-detect switch, and the WP pin connects to a write-protect switch.

Port outputs on the microcontroller drive 5V-tolerant inputs of buffers powered at +3.3V. The buffer's outputs in turn drive the CD, DataIn, and SCLK inputs on the MultiMediaCard. Pull-up resistors bring the logic-high buffer outputs close to +3.3V.

The Multimedia card's DataOut output drives an input of a buffer powered at +5V. The buffer has TTL-compatible input voltages. When DataOut is high, a pull-up resistor brings the voltage near 3.3V, which is well above the buffer's 2V minimum logic-high input requirement. The buffer's 5V-logic output drives input port pins on the microcontroller. In a similar way, the MultiMediaCard connector's CD and WP pins drive buffer inputs, and the corresponding buffer outputs connect to input port pins on the microcontroller.

Table 4-2: Pin functions for a MultiMediaCard in SPI mode.

Pin Number	Name	Description
1	CS	Chip Select input, active low
2	DataIn	Data input
3	VSS1	Power supply ground
4	VDD	Power supply voltage
5	SCLK	Clock input
6	VSS2	Power supply ground
7	DataOut	Data output

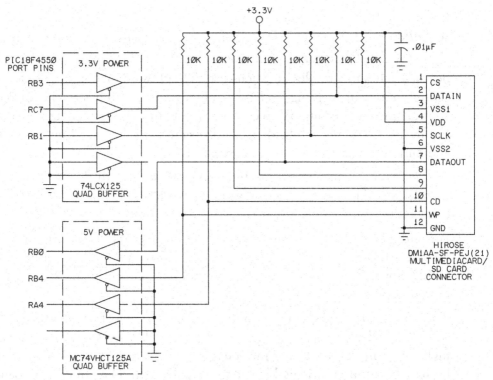

Figure 4-1: The pins on the MultiMediaCard/SD-Card connector connect to port pins on the PIC18F4550.

If the PIC18F4550 or another MultiMediaCard host is powered at 3.3V, the level-translation circuits are unneeded and the host can interface directly to the MultiMediaCard, but the maximum clock frequency (at Fosc) is 16 Mhz.

Host Programming

To communicate with a MultiMediaCard, the host uses the MultiMediaCard protocol to send commands, receive responses, and send and receive additional data as required by commands. On a lower level, the commands, responses, and data each consist of one or more bytes. This chapter explains how the individual bytes travel on the SPI bus. Chapter 5 describes the protocol for sending MultiMediaCard commands.

Configuring

SPI is a synchronous bus, where the host provides a clock signal that determines when the host and MultiMediaCard read and write data. The interface provides options for configuring the clock polarity and the phase, or timing, relationship between the clock and data bits. The clock polarity determines whether the clock is high or low when idle. The clock phase determines whether input data is valid on the rising or falling clock edge. For MultimediaCards, the clock line must be high when idle and data is valid on the rising clock edge.

SPI hosts are generally more flexible than SPI devices. Microcontrollers with SPI support typically provide configuration registers for selecting a clock polarity and phase to match a device's requirements.

Figure 4-2 and Table 4-3 show the timing requirements for MultiMediaCards. The cards latch data received on the DataIn line on SCLK's rising edge. The data must be valid 3 nanoseconds before and after the rising edge. When sending data on DataOut, the data is valid at least 5 nanoseconds before and after SCLK's rising edge. In practice, MultiMediaCards typically latch output data on SCLK's falling edge, so the data is valid for a longer period.

Data on the bus travels most significant bit first. Transmitting a byte requires eight clock cycles. The host must generate clock cycles when trans-

Table 4-3: Timing requirements for MultiMediaCards on a bus with 10 or fewer cards.

Parameter	Symbol	Minimum (nsec.)	Maximum (nsec.)
Clock low time	TWL	10	–
Clock high time	TWH	10	–
Clock rise time	TTLH	–	10
Clock fall time	TTHL	–	10
Input set-up time	TISU	3	–
Input hold time	TIH	3	–
Output set-up time	TOSU	5	–
Output hold time	TOH	5	–

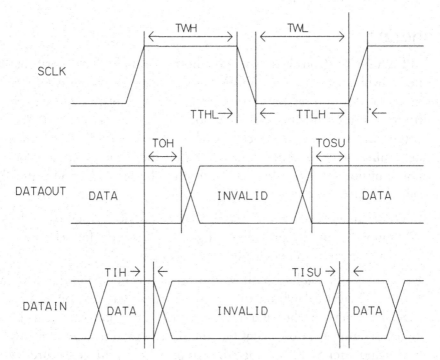

Figure 4-2: A MultiMediaCard data reads data on SCLK's rising edge and writes data that the MultiMediaCard host can read on SCLK's rising edge.

mitting bytes on DataIn, when receiving bytes on DataOut, and at other times as required by the MultiMediaCard specification.

Hardware Ports

The PIC18F4550 and other microcontrollers with hardware support for SPI hosts contain these components:

- Three port pins to provide the SCLK output, DataOut input, and DataIn output.
- One or more generic port pins to provide a firmware-controlled CS output for each device. If a host has many devices to control, a host can use an external decoder chip such as a 74HC138 to control the CS lines.
- One or more buffers to hold data waiting to transmit and received data.
- A clock source to drive the SCLK output.
- A shift register to clock data out on the DataIn line and clock data in on the DataOut line.
- Configuration registers to enable setting clock polarity and phase, setting the clock's frequency, and enabling the SPI port.

Many microcontrollers with SPI support also enable configuring the microcontroller as either a host (master) or device (slave). For MultiMediaCard communications, the microcontroller must be a host.

When the PIC18F4550's SPI port has been configured as a host, device firmware can send and receive data by bringing CS low and writing to the SPI buffer. Writing to the buffer causes SCLK to generate 8 clock cycles, latching a bit from the buffer onto DataIn on each cycle.

Each write operation also reads a byte from the DataOut line into the buffer. If there is no data to receive, firmware can ignore the received byte. To read a byte when there is no data to send, firmware can write a byte that holds the line in the idle state (FFh for MultiMediaCard communications). When eight bits have been transferred, the port hardware copies the byte read on DataOut from the shift register to the buffer, where firmware can access the value.

Firmware-controlled Ports

A microcontroller that doesn't have hardware SPI support can control all of the communications in firmware. In addition to toggling CS to select and deselect a card, the firmware must bring SCLK high and low as needed, write each bit to transmit at the appropriate time on DataIn, and read each received bit at the appropriate time on DataOut.

The MultiMediaCard SPI bus has no minimum required clock frequency or duty cycle except that the clock's high and low pulses must be at least 10 nanoseconds wide. Firmware can toggle SCLK as needed without having to worry about maintaining a frequency or duty cycle. The maximum SCLK frequency is 20 Mhz, and the maximum rise and fall times are 10 nanoseconds. (For buses with more than 10 MultiMediaCards, the maximum SCLK frequency is 5 Mhz and the maximum rise and fall times are 50 nanoseconds.)

Transferring Data

The code excerpts that follow show how the PIC18F4550's SPI port sends and receives data. Some of the information is specific to the chip, but other microcontrollers with SPI ports use similar architectures to implement SPI ports.

Default States

The host brings a card's CS line low to select the card. In MultiMediaCard communications, when CS is low and the DataIn output isn't transmitting, the host must hold DataIn high. When CS is low while the DataOut output isn't transmitting and the card isn't busy, the card holds DataOut high. When the clock is idle, the host must hold SCLK high. On completing a command and any responses to it, the host brings the card's CS line high to deselect the card.

SPI on the PIC18F4550

The PIC18F4550 has a Master Synchronous Serial Port (MSSP) module that can be configured as an SPI or I²C port. The MSSP manages the sending and receiving of data on an SPI or I²C bus. (I²C is another type of synchronous serial port used by serial EEPROMs and other peripheral chips.) When using SPI, the port can function as a host or device. Table 4-4 shows the port pins used by the chip's SPI port.

Registers

The PIC18F4550 has six registers that store information related to SPI communications.

The MSSP Status Register (SSPSTAT) contains status and control information relating to the port. Table 4-5 shows the functions of the SSPSTAT bits.

MSSP Control Register 1 (SSPCON1) contains additional status and control information relating to the port. Table 4-6 shows the functions of the SSPCON1 bits.

The Serial Receive/Transmit Buffer Register (SSPBUF) holds a received byte or a byte waiting to transmit.

The MSSP Shift Register (SSPSR) holds the bits in a byte being received or a byte that is transmitting. Firmware can't access the SSPSR.

In Peripheral Interrupt Enable Register 1 (PIE1), bit 3 is the master SPI interrupt enable bit. When the bit equals 1, the interrupt is enabled.

In Peripheral Interrupt Request (Flag) Register 1 (PIR1), bit 3 is the master SPI interrupt flag bit. When this bit equals zero, the SPI port is waiting to transmit or receive. When the bit equals 1, a transmit or receive operation is complete. Firmware that uses this interrupt should clear the bit in the interrupt-service routine that services the interrupt.

Microchip's MPLAB C18 C compiler provides a processor definition module for the PIC18F4550 (p18f4550.asm). The module defines names for the registers. These declarations from the compiler file p18F4550.h enable accessing SSPBUF and the bits in SSPCON1 and SSPSTAT:

```
extern volatile near unsigned char    SSPBUF;
extern volatile near unsigned char    SSPCON1;
extern volatile near unsigned char    SSPSTAT;
```

Table 4-4: The PIC18F4550's built-in SPI port uses three port pins (plus additional pins as needed for CS outputs).

Port	Bit	Signal on PIC18F4550	Connection to MultiMediaCard
PORTC	7	SDO	DataIn
PORTB	0	SDI	DataOut
PORTB	1	SCK	SCLK

```
extern volatile near struct {
  unsigned SSPM0:1;
  unsigned SSPM1:1;
  unsigned SSPM2:1;
  unsigned SSPM3:1;
  unsigned CKP:1;
  unsigned SSPEN:1;
  unsigned SSPOV:1;
  unsigned WCOL:1;
} SSPCON1bits;

extern volatile near struct {
  unsigned BF:1;
  unsigned UA:1;
  unsigned R_W:1;
  unsigned S:1;
  unsigned P:1;
  unsigned D_A:1;
  unsigned CKE:1;
  unsigned SMP:1;
} SSPSTATbits;
```

Configuring the Port

Before using the SPI port, firmware must also configure the port bits as inputs or outputs as appropriate and must configure the SPI port in the registers. The Microchip C18 compiler libraries include an OpenSPI function that performs these tasks. The function accepts three parameters: sync_mode sets the mode (bits 3..0 in SSPCON1), bus_mode sets the transmit mode (CKE) in SSPSTAT and clock polarity (CKP) in SSPCON1, and smp_phase sets the receive mode (SMP) in SSPSTAT.

Table 4-5: The SSPSTAT register contains configuration and status information for the SPI port.

Bit	Name	Description
0	BF	Receive buffer full. 1 = SSPBUF is full. 0 = SSPBUF is empty.
1..5	–	Unused in SPI mode.
6	CKE	Clock select. 1 = transmit occurs on the transition from active to idle clock state. 0 = transmit occurs on the transition from idle to active clock state.
7	SMP	Master mode: 1 = input data is sampled at the end of the data output time. 0 = input data is sampled in the middle of the data output time. Slave mode: 0

This statement opens the SPI port for MultiMediaCard communications:

```
OpenSPI(SPI_FOSC_64, MODE_11, SMPMID);
```

The compiler file spi.h defines the parameters passed to the function. SPI_FOSC_64 sets the sync_mode parameter to configure the port as an SPI master with the clock equal to Fosc/64. Fosc is the frequency of the microcontroller's OSC1/CLKI input. The clock speed must be less than or equal to 400 kHz until the MultiMediaCard has initialized and the host has read the card's CSD register. A setting of Fosc/64 meets this requirement if Fosc is 25 Mhz or less.

MODE_11 sets the bus_mode parameter with CKE = 0 and CKP = 1, so the clock's idle state is high and bits transmit on high-to-low clock transitions.

SMPMID sets the smp_phase parameter with SMP = 0 to cause the chip to sample DataOut in the middle of the clock cycle (on low-to-high clock transitions).

Writing a Byte

After configuring and enabling the port, device firmware can send a byte by writing the value to SSPBUF. The shift register clocks the bits out on the SDO/DataIn line without further intervention by firmware. When the byte has been written, the BF bit in SSPSTAT equals zero. Any attempt to write to SSPBUF while the register is sending data results in a collision. On a col-

Table 4-6: The SSPCON1 register contains configuration and status information for the SPI port.

Bit	Name	Description
3..0	SSPM3.. SSPM0	Synchronous serial port mode select: 0101: slave, clock = SCK input, /SS disabled 0100: slave, clock = SCK input, /SS enabled 0011: master, clock = (TMR2 output) / 2 0010: master, clock = FOSC / 64 0001: master, clock = FOSC / 16 0000: master, clock = FOSC / 4
4	CKP	Clock polarity: 1 = clock idle state is high; 0 = clock idle state is low.
5	SSPEN	Synchronous serial port enable. 1= enabled; 0 = disabled.
6	SSPOV	Receive overflow. Slave mode: 1 = overflow. 0 = no overflow. Master mode: 0.
7	WCOL	Write collision detect. 1 = SSPBUF was written to while transmitting. 0 = no collision.

lision, the byte being sent continues to transmit, but the attempted new write operation fails and the WCOL bit in SSPCON1 is set to 1. After writing a byte, device firmware should check WCOL to verify that the write was successful and if not, clear the bit and try again.

Microchip's C18 compiler libraries include a WriteSPI function, which writes a byte to the SPI bus. The function accepts a byte to write (data_out), writes the byte to SSPBUF, and checks WCOL. If there was no collision, the function waits for the byte to transmit. A return value of zero means the write was successful.

```
unsigned char WriteSPI( unsigned char data_out )
{
    // Write the passed byte to the SPI buffer.

    SSPBUF = data_out;

    if ( SSPCON1 & 0x80 )

    // WCOL = 1, so there was a write collision.

        return ( -1 );
```

```
    else
    {
      // No collision occurred.
      // When the BF bit in SSPSTAT = 1, the transmit operation is complete.

      while (!SSPSTATbits.BF);
    }
    // Success.

    return ( 0 );
}
```

Reading a Byte

When receiving a byte, the shift register stores bits received on SDI/DataOut. When a byte has been received, the port hardware copies the byte to SSPBUF. The BF bit SSPSTAT is set to 1 and the SPI interrupt flag in PIR1 is set to 1 to indicate that a byte has arrived. Firmware can detect received data with the SPI interrupt or by polling BF. After the hardware copies a received byte to SSPBUF, the shift register can begin receiving another byte. Reading a byte from SSPBUF clears the BF bit. Firmware must clear the interrupt flag.

Microchip's C18 compiler libraries include a ReadSPI function, which reads a byte from the SPI bus. However, the function isn't usable for MultiMediaCard communications because ReadSPI holds DataIn low while reading a byte, and MultiMediaCards require DataIn to be high. The ReadMedia function reads a byte while holding DataIn high:

```
byte ReadMedia(void)
{
    // Write FFh to the SPI buffer to hold the MultiMediaCard's DataIn line high
    // while reading a byte.

    SSPBUF = 0xFF;

    // When the BF bit in SSPSTAT = 1, SSPBUF contains a byte read from the bus.

    while (!SSPSTATbits.BF);

    return(SSPBUF);
}
```

5

MultiMediaCard Protocol

SPI provides a protocol for sending and receiving bytes, but the interface assumes nothing about the contents of the bytes being transferred. The MultiMediaCard specification defines commands to use in SPI communications. The host uses the commands to retrieve information about a card and its status, to send control information to a card, and to read and write data in the card's storage media. This chapter introduces the MultiMediaCard commands and shows how to implement the commands in firmware. A host can use the same commands and firmware to access SD Cards.

Command and Response Formats

Each MultiMediaCard command has a defined format for the command, a response, and any additional data the command sends or requests. On the SPI bus, the DataIn line carries commands and data sent by the host, and the DataOut line carries responses and data sent by the MultiMediaCard.

The information that travels on the bus includes commands, command responses, and tokens that contain data and error indications.

Commands

Each MultiMediaCard command is 48 bits. Table 5-1 shows the format of the commands.

The command index is a number that identifies the command. Each command also has a name consisting of "CMD" followed by the index value (CMD0, CMD1, and so on) and a descriptive abbreviation. For example, the descriptive abbreviation for CMD17 is READ_SINGLE_BLOCK.

The command argument is a 32-bit value that can provide supplementary information required to carry out a command. For example, the argument for READ_SINGLE_BLOCK is the beginning address of the block to read. For commands that don't require arguments, the host sends stuff bits of zero.

The CRC value is seven bits that the MultiMediaCard controller can use to verify that a command arrived without error.

The transmission bit is set to 1. The start bit and end bit mark the beginning and end of the command.

Response Types

On receiving a command and argument, a MultiMediaCard returns a response. The MultiMediaCard specification defines six response types with each command having a designated response type. Most commands use response type R1 or R1b. A few use R2 or R3. Only I/O cards use types R4 and R5.

These are the response types a mass-storage device uses on an SPI bus.

R1

Response type R1 is a single byte. A value of 00h means that the command completed without error. On error, one or more of the bits are set:

Bit 0: The card is in the idle state and is initializing.

Bit 1: An erase sequence was cleared before executing the command because an out-of-erase-sequence command was received.

Table 5-1: MultiMediaCard commands have 48 bits.

Bit(s)	Field Width (bits)	Value	Description
0	1	End bit	Always 1
1..7	7	CRC	Error-detect value
8..39	32	Command argument	Additional information or stuff bits (zeros)
40..45	6	Command index	Identifies the command
46	1	Transmission bit	Always 1 for commands
47	1	Start bit	Always zero

Bit 2: An illegal or unsupported command code was received.

Bit 3: CRC error.

Bit 4: An error occurred in the sequence of erase commands.

Bit 5: The device received an address that doesn't match the expected block length.

Bit 6: The command's argument was out of range.

Bit 7: Always zero.

The RESPONSE_1 union defines a byte or eight bits that can hold an R1 response:

```
typedef union
{
   byte _byte;
   struct
   {
      unsigned IN_IDLE_STATE:1;
      unsigned ERASE_RESET:1;
      unsigned ILLEGAL_CMD:1;
      unsigned CRC_ERR:1;
      unsigned ERASE_SEQ_ERR:1;
      unsigned ADDRESS_ERR:1;
      unsigned PARAM_ERR:1;
      unsigned B7:1;
   };
} RESPONSE_1;
```

R1b

Response type R1b is identical to the R1 response format except the response byte is followed by one or more bytes that indicate busy status. The card returns zeroes continuously while busy and returns a non-zero byte when ready to receive another command. In other words, DataOut remains low to indicate busy and goes high when no longer busy.

R2

In SPI mode, response type R2 is used only for the SEND_STATUS command. The response is two bytes. The first byte is identical to the R1 format. The second byte contains eight status bits. On error, one or more of the bits are set:

Bit 0: The user has locked the card.

Bit 1: The host has attempted to erase a write-protected block or a sequence or password error occurred during a card lock/unlock operation.

Bit 2: General or unknown error.

Bit 3: Internal card-controller error.

Bit 4: A card's internal error-correction code was applied but failed to correct the data.

Bit 5: The command tried to write to a write-protected block.

Bit 6: The selection of erase groups was invalid.

Bit 7: The command argument was out of range, or the command is attempting to change the ROM section, or the command is attempting to reverse the copy bit or permanent write-protect bit in the CSD register.

The RESPONSE_2 union defines a word, bytes, or bits that can hold an R2 response:

```
typedef union
{
  word _word;
  struct
  {
    byte     _byte0;
    byte     _byte1;
  };
  struct
  {
    unsigned IN_IDLE_STATE:1;
    unsigned ERASE_RESET:1;
    unsigned ILLEGAL_CMD:1;
    unsigned CRC_ERR:1;
    unsigned ERASE_SEQ_ERR:1;
    unsigned ADDRESS_ERR:1;
    unsigned PARAM_ERR:1;
    unsigned B7:1;
    unsigned CARD_IS_LOCKED:1;
    unsigned WP_ERASE_SKIP_LK_FAIL:1;
    unsigned ERROR:1;
    unsigned CC_ERROR:1;
    unsigned CARD_ECC_FAIL:1;
    unsigned WP_VIOLATION:1;
    unsigned ERASE_PARAM:1;
    unsigned OUTRANGE_CSD_OVERWRITE:1;
  };
} RESPONSE_2;
```

R3

Response type R3 is five bytes. In SPI mode, the only command that uses this response type is READ_OCR, which requests the contents of the operation conditions register. The first byte is identical to the R1 format. The next four bytes are the contents of the register.

Token Formats

Commands that send or request blocks of data use structures called tokens to hold the data and MultiMediaCard responses. There are three types of tokens: data, data_response, and data_error.

Data

Data blocks being sent to or from a MultiMediaCard's storage media travel in data tokens. In SPI mode, each data token consists of a Start Block token (1 byte) followed by the data block (1 or more bytes) and a CRC value (2 bytes). Table 5-2 shows the values for Start Block tokens and the Stop Tran token, which a host can send to end a command that is writing multiple blocks. Note that FEh is the Start Block token for all operations except multiple block writes.

Data_response

After receiving a data token, the MultiMediaCard returns a 1-byte data_response token. These are the values of the bits in the data_response token:

Bit 0: 1.
Bits 3..1: Status
      010 = Data accepted
      101 = CRC error
      110 = Write error
Bit 4: 0.
Bits 5..7: Don't care.

To determines if the data was accepted, firmware can logically AND the data_response byte with 0Fh. If the result is 05h, the data was accepted.

Table 5-2: A Start Block data token precedes a block of data being sent to or from the storage media. A Stop Tran data token requests to end a multiple-block write.

Token Type	Transaction Type	Value (hex)
Start Block	Single block read	FE
	Multiple block read	FE
	Single block write	FE
	Multiple block write	FC
Stop Tran	Multiple block write (end)	FD

Data_error

When unable to return a requested data token, a MultiMediaCard returns a data-error token. These are the values of the bits in the data_error token:

Bit 0: General or unknown error.

Bit 1: Internal card controller error.

Bit 2: A card's internal error-correction code was applied but failed to correct the data.

Bit 3: The command's argument was out of range.

Bit 4: The user has locked the card.

Bits 5..7: Zero.

The Commands

A MultiMediaCard host with an SPI interface can use most of the commands defined in the MultiMediaCard specification.

Classes

The specification defines ten classes of commands (Table 5-3). A single command can be in multiple classes. For example, both the block-read and block-write classes include the SET_BLOCK_LEN command, which sets the length of a data block. SPI mode doesn't support commands in the stream-read and stream-write classes, where transmitted data isn't in blocks of a defined size, or commands in the I/O-mode class, which supports

Table 5-3: The MultiMediaCard protocol includes ten classes of commands.

Class Number	Class Name	SPI Support?
0	basic	yes
1	stream read	no
2	block read	yes
3	stream write	no
4	block write	yes
5	erase	yes
6	write protection	yes
7	lock card	yes
8	application specific	yes
9	I/O mode	no

non-storage functions. SPI mode supports everything a mass-storage device requires, however.

All MultiMediaCards support all of the commands in the basic class. These commands carry out basic status and control functions. MultiMediaCards using SPI also support commands in the block-read, block-write, erase, write-protection, lock-card, and application-specific classes.

A host needs to support only the commands required to carry out its purpose. Some commands are required to initialize the card. USB mass-storage communications read and write blocks of data, so a MultiMediaCard host in a USB mass-storage device uses block-read and block-write commands to access the MultiMediaCard's storage media.

The descriptions that follow apply to a MultiMediaCard host using the SPI bus. A host using the MultiMediaCard bus can accomplish the same things, but the command and response formats and protocols vary as described in the MultiMediaCard specification.

Commands Used by Mass-storage Devices

Table 5-4 shows basic-class commands that flash-memory MultiMediaCard hosts typically support in USB mass-storage devices.

Table 5-5 shows commands used in reading and writing blocks of data. The commands that read or write data require a starting address to read or write.

Table 5-4: Mandatory basic-class commands for a MultiMediaCard.

Index	Abbreviation	Argument	Response	Description
CMD0	GO_IDLE_STATE	none	R1	Reset the card to the idle state.
CMD1	SEND_OP_COND	none	R1	Activate the card's initialization process.
CMD9	SEND_CSD	none	R1	Request the contents of the CSD register. The register's contents follow the response token.
CMD10	SEND_CID	none	R1	Request the contents of the CID register. The register's contents follow the response token.
CMD13	SEND_STATUS	none	R2	Request status information
CMD58	READ_OCR	none	R3	Read the operation conditions register. The register's contents are in the response token.
CMD59	CRC_ON_OFF	31..1: stuff bits; 0: CRC option	R1	Bit 0 = 1: use CRC. Bit 0 = 0: ignore CRC.

This value is the offset of the byte within the media, with the bytes numbered sequentially from zero. To convert a logical block address (LBA) to a byte address, multiply the LBA by the media's block, or sector, size (typically 512).

Registers

Some commands read or write to registers in the MultiMediaCard. Table 5-6 shows the three MultiMediaCard registers used in SPI communications. The MultiMediaCard bus supports two additional registers for storing a card address and providing data to improve bus performance. These registers are unneeded and unavailable in SPI mode.

Sending Commands

Most MultiMediaCard commands are in one of three categories: commands that transmit no data blocks to or from the storage media, commands where the MultiMediaCard host sends data to the storage media, and commands where the MultiMediaCard host receives data from the storage media. For

Table 5-5: Block read and write commands used by mass-storage devices.

Index	Abbreviation	Argument	Response	Description
CMD12	STOP_TRANSMISSION	00000000h	R1b	Stop multiple block read.
CMD15	SET_BLOCK_LEN (not supported in SPI mode)	Block length	R1	Set the block size in bytes for block read and block write.
CMD17	READ_SINGLE_BLOCK	Starting address to read	R1	Read a block of data.
CMD18	READ_MULTIPLE_BLOCK	Starting address to read	R1	Read multiple blocks of data.
CMD23	SET_BLOCK_COUNT (not supported in SPI mode)	31..16: 0000h; 15..0: number of blocks	R1	Set the number of blocks to transfer in a multiple-block read or write command.
CMD24	WRITE_SINGLE_BLOCK	Starting address to write to	R1	Write a block of data.
CMD25	WRITE_MULTIPLE_BLOCK	Starting address to write to	R1	Write multiple blocks of data.

each command, the host sends a command block and the device sends a response. For some commands, the device follows the response with one or more data tokens. For other commands, the host follows the response with one or more data tokens, and the device sends a response after receiving each data token.

Timing Considerations

Communications on the SPI bus must meet the timing and clocking requirements in the MultiMediaCard specification. The host must generate clock cycles when sending a command or data, when receiving a response or data token from a card, and when waiting for a response or data token from a card. The host also must generate 8 clock cycles after all of a command's communications are complete.

When generating clock cycles and not transmitting a command or data, the host must hold DataIn high. A PIC18F4550 host can send eight clock

Table 5-6: MultiMediaCards have five configuration and status registers. Two of the registers are unused in SPI mode.

Abbrevia-tion	Name	Size (bytes)	Purpose
OCR	Operation Conditions Register	4	Bits 30..0 specify allowed power-supply voltages. Bit 31 is a status bit that equals 1 when the power-up procedure has completed.
CID	Card Identification	16	Contains manufacturer and card identification numbers, product name, revision, serial number, and manufacturing date.
CSD	Card Specific Data	16	Provides card-specific information. Includes data relating to timing, data formats, electrical specifications, write protection, and error detecting.

cycles while holding DataIn high by writing FFh to the SPI buffer (SSP-BUF). This macro generates eight clock cycles while holding DataIn high by calling the WriteSPI library function:

```
#define mSend8ClkCycles()     WriteSPI(0xFF);
```

Figure 5-1 shows the timing for block-read and block-write commands for MultiMediaCards on an SPI bus. The following descriptions refer to the signals and times in the diagram.

A host can send a command immediately on bringing CS low to select the card (NCS).

After receiving a command, a card delays between 8 and 64 clock cycles before sending a response (NCR).

In a read operation, after sending a response, a card delays between 8 clock cycles and a card-specific access time before sending the requested data token (NAC). For commands where the card sends multiple data tokens, the same wait time applies for the time between data tokens. The card-specific time is determined by values in the CSD register and the SCLK frequency. Firmware that is waiting for a response can time out after any value equal to or greater than the card-specific time.

Commands that request the contents of the CSD and CID registers are similar in structure to commands that read from the storage media. A difference is that the card delays just zero to eight cycles between the response token and the register data.

In a write operation, after sending a command and receiving a response, the host generates at least 8 clock cycles before sending a data token (NWR). There is no maximum number of clock cycles before the data token. The card's response follows the data token immediately. The host then waits for the DataOut line to return high to indicate that the card has programmed

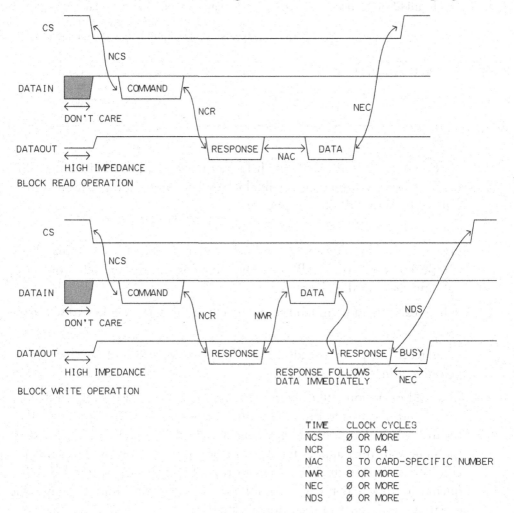

Figure 5-1: Timing for block-read and block-write commands.

the received data into the storage media. There is no specified maximum time to wait for DataOut to return high.

After a command completes, the host generates at least 8 clock cycles before sending a new command. There is no maximum number of clock cycles before the next command. The host can bring CS high on the last clock transition of the last byte that is part of the command's communications (before the final 8 clock cycles) or any time after this (NEC and NDS). In a block-write operation, the host can bring CS high while the card is busy programming, and bring CS low again later to verify that DataOut is high, indicating that the write operation completed.

Commands with No Data Transfer

On an SPI bus, a command with no data transfer has these steps:

1. The host brings CS low.

2. The host sends the 48-bit command and continues to generate clock cycles.

3. After receiving the command followed by 8 to 64 clock cycles, the card sends the command's response.

4. The host can bring CS high any time after receiving the response.

5. The host generates 8 clock cycles to complete the command.

Commands that Read Data from the Storage Media

On an SPI bus, a command that requests a single data block from the storage media has these steps:

1. The host brings CS low.

2. The host sends the 48-bit command and continues to generate clock cycles.

3. After receiving the command followed by 8 to 64 clock cycles, the card sends the command's response.

4. The host continues to generate clock cycles.

5. After between 8 clock cycles and the card-specific access time, the card sends the requested data block. On error, the card sends a data_error token instead of a data token.

6. The host can bring CS high at any time after receiving the data block or a data_error token.

7. The host generates 8 clock cycles to complete the command.

In a command that reads multiple blocks, step 5 repeats as many times as needed to transfer the data blocks. Steps 6 and 7 occur when any of the following is true: the card has sent the requested number of data blocks, the card has sent a data_error token, or the host has sent a STOP_TRANSMISSION command (CMD12).

Commands that Write Data to the Storage Media

On an SPI bus, a command that writes a single data block to the storage media has these steps:

1. The host brings CS low.

2. The host sends the 48-bit command followed by clock cycles.

3. After between 8 and 64 clock cycles, the card sends the command's response.

4. After 8 or more clock cycles, the host sends a data block in a data token and continues to generate clock cycles.

5. The card sends a data_response token immediately after receiving the data token. If the card received the data token without error, the card follows the data_response token with continuous busy tokens (by holding DataOut low) until the controller has finished programming the data block into the storage media. The card then brings DataOut high.

6. The host can bring CS high any time after writing the data tokens or receiving a data_error token. If the host brings CS high before DataOut goes high, the host must bring CS low again and read DataOut to verify that the write operation completed

7. The host generates 8 clock cycles to complete the command.

In a command that writes multiple blocks, steps 4 and 5 repeat as many times as needed to transfer the data blocks. After DataOut goes high to indicate that the card has programmed the previous block, the host generates at least 8 clock cycles before sending the next data block. The transfer ends when any of the following is true: the card has received and programmed the specified number of data blocks, the card has sent an error indication in a data_response token, or the host has sent a Stop Tran data token instead of a data block.

The host can check the result of a write operation by sending CMD13 (SEND_STATUS). The card returns a response that contains the status information.

Application Example

The example that follows uses the Microchip PIC18F4550 microcontroller circuit introduced in Chapter 4. The code shows how to detect a MultiMediaCard, initialize communications, and read and write data in the card's storage media.

Detecting and Selecting a Card

As the circuit in Chapter 4 showed, firmware can use spare port bits to control a MultiMediaCard's CS input and monitor a card connector's card-detect (CD) and write-protect (WP) pins. The host brings CS low to enable communications in SPI mode. The card-detect and write-protect pins connect to switches in the card connector, with one switch terminal connected to the ground pin and the other terminal brought out to the CD or WP connector pin. The card-detect switch is open when no card is present and closed when a card is present. The write-protect switch is open if the card's write-protect tab is in the write-protect position or the card isn't present. The switch is closed if the tab is in the write-enable position or the card doesn't have a write-protect tab. Only full-size SD Cards have write-protect tabs, though full-size adapters with tabs enable other card types to provide a write-protect signal.

Hirose DM1 series sockets are an example of SD-Card/MultiMediaCard sockets that have card-detect and write-protect switches. To monitor the state of a switch, connect it to a port pin with a pull up. The port pin is high when the switch is open and low when the switch is closed.

On the PIC18F4550, each I/O port has three registers. A TRIS register sets the direction of the port's bits (0 = output, 1 = input). Firmware can use the Port and LAT registers to read and write to the port. Reading the Port register returns the current state of the port's pins. Firmware can write to the port by writing to either the Port or LAT register. Writing to the Port register latches the value to the port pins. The LAT register simplifies writes to individual bits. The register always contains the last value written to the port. To change a single bit on the port, firmware can write to the bit in the register, and the write operation causes the chip to write the register's contents, including the just-written bit, to the port pins.

In Chapter 4's circuit, CS connects to PORTB, bit 3 on the microcontroller. The card-detect pin connects to PORTB, bit 4, and the write-protect pin connects to PORTA, bit 4. The code below provides application-specific names for the port bits and their direction bits. The Microchip C18 compiler files p18f4550.asm and p18f4550.h define the locations of the registers.

```
#define SDC_CS            LATBbits.LATB3
#define SDC_CS_DIR        TRISB3
#define MEDIA_CD          RB4
#define MEDIA_CD_DIR      TRISB4
#define MEDIA_WD          RA4
#define MEDIA_WD_DIR      TRISA4
```

The SocketInitialize function initializes a MultiMediaCard socket by setting the direction of the card-detect, CS, and write-protect bits and setting CS high to deselect the card:

```
void SocketInitialize(void)
{
    MEDIA_CD_DIR = INPUT;
    SDC_CS_DIR = OUTPUT;
    MEDIA_WD_DIR = INPUT;
    SDC_CS = 1;
}
```

The DetectSDCard function returns the state of the card-detect pin:

```
int DetectSDCard(void)
{
    if (MEDIA_CD)
        return 0;    // Card not present.
    else
        return 1;    // Card is present.
}
```

Sending a Command

For each supported MultiMediaCard command, device firmware needs to know the command index, the response type, the CRC value to send in the command, and whether the command's six bytes are followed by more data. The code below stores this information about commands using an enumeration, a series of defines, and a table in ROM.

Storing Command Information

The sdmmc_cmd enumeration assigns a value to each command:

```
typedef enum
{
    GO_IDLE_STATE,
    SEND_OP_COND,
    SEND_CSD,
    SEND_CID,
    STOP_TRANSMISSION,
    SEND_STATUS,
    SET_BLOCKLEN,
    READ_SINGLE_BLOCK,
    READ_MULTI_BLOCK,
    WRITE_SINGLE_BLOCK,
    WRITE_MULTI_BLOCK,
    TAG_SECTOR_START,
    TAG_SECTOR_END,
    UNTAG_SECTOR,
    TAG_ERASE_GRP_START,
    TAG_ERASE_GRP_END,
    UNTAG_ERASE_GRP,
    ERASE,
    LOCK_UNLOCK,
    SD_APP_OP_COND,
    APP_CMD,
    READ_OCR,
    CRC_ON_OFF
}sdmmc_cmd;
```

A table in ROM holds additional information about the commands. For each command, the table below stores a command name, CRC value, response type, and whether or not the command is followed by more data. Firmware can identify an entry in the table by specifying a command from the enumeration above. For example, SEND_CSD is the third enumeration constant in the enumeration, and cmdSEND_CSD is the third entry in the table.

```
#define MOREDATA   !0
#define NODATA      0

const rom typSDC_CMD sdmmc_cmdtable[] =
{
    // command name               CRC    response type      more data?

    {cmdGO_IDLE_STATE,            0x95,  R1,                NODATA},
    {cmdSEND_OP_COND,             0xF9,  R1,                NODATA},
    {cmdSEND_CSD,                 0xAF,  R1,                MOREDATA},
    {cmdSEND_CID,                 0x1B,  R1,                MOREDATA},
    {cmdSTOP_TRANSMISSION,        0xC3,  R1,                NODATA},
    {cmdSEND_STATUS,              0xAF,  R2,                NODATA},
    {cmdSET_BLOCKLEN,             0xFF,  R1,                NODATA},
    {cmdREAD_SINGLE_BLOCK,        0xFF,  R1,                MOREDATA},
    {cmdREAD_MULTI_BLOCK,         0xFF,  R1,                MOREDATA},
    {cmdWRITE_SINGLE_BLOCK,       0xFF,  R1,                MOREDATA},
    {cmdWRITE_MULTI_BLOCK,        0xFF,  R1,                MOREDATA},
    {cmdTAG_SECTOR_START,         0xFF,  R1,                NODATA},
    {cmdTAG_SECTOR_END,           0xFF,  R1,                NODATA},
    {cmdUNTAG_SECTOR,             0xFF,  R1,                NODATA},
    {cmdTAG_ERASE_GRP_START,      0xFF,  R1,                NODATA},
    {cmdTAG_ERASE_GRP_END,        0xFF,  R1,                NODATA},
    {cmdUNTAG_ERASE_GRP,          0xFF,  R1,                NODATA},
    {cmdERASE,                    0xDF,  R1b,               NODATA},
    {cmdLOCK_UNLOCK,              0x89,  R1b,               NODATA},
    {cmdSD_APP_OP_COND,           0xF5,  R1,                NODATA},
    {cmdAPP_CMD,                  0x73,  R1,                NODATA},
    {cmdREAD_OCR,                 0x25,  R3,                NODATA},
    {cmdCRC_ON_OFF,               0x25,  R1,                NODATA}
};
```

In a command's first byte, bit 7 = 0, bit 6 = 1, and bits 5..0 are the command index. In other words, the first byte in the command equals the command index + 40h.

The code below provides values for the first bytes in MultiMediaCard commands:

```
              // command                 first byte   command index
#define    cmdGO_IDLE_STATE           0x40       // 0
#define    cmdSEND_OP_COND            0x41       // 1
#define    cmdSEND_CSD                0x49       // 9
#define    cmdSEND_CID                0x4a       // 10
#define    cmdSTOP_TRANSMISSION       0x4c       // 12
#define    cmdSEND_STATUS             0x4d       // 13
#define    cmdSET_BLOCKLEN            0x50       // 16
#define    cmdREAD_SINGLE_BLOCK       0x51       // 17
#define    cmdREAD_MULTI_BLOCK        0x52       // 18
#define    cmdWRITE_SINGLE_BLOCK      0x58       // 24
#define    cmdWRITE_MULTI_BLOCK       0x59       // 25
#define    cmdTAG_SECTOR_START        0x60       // 32
#define    cmdTAG_SECTOR_END          0x61       // 33
#define    cmdUNTAG_SECTOR            0x62       // 34
#define    cmdTAG_ERASE_GRP_START     0x63       // 35
#define    cmdTAG_ERASE_GRP_END       0x64       // 36
#define    cmdUNTAG_ERASE_GRP         0x65       // 37
#define    cmdERASE                   0x66       // 38
#define    cmdSD_APP_OP_COND          0x69       // 41
#define    cmdLOCK_UNLOCK             0x71       // 49
#define    cmdAPP_CMD                 0x77       // 55
#define    cmdREAD_OCR                0x7a       // 58
#define    cmdCRC_ON_OFF              0x7b       // 59
```

Command and Response Structures

Each 48-bit command can be accessed as six generic bytes, a command byte plus four address bytes and CRC byte, or a command byte plus a 4-byte address, a 7-bit CRC value, and an end bit.

The CMD_PACKET union provides these options:

```
typedef union
{
  struct
  {
    byte field[6];
  };
  struct
  {
    byte crc;
    byte addr0;  // LSB
    byte addr1;
    byte addr2;
    byte addr3;  // MSB
    byte cmd;
  };
  struct
  {
    unsigned END_BIT:1;
    unsigned CRC7:7;
    dword address;
    byte command;
  };
} CMD_PACKET;
```

The SDC_RESPONSE union can hold a RESPONSE_1 or RESPONSE_2 structure as defined earlier in this chapter:

```
typedef union
{
  RESPONSE_1 r1;
  RESPONSE_2 r2;
} SDC_RESPONSE;
```

Error Codes

The SDC_Error enumeration names various MultiMediaCard communication errors:

```
typedef enum
{
    sdcValid = 0,                  // No error
    sdcCardInitCommFailure,        // Communication hasn't been established with the card.
    sdcCardNotInitFailure,         // Card did not initialize.
    sdcCardInitTimeout,            // Card initialization timed out.
    sdcCardTypeInvalid,            // Card type was not able to be defined.
    sdcCardBadCmd,                 // Card did not recognize the command.
    sdcCardTimeout,                // Card timed out during a read, write or erase sequence.
    sdcCardCRCError,               // A CRC error occurred during a read.
    sdcCardDataRejected,           // CRC did not match.
    sdcEraseTimedOut               // Erase timed out.
}SDC_Error;
```

A Function for Sending Commands

The SendSDCCmd function sends a command on the SPI bus and returns an SDC_RESPONSE structure. The function accepts a byte that corresponds to an entry in the command table (cmd) and a 4-byte command argument (address). The function calls the ReadMedia and WriteSPI functions introduced in Chapter 4.

The function ends after sending a command and receiving a response. If the response will be followed by data to or from the card, the function leaves CS low. Firmware can then call another function (SectorWrite or SectorRead, presented later in this chapter) to send or receive data.

```
SDC_RESPONSE SendSDCCmd(byte cmd, dword address)
{
    CMD_PACKET      CmdPacket;
    byte            index;
    SDC_RESPONSE    response;
    word            timeout = 9;

    // Bring the card's chip-select line low.

    SDC_CS = 0;
```

113

```
// Store a command byte, address, and CRC value in the CMD_PACKET structure.

CmdPacket.cmd = sdmmc_cmdtable[cmd].CmdCode;
CmdPacket.address = address;
CmdPacket.crc = sdmmc_cmdtable[cmd].CRC;

// Send the command byte, address bytes, and CRC byte.
// The WriteSPI library function writes a byte on the SPI bus.

WriteSPI(CmdPacket.cmd);
WriteSPI(CmdPacket.addr3);
WriteSPI(CmdPacket.addr2);
WriteSPI(CmdPacket.addr1);
WriteSPI(CmdPacket.addr0);
WriteSPI(CmdPacket.crc);

// Is the command's response type R1 or R1b?

if (sdmmc_cmdtable[cmd].responsetype == R1 ||
    sdmmc_cmdtable[cmd].responsetype == R1b)
{
    do
    {
        // Read a byte from the card until the byte doesn't equal FFh or a timeout occurs.

        response.r1._byte = ReadMedia();
        timeout--;

    } while ((response.r1._byte == 0xFF) && (timeout != 0));
}
// Is the command's response type R2?

else if (sdmmc_cmdtable[cmd].responsetype == R2)
{
    do
    {
        // read the first bye of the response.
        // _byte0 transmits first.

        response.r2._byte0 = ReadMedia();
        timeout--;

    } while ((response.r2._byte0 == 0xFF) && (timeout != 0));
```

```
      // If the first byte was read, read the second byte.

      if (response.r2._byte0 != 0xFF)
         response.r2._byte1 = ReadMedia();
      }
   // Is the response type R1b?

   if (sdmmc_cmdtable[cmd].responsetype == R1b)
   {
      // The R1b response byte has been read.
      // Wait for not busy status by reading from the card until a byte doesn't equal 00h
      // or a timeout occurs..

       response.r1._byte = 0x00;

      for (index = 0; index < 0xFF && response.r1._byte == 0x00; index++)
      {
         timeout = 0xFFFF;

         do
         {
            response.r1._byte = ReadMedia();
            timeout--;

         } while ((response.r1._byte == 0x00) && (timeout != 0));
      }
   }
   // Generate 8 clock cycles.

   mSend8ClkCycles();

   // If no more data is expected for this command, deselect the card.

   if (!(sdmmc_cmdtable[cmd].moredataexpected))

      SDC_CS = 1;

   return(response);
}
```

Reading the CSD Register

When initializing communications, the host must read the card's CSD register. The CSD union below defines the contents of the CSD register as 4 dwords or 16 bytes. For brevity, I didn't include a union component with a field for each of the CSD's 37 items.

```
typedef union
{
  struct
  {
    DWORD _u320;
    DWORD _u321;
    DWORD _u322;
    DWORD _u323;
  };
  struct
  {
    byte _byte[16];
  };
} CSD;
```

The CSDRead function issues the SEND_CSD command and waits for the card to send the register's 16 bytes. Much of the function is similar to the SendSDCCmd function above. A difference is that the function retrieves data from the card after sending the command.

```
#define CSD_SIZE              16
#define DATA_START_TOKEN      0xFE  // The Start Block token

CSD gblCSDReg;

SDC_Error CSDRead()
{
  dword          address = 0x00;
  byte           cmd = SEND_CSD;
  CMD_PACKET     CmdPacket;
  byte           data_token;
  word           index;
  SDC_RESPONSE   response;
  SDC_Error      status = sdcValid;
  word           timeout = 0x2ff;
```

```
// Select the card.

SDC_CS = 0;

// Store a command byte, address, and CRC value in the CMD_PACKET structure.

CmdPacket.cmd = sdmmc_cmdtable[cmd].CmdCode;
CmdPacket.address = address;
CmdPacket.crc = sdmmc_cmdtable[cmd].CRC;

// Send the command byte, address bytes, and CRC byte.
// The WriteSPI library function writes a byte on the SPI bus.

WriteSPI(CmdPacket.cmd);
WriteSPI(CmdPacket.addr3);
WriteSPI(CmdPacket.addr2);
WriteSPI(CmdPacket.addr1);
WriteSPI(CmdPacket.addr0);
WriteSPI(CmdPacket.crc);

// Read a byte from the card until the byte doesn't equal FFh or a timeout occurs.

do
{
    response.r1._byte = ReadMedia();
    timeout--;

} while ((response.r1._byte == 0xFF) && (timeout != 0));

// A response of 00h means the command was accepted.

if (response.r1._byte != 0x00)
{
   status = sdcCardBadCmd;
}
```

```
        else
        {
            index = 0x2FF;

            //Wait for the data_start token or a timeout.

            do
            {
                data_token = ReadMedia();
                index--;

            } while ((data_token == SDC_FLOATING_BUS) && (index != 0));

            if ((index == 0) || (data_token != DATA_START_TOKEN))

                status = sdcCardTimeout;

            else
            {
                // A data start token was received.
                // Read the CSD register's 16 bytes.

                for (index = 0; index < CSD_SIZE; index++)
                {
                    gblCSDReg._byte[index] = ReadMedia();
                }
            }
            // Generate 8 clock cycles to complete the command.

            mSend8ClkCycles();
        }
        // Deselect the card.

        SDC_CS = 1;
        return(status);
    }
```

Reading a Sector

MultiMediaCard firmware reads data from the storage media in sectors, which are typically 512 bytes. The SectorRead function and related code below perform this function. The function accepts a 32-bit LBA that identifies the sector to read (sector_addr) and a pointer to a buffer that will store the data read from the card (buffer). The function returns a status code.

```
// This macro writes FFh twice to clock in two CRC bytes.

#define mReadCRC()          WriteSPI(0xFF); WriteSPI(0xFF);

#define SDC_FLOATING_BUS    0xFF
#define SDC_BAD_RESPONSE    SDC_FLOATING_BUS
#define SDC_SECTOR_SIZE     512

SDC_Error SectorRead(dword sector_addr, byte* buffer)
{
    byte            data_token;
    word            index;
    SDC_RESPONSE    response;
    SDC_Error       status = sdcValid;

    // Issue a READ_SINGLE_BLOCK command.
    // Specify the address of the first byte to read in the media.
    // To obtain the address of a sector's first byte,
    // shift the sector address left 9 times to multiply by 512 (sector size).

    response = SendSDCCmd(READ_SINGLE_BLOCK, (sector_addr << 9));

    // A response of 00h indicates success.

    if (response.r1._byte != 0x00)
    {
        status = sdcCardBadCmd;
    }
    else
    {
        // The command was accepted.

        index = 0x2FF;
```

```
    do
    {
        // Read from the card until receiving a response or a timeout.

        data_token = ReadMedia();
        index--;

    } while ((data_token == SDC_FLOATING_BUS) && (index != 0));

    if ((index == 0) || (data_token != DATA_START_TOKEN))

        // The card didn't send a data start token.

        status = sdcCardTimeout;

    else
    {
        // The card sent a data start token.
        // Read a sector's worth of data from the card.

        for (index = 0; index < SDC_SECTOR_SIZE; index++)
        {
            buffer[index] = ReadMedia();
        }
        // Read the CRC bytes.

        mReadCRC();
    }
    // Generate 8 clock cycles to complete the command.

    mSend8ClkCycles();
}
// Deselect the card.

SDC_CS = 1;

return(status);
}
```

Writing a Sector

MultiMediaCard firmware writes data to the storage media in sectors. The SectorWrite function and related code below perform this function. The function calls the ReadMedia and WriteSPI functions from Chapter 4 and the SendSDCCmd function above.

```
// This macro writes FFh twice to send two CRC bytes.
// The code assumes CRC values are ignored (the default in SPI mode).

#define mSendCRC()          WriteSPI(0xFF); WriteSPI(0xFF);

#define DATA_ACCEPTED       0b00000101

SDC_Error SectorWrite(dword sector_addr, byte* buffer)
{
    byte                data_response;
    word                index;
    SDC_RESPONSE        response;
    SDC_Error           status = sdcValid;

    // Issue a WRITE_SINGLE_BLOCK command.
    // Pass the address of the first byte to write in the media.
    // To obtain the address of a sector's first byte,
    // shift the sector address left 9 times to multiply by 512 (sector size).

    response = SendSDCCmd(WRITE_SINGLE_BLOCK, (sector_addr << 9));

    // A response of 00h indicates success.

    if (response.r1._byte != 0x00)

        status = sdcCardBadCmd;
```

```
    else
    {
        // The command was accepted.
        // Send a data start token.

        WriteSPI(DATA_START_TOKEN);

        // Send a sector's worth of data.

        for(index = 0; index < 512; index++)

            WriteSPI(buffer[index]);

        // Send the CRC bytes.

        mSendCRC();

        // Read the card's response.

        data_response = ReadMedia();

        if ((data_response & 0x0F) != DATA_ACCEPTED)
        {
            status = sdcCardDataRejected;
        }
        else
        {
            // The card is writing the data into the storage media.
            // Wait for the card to return non-zero (not busy) or a timeout.

            index = 0;

            do
            {
                data_response = ReadMedia();
                index++;

            } while ((data_response == 0x00) && (index != 0));
```

```
    if (index == 0)

        // The write timed out.

        status = sdcCardTimeout;
    }
    // The write was successful.
    // Generate 8 clock cycles to complete the command.

    mSend8ClkCycles();
}
// Deselect the card.

SDC_CS = 1;

return(status);
}
```

Initializing Communications

Before accessing a card's media. the card's host must initialize communications by sending a sequence of commands. Initializing a card consists of the following actions by the host:

1. Configure the SPI port with a clock frequency of 400 kHz or less.

2. Enable the SPI port.

3. With CS high and DataIn high, generate clock cycles for the maximum of the power-supply ramp-up time, 1 millisecond, or 74 clock cycles. With a 400-kHz clock, 1 millisecond requires 400 clock cycles. The power-supply ramp-up time is the time required for the supply to rise from the minimum valid supply voltage to the supply voltage the card will use.

4. Issue the GO_IDLE_STATE command to select SPI mode.

5. Issue the SEND_OP_COND command repeatedly until the card responds or a timeout.

6. Issue the SEND_CSD command to read the CSD register.

The card is now ready for use in SPI mode. Firmware can perform these additional actions as desired:

Increase the SPI port's clock frequency. The CSD register specifies the card's maximum data-transfer rate.

Issue the CRC_ON_OFF command to enable CRC checking in the card.

If necessary, issue the SET_BLOCK_LEN command to change the block length for media reads and writes. The default is 512 bytes.

Read and store the state of the write-protect tab.

Issue block-read and block-write commands to access the media's contents.

Cards in MultiMediaCard-bus mode always use the CRC values. In SPI mode, the card ignores the CRC values unless the host has issued a CRC_ON_OFF command to enable CRC. All cards are in MultiMediaCard-bus mode until the host issues a GO_IDLE_STATE command to switch the card to SPI mode. So the GO_IDLE_STATE command must have a valid CRC value, but for all following commands in SPI mode, the host can use any stuff bits for the CRC if desired.

Card Information

The SDCSTATE union below is a byte that identifies the device as an SD Card/MultiMediaCard and indicates if the card is write-protected:

```
typedef union _SDCstate
{
  struct
  {
    byte isSDMMC : 1;    // set for an SD Card or MultiMediaCard
    byte isWP   : 1;     // set if write protected
  };
  byte _byte;

} SDCSTATE;
```

The IsWriteProtected function returns true if the card has a write-protect tab that is set to write protect.

```
byte IsWriteProtected(void)
{
   if (MEDIA_WD) return TRUE;
   else return FALSE;
}
```

Delay Timer

A function that returns after a specific delay time is often useful for tasks such as waiting for hardware to initialize. The Delayms function uses an on-chip hardware timer to delay the number of milliseconds passed to the function. When the time has elapsed, the function returns. This function is very specific to the PICMicro architecture and accesses registers defined in the compiler file p18f4550.h. Firmware for other chips can perform equivalent functions using hardware timers in the chips.

```
#define SYSTEM_CLOCK          (dword) 20000000 // Set to Fosc frequency.
#define CLKSPERINSTRUCTION    (byte) 4
#define TMR1PRESCALER         (byte) 8
#define TMR1OVERHEAD          (byte) 5
#define MILLISECDELAY         (word)((SYSTEM_CLOCK / CLKSPERINSTRUCTION /
                              TMR1PRESCALER / (word)1000) - TMR1OVERHEAD)
void Delayms(byte milliseconds)
{
   T1CON = 0xB0;  // Initialize the timer 1 control register.
   TMR1IE = 1;    // Enable the timer 1 overflow interrupt.

   do {
     TMR1H = high(0xFFFF - MILLISECDELAY); // Load the timer registers.
     TMR1L = low(0xFFFF - MILLISECDELAY);

     TMR1IF = 0;        // Clear the overflow flag.
     TMR1ON = 1;        // Start the timer.
     while (!TMR1IF){;} // Wait for timer overflow.
     TMR1ON = 0;        // Stop the timer.
     Nop();             // Additional delay for accuracy.
     Nop();             // Additional delay for accuracy.
     milliseconds--;    // Decrement the number of milliseconds to delay.

   // Quit after the specified number of milliseconds has elapsed.
   } while (milliseconds > 0);
```

Error:
// On error or completion of the delay, turn off the timer and disable its interrupt.

```
TMR1ON = 0;
TMR1IE = 0;
}
```

A Function for Initializing

The MediaInitialize function performs initialization tasks and returns status in an SDC_Error structure. The function accepts a pointer to an SDC-STATE structure and sets the states of the structure's two members. The function uses the 512-byte msd_buffer array introduced in Chapter 3 to hold data read from the card's storage media. The function calls the Open-SPI function from Chapter 4.

```
SDC_Error MediaInitialize(SDCSTATE *Flag)
{
    SDC_Error        CSDstatus = sdcValid;
    SDC_RESPONSE     response;
    SDC_Error        status = sdcValid;
    word             timeout;

    Flag -> _byte = 0x0;

    // Deselect the card.

    SDC_CS = 1;

    // Open the SPI port.
    // Clock speed must be <= 400 kHz until the card is initialized
    // and the CSD register has been read.
    // MultiMediaCards require CKE = 0, CKP = 1,
    // and sampling DataOut in the middle of a clock cyle.

    OpenSPI(SPI_FOSC_64, MODE_11, SMPMID);

    // Allow the card time to initialize.

    Delayms(100);
```

```
// Generate clock cycles for 1 millisecond as required by the MultiMediaCard spec.

for (timeout = 0; timeout < 50; timeout++)

    mSend8ClkCycles();

// Select the card.

SDC_CS = 0;
Delayms(1);

// Issue the GO_IDLE_STATE command to select SPI mode.

response = SendSDCCmd(GO_IDLE_STATE, 0x0);

if (response.r1._byte == SDC_BAD_RESPONSE)
{
    status = sdcCardInitCommFailure;
    goto InitError;
}
// A response of 01h means the card is in the idle state and is initializing.

if (response.r1._byte != 0x01)
{
    status = sdcCardNotInitFailure;
    goto InitError;
}
// Issue the SEND_OP_COND command until the card responds or a timeout.

timeout = 0xFFF;

do
{
    response = SendSDCCmd(SEND_OP_COND, 0x0);
    timeout--;

} while (response.r1._byte != 0x00 && timeout != 0);

if (timeout == 0)
{
    status = sdcCardInitTimeout;
    goto InitError;
}
```

```
    else {

        // The command succeeded.
        // Read the CSD register.

        CSDstatus = CSDRead();

        if (!CSDstatus)

            // The response was zero. The CSD was read successfully.
            // OK to increase the clock speed.

            OpenSPI(SPI_FOSC_4, MODE_11, SMPMID);

        else

            // Unable to read the CSD.

            status = sdcCardTypeInvalid;
    }
    // Issue the SET_BLOCKLEN command to set the block length to 512.
    // (Optional, since this is the default.)

    SendSDCCmd(SET_BLOCKLEN, 512);

    // Set a bit in the SDCSTATE structure if the card is write-protected.

    if (IsWriteProtected())

        Flag -> isWP = TRUE;

    // Read sector zero from the card into msd_buffer until success or a timeout.
    // Some cards require multiple attempts.

    for (timeout = 0xFF;
        timeout > 0 && SectorRead(0x0, (byte*)msd_buffer) != sdcValid;
        timeout--)
```

```
    // The attempt to read timed out.

    if (timeout == 0)
    {
        status = sdcCardNotInitFailure;
        goto InitError;
    }
    return(status);

InitError:

// On error or success, deselect the device.

SDC_CS = 1;

return(status);
}
```

6

SCSI Commands

SCSI commands originated as a protocol for devices that use the Small Computer Systems Interface (SCSI) parallel interface. The commands provide a framework for obtaining information about a storage device, controlling the device's operation, and reading and writing blocks of data in the storage media. Storage devices that use other hardware interfaces, including USB, also use SCSI commands to perform these operations.

About the Commands

The SCSI commands cover a wide range of device types and functions. Most devices need to support only a small number of the commands.

Specifications

As Chapter 3 explained, each command travels in a structure called the command descriptor block (CDB), or command block for short. The first byte of the CDB is the code that identifies the command. Several sources provide specifications for commands used by mass-storage devices.

The INCITS Technical Committee T10 (www.t10.org) has these specifications:

SCSI Architectural Model (SAM). Defines a reference model that applies to all SCSI devices. The current version is SAM-3.

SCSI Primary Commands (SPC). Defines commands that apply to all SCSI devices. The current version is SPC-3.

SCSI Block Commands (SBC). Defines commands used by hard drives, flash drives, and other direct-access block devices. The current version is SBC-3.

Multi-Media Commands (MMC). Defines commands used by CD and DVD drives. The current version is MMC-4.

INCITS Technical Committee T13 (www.t13.org) has this specification:

ATA/ATAPI. Defines commands used by CD and DVD drives. The current version is ATA/ATAPI - 7.

The SFF Committee (www.sffcommittee.com) has these specifications:

ATA Packet Interface for CD-ROMs (SFF-8020i). An earlier version of the ATA/ATAPI specification.

ATAPI Removable Rewritable Media Devices (SFF-8070i). Commands that apply to some floppy drives.

Working drafts of the documents from INCITS are available from www.t10.org and www.t13.org. Approved standards are ANSI documents sold by Global Engineering Documents (www.global.ihs.com).

Rather than repeating every detail about the command blocks from the specifications, this chapter is more of a companion guide to the specification documents. The guide explains the purpose and use of common commands and provides application hints for implementing the commands in device firmware.

Which Commands to Implement?

A question many firmware programmers have is which SCSI commands a device must implement. Each device specifies a command set in the response to a SCSI INQUIRY command, and the command set's specification lists mandatory commands. For example, a device that returns an

INQUIRY response with PERIPHERAL DEVICE TYPE = 00h (direct access block device) and VERSION = 05h (SPC-3) should implement all commands defined as mandatory in the SPC-3 specification and all mandatory commands in a SCSI block commands specification such as SBC-2 or SBC-3. Table 6-1 shows the mandatory commands and some optional commands for devices that use SCSI block commands. In practice, however, many devices don't implement every mandatory command.

The USB-IF is developing a USB Mass Storage Class Compliance Test Specification, which names required and optional SCSI and multimedia commands for different peripheral device types. At this writing, a preliminary version of the specification is available from the USB-IF. Also available is a preliminary version of the USB-IF's Command Verifier software (USBCV) with mass-storage compliance tests. Check usb.org for the latest versions.

It's also useful to learn what commands your device's host(s) typically use and to be sure to implement those commands in your device. Some developers concentrate on supporting these commands rather than implementing every command a specification dictates. To learn what commands a host issues, use a bus analyzer to observe bus traffic when your device or similar devices are attached to a host.

In practice, to enable communications, a device should implement at minimum these SCSI commands:

INQUIRY

READ CAPACITY(10)

READ(10)

REQUEST SENSE

TEST UNIT READY

WRITE(10) (for writable devices)

A specific host or device is likely to require commands in addition to these, however. When a device claims to implement a command set, it's reasonable for a host to assume that the device supports all commands declared as mandatory in that command set.

Table 6-1: Mandatory SCSI commands and common optional SCSI commands for USB mass-storage devices that comply with SBC-2 or SBC-3.

Command	Code (hex)	Required?	Document
FORMAT UNIT	04	yes	SBC
INQUIRY	12	yes	SPC
MODE SELECT(6)	15	no	SPC
MODE SELECT(10)	55	no	SPC
MODE SENSE(6)	1A	no	SPC
MODE SENSE(10)	5A	no[1]	SPC
PREVENT ALLOW MEDIUM REMOVAL	1E	no	SPC
READ(6)	08	yes[2]	SBC
READ(10)	28	yes	SBC
READ(12)	A8	no	SBC
READ CAPACITY(10)	25	yes	SBC
READ FORMAT CAPACITIES	23	no	MMC
READ TOC/PMA/ATIP	43	no	MMC
REPORT LUNS	A0	yes (SPC-3)	SPC
REQUEST SENSE	03	yes	SPC
SEND DIAGNOSTIC	1D	yes	SPC
START STOP UNIT	1B	no	SBC
SYNCHRONIZE CACHE(10)	35	no	SBC
TEST UNIT READY	00	yes	SPC
VERIFY(10)	2F	no	SBC
WRITE(6)	0A	yes[2]	SBC
WRITE(10)	2A	no	SBC
WRITE(12)	AA	no	SBC

[1]Required for some bootable devices.

[2]Application clients should migrate to READ(10) and WRITE(10).

On receiving an unsupported command, a device must not crash or hang. The correct response to an unsupported command is this:

- Return 01h (command failed) in the CSW 's bCSWStatus field.
- In the sense data, set the SENSE KEY parameter to 05h (ILLEGAL REQUEST) and set the ADDITIONAL SENSE CODE parameter to 20h (INVALID COMMAND OPERATION CODE), as described below.

Sense Data

On experiencing a problem in executing a command or on receiving an unsupported command, a device fills a structure with status information and sets bCSWStatus in the CSW to 01h (command failed). The status information is called the sense data. A REQUEST SENSE command can request the sense data, which the device returns in the data-transport phase.

A device can also use sense data to announce other events that require attention by the host, such as the inserting of removable media. To signal the event, the device sets the SENSE KEY field in the sense data to 06h (UNIT ATTENTION).

The contents of the returned sense-data structure vary with the command, the device type, and whether the DESC bit in the REQUEST SENSE command block requests fixed-format sense data (0) or descriptor-format sense data (1). Fixed-format sense data uses a single defined structure to return status information (Table 6-2). The format of descriptor-format sense data varies with the descriptors being sent. Each descriptor is a structure with a type of status information such as command-specific information, information relating to an exception condition, or information relating to block commands.

(In true SCSI communications, the device returns a status code after each command, and a status of CHECK CONDITION indicates that the SCSI host should issue a REQUEST SENSE command. USB communications use the status code in the CSW instead.)

Table 6-2: Fixed-format Sense Data has a defined structure.

Byte	Description
0	bit 7: VALID. Set to 1 if the INFORMATION field contains valid information. bits 6..0: RESPONSE CODE. Set to 70h for information on current errors. Set to 71h for information on deferred errors (used with commands that use caching).
1	Obsolete.
2	Bit 7: FILEMARK. Used by streaming devices. Bit 6: EOM. End of medium. Used by streaming devices. Bit 5: ILI: Incorrect length indicator. Used with READ LONG, WRITE LONG, and stream READ commands. Bit 4: Reserved Bits 3..0: SENSE KEY. Contains information describing the error.
3..6	INFORMATION. Device-specific or command-specific information.
7	ADDITIONAL SENSE LENGTH. The number of additional sense bytes that follow this field. Maximum 244.
8..11	COMMAND-SPECIFIC INFORMATION
12	ADDITIONAL SENSE CODE (ASC). Provides additional information about the error. Set to zero if unused.
13	ADDITIONAL SENSE CODE QUALIFIER (ASCQ). Provides additional information related to the additional sense code. Set to zero if unused.
14	FIELD REPLACEABLE UNIT CODE. Identifies a failed component. Set to zero if there is no component to identify.
15..17	If byte 15, bit 7 (SKSV) equals 1, the remainder of the field contains SENSE KEY SPECIFIC information.
18..n	Additional sense bytes (optional). Vendor specific.

Fixed-format Sense Data

The RequestSenseResponse union enables accessing fixed-format sense data as 18 generic bytes or as a structure with a series of named members:

```
typedef union {
  struct
  {
    byte _byte[18];
  };
  struct
  {
    unsigned ResponseCode:7;
    unsigned VALID:1;
    byte Obsolete;
    unsigned SenseKey:4;
    unsigned Resv:1;
    unsigned ILI:1;
    unsigned EOM:1;
    unsigned FILEMARK:1;
    DWORD Information;
    byte AddSenseLen;
    DWORD CmdSpecificInfo;
    byte ASC;
    byte ASCQ;
    byte FRUC;
    byte SenseKeySpecific[3];
  };
} RequestSenseResponse;
```

Setting Default Values

The ResetSenseData function sets the values in the RequestSenseResponse structure gblSenseData to default values:

```
RequestSenseResponse gblSenseData;

void ResetSenseData(void)
   {
   gblSenseData.ResponseCode =           0x70;
   gblSenseData.VALID =                  0x0;
   gblSenseData.Obsolete =               0x0;
   gblSenseData.SenseKey =               0x0;
   gblSenseData.Resv =                   0x0;
   gblSenseData.ILI =                    0x0;
   gblSenseData.EOM =                    0x0;
   gblSenseData.FILEMARK =               0x0;
   gblSenseData.Information._dword =     0x0;
   gblSenseData.AddSenseLen =            0x0a;
   gblSenseData.CmdSpecificInfo._dword = 0x0;
   gblSenseData.ASC =                    0x0;
   gblSenseData.ASCQ =                   0x0;
   gblSenseData.FRUC =                   0x0;
   gblSenseData.SenseKeySpecific[0] =    0x0;
   gblSenseData.SenseKeySpecific[1] =    0x0;
   gblSenseData.SenseKeySpecific[2] =    0x0;
   }
```

The sense codes can have assigned friendly names:

```
#define S_NOT_READY                                  0x2
#define S_MEDIUM_ERROR                               0x3
#define S_ILLEGAL_REQUEST                            0x5
#define S_UNIT_ATTENTION                             0x6
#define ASC_LOGICAL_BLOCK_ADDRESS_OUT_OF_RANGE       0x21
#define ASCQ_LOGICAL_BLOCK_ADDRESS_OUT_OF_RANGE      0x00
#define ASC_MEDIUM_NOT_PRESENT                       0x3a
#define ASCQ_MEDIUM_NOT_PRESENT                      0x00
#define ASC_PERIPHERAL_DEVICE_WRITE_FAULT            0x03
#define ASCQ_PERIPHERAL_DEVICE_WRITE_FAULT           0x00
#define ASC_UNRECOVERED_READ_ERROR                   0x11
#define ASCQ_UNRECOVERED_READ_ERROR                  0x00
#define ASC_WRITE_PROTECTED                          0x27
#define ASCQ_WRITE_PROTECTED                         0x00
```

Primary Commands

Each of the commands below is documented in the SCSI Primary Commands (SPC) specification.

INQUIRY

The INQUIRY command requests a structure containing information about the device. A device should be able to return the structure even when the media isn't ready to respond to other commands. All SBC devices must support the INQUIRY command.

The data returned by the device in the data-transport phase is at least 36 bytes (Table 6-3). The data identifies the peripheral device type (PDT) and SPC version number and contains a vendor identification number, product identification number, product revision number, and other information about the device's abilities and supported protocols.

Table 6-4 lists common PDTs and their codes from the SCSI Primary Commands document. Hard drives and flash-memory cards are type 00h: direct-access block device. Devices with PDT = 0Eh use the reduced block command (RBC) set, which is intended for block devices that have fewer requirements and options compared to SBC devices. RBC might sound appealing for some applications, but in practice the type is rarely used in part because Windows doesn't provide a driver for it. If you need to provide a vendor-specific RBC driver, you may as well define the device as vendor specific in the descriptors. That way, you'll avoid confusion with any RBC drivers a user may have loaded for another purpose.

As Chapter 3 explained, if the interface descriptor's bInterfaceSubClass doesn't equal 06h (SCSI transparent command set), the PDT should match the declared bInterfaceSubClass.

Note that the RMB parameter (bit 7 of byte 1) reports whether the device has removable media. USB flash drives (thumb drives, pen drives, and similar devices) are removable devices with fixed media. However, some Microsoft documentation recommends that flash drives declare that they have removable media (RMB = 1), and many flash drives do so.

Table 6-3: The response to an INQUIRY command is at least 36 bytes. The SPC specification has more details on these fields.

Byte	Description
0	Bits 7..5: PERIPHERAL QUALIFIER (000 = a device is connected to this logical unit) Bits 4..0: PERIPHERAL DEVICE TYPE (PDT)
1	Bit 7: RMB (0 = non-removable media; 1 = removable media) Bits 6..0: reserved
2	VERSION of SPC standard (5 = SPC-3; 4 = SPC-2)
3	Bits 7..6: obsolete Bit 5: NORMACA (normal ACA bit support) Bit 4: HISUP (hierarchical addressing support) Bits 3..0: response data format (must = 2)
4	ADDITIONAL LENGTH (the number of additional bytes in the response - 1). Equal to (response length - 5). Set to 1Fh if returning 36 (24h) bytes.
5	Bit 7: SCCS (0 = no embedded storage array controller component present) Bit 6: ACC (0 = no access controls coordinator present) Bits 5..4: TPGS (0 = no support or vendor-specific support for asymmetric logical unit access) Bit 3: 3PC ((0 = no support for third-party copy commands) Bits 2..1: reserved Bit 0: PROTECT (0 = no support for protection information)
6	Bit 7: BQUE (0 = no support for basic task management) Bit 6: ENCSERV (0 = no support for embedded enclosure services) Bit 5: VS (vendor specific) Bit 4: MULTIP (0 = device has a single port) Bit 3: MCHNGR (0 = no support for media changer) Bits 2..1: obsolete Bit 0: ADDR16 (not used with USB interface)
7	Bit 7..6: obsolete Bit 5: WBUS16 (not used with USB interface) Bit 4: SYNC (not used with USB interface) Bit 3: LINKED (0 = no support for linked commands) Bit 2: obsolete Bit 1: CMDQUE (0 = no support for full task management) Bit 0: VS (vendor specific)
8..15	T10 VENDOR IDENTIFICATION, MSB first
16..31	PRODUCT IDENTIFICATION, MSB first
32..35	PRODUCT REVISION LEVEL, MSB first

Table 6-4: Some of the Peripheral Device Types (PDTs) defined in the SCSI Primary Commands document.

PDT (hex)	Peripheral Device Type	Specification[1]
00	Direct-access block device. Magnetic and flash drives.	SBC-2
05	CD/DVD device	MMC-4
07	Optical memory device (non-CD optical disk)	SBC
0E	Reduced block command (RBC) (simplified) direct-access device	RBC

[1]Devices can use a later edition of a specification if available.

A vendor identification number is available at no charge from the T10 Technical Committee. The number consists of eight or fewer characters in the range 21h–7Eh.

Following the first 36 bytes are optional fields with additional data, including areas that vendor-specific drivers can use to obtain vendor-specific information. Device firmware shouldn't assume that the host will always request exactly 36 bytes. The thirteen cases in Chapter 3 describe what a device should do if it has more or fewer bytes to return than the host requests.

The Response

An InquiryResponse structure can hold the data a device returns in response to an INQUIRY command:

```
typedef struct
{
    byte Peripheral;
    byte Removvble;
    byte Version;
    byte Response_Data_Format;
    byte AdditionalLength;
    byte Sccstp;
    byte bqueetc;
    byte CmdQue;
    char vendorID[8];
    char productID[16];
    char productRev[4];
} InquiryResponse;
```

The InquiryResponse data normally doesn't change, so a device can store the data in ROM:

```
const rom InquiryResponse inq_resp = {
    0x00,              // direct access block device, connected
    0x80,              // device is removable
    0x04,              // SPC-2 compliance
    0x02,              // response data format
    0x1F,              // additional response bytes - 1
    0x00,              // additional fields, none set
    0x00,              // additional fields, none set
    0x00,              // additional fields, none set
    "Microchp",        // 8 -byte T10-assigned Vendor ID
    "Mass Storage   ", // 16-byte product identification
    "0001"             // 4-byte product revision level
};
```

Sending the Response

The MSDInquiryHandler function copies an InquiryResponse structure to msd_buffer (defined in Chapter 3) for sending to the host and sets the CSWDDataResidue and CSWStatus fields of the command's CSW.

The function calls the memcopypgm2ram function provided with the Microchip C18 compiler. The function copies the response data from program memory into RAM.

```
void MSDInquiryHandler(void)
{
    byte   i;
    byte   *buffer;

    // Copy sizeof(InquiryResponse) bytes from program memory beginning at
    // &inq_resp to RAM beginning at &med_buffer[0].

    memcpypgm2ram
        ((byte *)&msd_buffer[0],
        (byte *)&inq_resp,
        sizeof(InquiryResponse));

    msd_csw.dCSWDataResidue = sizeof(InquiryResponse);
    msd_csw.bCSWStatus = 0x00;
    return;
}
```

MODE SELECT

A host can use the MODE SELECT command to specify parameters relating to the storage media, a logical unit, or the device itself. The information is in structures called block descriptors and mode pages. There are two commands that differ in the size and format of the mode-parameter header that precedes any block descriptors and mode pages being sent. MODE SELECT(6) has a 4-byte header, and MODE SELECT(10) has an 8-byte header. Support for MODE SELECT is optional unless the device also supports MODE SENSE as explained below.

Mode page 08h is the caching mode page. The Windows mass-storage driver attempts to read the page and if supported, send a page to disable caching unless the user has selected *optimize for performance* for the volume in Device Manager > Properties > Policies.

MODE SENSE

The MODE SENSE commands are the complements to the MODE SELECT commands. A host can use MODE SENSE to request parameters relating to the storage media, a logical unit, or the device itself. As with MODE SELECT, there are two commands that differ in the size and format of the mode-parameter header that precedes any block descriptors and mode pages being returned. MODE SENSE(6) has a 4-byte header, and MODE SENSE(10) has an 8-byte header.

The SPC specification says that a device that supports a MODE SENSE command should support the corresponding MODE SELECT command, and a device that supports a MODE SELECT command should support the corresponding MODE SENSE command. The MODE SENSE command is optional for many SBC devices, but Windows and other hosts use this command to request information from devices. Bootable devices must support MODE SENSE(10).

Each MODE SENSE command block contains a page code and a subpage code that together specify what information the host is requesting. The SBC specification defines a variety of mode pages. When SUBPAGE CODE = 00h, the mode page uses the page_0 format. The page includes fields for the page code, page length, and mode parameters. For other subpage codes, the mode page uses the subpage format, which adds a field for a subpage code.

When communicating with direct-access block devices (PDT = 00h), the Windows mass-storage driver and other hosts commonly request these mode pages:

PAGE CODE = 3Fh requests all supported mode pages.

PAGE CODE = 1Ch requests the informational exceptions control mode page. This page contains information about how the device reports exception conditions due to vendor-specific events and conditions that result from scans or self-tests a device performs in the background (using no bus bandwidth).

PAGE CODE = 08h requests the caching mode page, which defines parameters that relate to a device's use of its cache.

PAGE CODE = 05h is the flexible disk mode page (FDMP), which contains parameters needed to convert between LBA and CHS addressing. Some hosts refuse to try booting from devices that lack this page, possibly because the boot code uses CHS addressing. The USB bootability specification requires support for this page in all bootable devices with a PDT other than 05h (CD/DVD drive). The bootability specification redefines mode page 05h as a simplified version of the page defined in the original SBC specification. (Note that the mode page is listed as obsolete in SBC-2 and later but the USB version of the page is required for bootable USB devices.)

A response to a MODE SENSE command begins with a mode parameter header (Table 6-5). Note that in byte 2, bit 7, an SBC device informs the host whether the media is write-protected.

Following the header, an SBC device may send a mode parameter block descriptor that specifies the number of logical blocks in the media and the block size. A response can also contain one or more mode pages and/or mode subpages.

On receiving a MODE SENSE command for an unsupported mode page, a device should fail the command and return SENSE KEY = ILLEGAL REQUEST and ADDITIONAL SENSE CODE = INVALID FIELD IN COMMAND PACKET. Some devices with no data to send respond by sending just the header. In response to a MODE SENSE(6) command, a device with no data to return can return the header with MODE DATA LENGTH = 3 and BLOCK DESCRIPTER LENGTH = 0.

Table 6-5: The data-transport phase in a MODE SENSE(6) command begins with this header.

Byte	Description
0	MODE DATA LENGTH. The number of bytes that follow.
1	MEDIUM TYPE. 00h for SBC devices.
2	DEVICE-SPECIFIC PARAMETER. For SBC devices: bit 7: WP. Set to 1 if the media is write-protected. bits 6..4: reserved bit 4: DPOFUA. Set to 1 if the device supports the DPO and FUA bits (used in caching) bits 3..0: reserved
3	BLOCK DESCRIPTOR LENGTH. The length in bytes of all block descriptors in the mode parameter list.

The MSDModeSenseHandler function prepares a response to a MODE SENSE(6) command, writing data to return into msd_buffer and setting fields in the command's CSW:

```
void MSDModeSenseHandler()
{
    // Set values to return, from SPC spec, section 7.4.3 and SBC spec, section 6.3.1.

    msd_buffer[0] = 0x03; // The number of bytes that follow.
    msd_buffer[1] = 0x00; // The media type is SBC.
    msd_buffer[2] = 0x00; // Not write-protected, no cache-control-bit support.
    msd_buffer[3] = 0x00; // No mode-parameter block descriptors.

    msd_csw.bCSWStatus=0x0;
    msd_csw.dCSWDataResidue=0x04;
    return;
}
```

PREVENT ALLOW MEDIUM REMOVAL

The PREVENT ALLOW MEDIUM REMOVAL command requests the device to prevent or allow users to remove the storage media from the device. A 2-bit PREVENT field in the command is set to 00b to allow media removal or 01b to prohibit removal. The command has no data-transport phase. Support for this command is optional. Of course, many devices have non-removable media or use flash-memory cards or other media with no mechanism to prevent removal.

Flash drives that fail this command when PREVENT = 01 have improved performance. When the command fails, Windows doesn't enable write caching. Write caching causes Windows to launch multiple threads that cause random writes, which result in slow write performance on flash media.

REPORT LUNS

The REPORT LUNS command requests a list of the numbers of all logical units that are present and that match the peripheral device type returned in response to an INQUIRY command. The response can also optionally include the numbers of logical units that currently have no device present. A device should be able to respond to this command without having to access the media and even when the device isn't ready to respond to other commands. The SBC-2, SBC-3, and SPC-3 specifications all list this command as mandatory. The command is optional in SPC-2, however.

REQUEST SENSE

The REQUEST SENSE command requests a structure containing sense data. The specification says that the ALLOCATION LENGTH parameter in the request should always equal 252 bytes to enable devices to return all of their sense data, including vendor-specific data. Windows hosts typically request just the first 18 bytes, however. For this reason, device vendors often use vendor-specific control requests to obtain additional sense data if needed. The REQUEST SENSE command is mandatory for SBC devices.

The command descriptor block for this command is 6 bytes. However, the Windows driver sets bCBWCBLength in the CBW to 0Ch instead of 06h. This incorrect value doesn't affect the number of bytes that transmit on the bus because the CBW is always 31 bytes with 16 bytes reserved for the command descriptor block. Device firmware should accept the incorrect value and ignore the additional declared 6 bytes.

The MSDRequestSenseHandler function copies data from the gblSense-Data array into msd_buffer for returning to the host. The function also sets values in the CSW.

```
void MSDRequestSenseHandler(void)
{
    byte i;
    for (i = 0; i < sizeof(RequestSenseResponse); i++)
        msd_buffer[i] = gblSenseData._byte[i];

    msd_csw.dCSWDataResidue = sizeof(RequestSenseResponse);
    msd_csw.bCSWStatus = 0x0; // success
    return;
}
```

SEND DIAGNOSTIC

The SEND DIAGNOSTIC command requests the device to test itself, a logical unit, or both. For SBC devices, support for a default, vendor-specific self test is mandatory. The host requests the default test by setting SELF-TEST = 1, SELF-TEST CODE = zero, and PARAMETER LIST LENGTH = zero. On receiving the command, a device begins the self test in the background (without using bus bandwidth). On completion of the test, the device returns a CSW with status information.

While a background test is in progress, on receiving most commands, the device should suspend testing within two seconds and respond to the command. SBC devices don't need to service FORMAT UNIT or START STOP UNIT commands while self-testing. To terminate testing, a host can issue a SEND DIAGNOSTIC command with SELF-TEST CODE = 100b.

Hosts rarely use this command. Some devices support the command by returning success immediately, without performing a test.

TEST UNIT READY

The host issues a TEST UNIT READY command to find out if a storage device is ready for use. The command has no data-transport phase. If the media isn't ready, the device updates its sense data and returns a CSW with the bCSWStatus field set to 01h to indicate that the command failed. The host can then request sense data by issuing a REQUEST SENSE command. All SBC devices must support this command.

For devices with removable media, some hosts issue periodic TEST UNIT READY commands to find out if the media is still present. A successful TEST UNIT READY response doesn't guarantee that the next READ or WRITE command will succeed, however. Instead of periodic TEST UNIT READY commands, a host can just attempt to read or write to the media as needed. If the media has been removed, the READ or WRITE command fails, and a REQUEST SENSE command can obtain the reason.

The MSDTestUnitReadyHandler function resets the sense data in the gblSenseData structure and calls the DetectSDCard function from Chapter 5 to determine if a MultiMediaCard or SD Card is present. If a card isn't detected, the function sets data in the appropriate fields in the Request-SenseResponse structure. The function also sets the CSWStatus and CSW-DataResidue fields in the CSW.

```
void MSDTestUnitReadyHandler()
{
    msd_csw.bCSWStatus=0x0;
    ResetSenseData();
    if (!DetectSDCard()) {
        gblSenseData.SenseKey = S_UNIT_ATTENTION;
        gblSenseData.ASC = ASC_MEDIUM_NOT_PRESENT;
        gblSenseData.ASCQ = ASCQ_MEDIUM_NOT_PRESENT;
        msd_csw.bCSWStatus = 0x01;
    }
    msd_csw.dCSWDataResidue = 0x00;
    return;
}
```

Block Commands

Each of the commands below is documented in the SCSI Block Commands (SBC) specification.

FORMAT UNIT

The FORMAT UNIT command requests a device to divide its storage media into logical blocks that applications can access. If the host previously sent a MODE SELECT command, the device should use the number of blocks and block length specified in that command. Otherwise the device should use its current number of blocks and block length.

A device that uses MultiMediaCards or other formatted, removable media might have no need to format its media, but the SBC specification lists the command as mandatory. A host can use the command as a fast and reliable method to erase the media.

READ

The READ and WRITE commands are where a host accesses a device's storage media. The host issues a READ command to request to read a block of data from the device's storage media. In the command block, the LOGICAL BLOCK ADDRESS field specifies the LBA of the first requested block, and the TRANSFER LENGTH field contains the number of requested blocks.

There are five READ commands: READ(6), READ(10), READ(12), READ(16), and READ(32). The commands vary in the sizes of the logical-block-address and transfer-length fields and in the quantity and type of status and control information included in the command block. READ(6) and READ(10) are mandatory for SBC devices. The specification recommends migrating all code from READ(6) to READ(10), but a host might still attempt to use READ(6). The Windows USB mass-storage driver uses READ(10).

On receiving a READ(10) command, a device should send the contents of the requested blocks to the host in the data-transport phase. The device doesn't have to know or care what is in the requested blocks. All the device needs is a block number and the number of blocks to return.

The MSDReadHandler function reads the block address and the number of bytes to transfer specified in the CBW, handles any detected errors, sets fields on the CSW, and calls the MSDDataIn function from Chapter 3 to send the requested data.

The MSDReadHandler function uses the variable gblNumBLKS, which contains the number of blocks in the volume. The section describing the READ CAPACITY command later in this chapter shows how to obtain the value.

```
byte *ptrNextData;

void MSDReadHandler()
{
    byte        Flags;
    word        i;
    DWORD       LBA;
    dword       sectorNumber;
    SDC_Error   status;
    WORD        TransferLength;

    /// The command block stores the MSB first. Device firmware stores the LSB first.
    // The starting LBA to read is in bytes 2-5 of the command block.

    LBA.v[3] = gblCBW.CBWCB[2];
    LBA.v[2] = gblCBW.CBWCB[3];
    LBA.v[1] = gblCBW.CBWCB[4];
    LBA.v[0] = gblCBW.CBWCB[5];

    // The number of blocks to transfer is in bytes 7 and 8 of the CBW.

    TransferLength.v[1] = gblCBW.CBWCB[7];
    TransferLength.v[0] = gblCBW.CBWCB[8];

    // The data-transport phase is device to host.

    Flags = gblCBW.CBWCB[1];

    // Set default values in the CSW.

    msd_csw.bCSWStatus = 0x0;  // Success.
    msd_csw.dCSWDataResidue = 0x0;

    if (LBA._dword + TransferLength._word > gblNumBLKS._dword) {

        // The requested blocks extend beyond the available blocks In the media.
        // Set bCSWStatus to "command failed."
        // Store sense data to describe the error.

        msd_csw.bCSWStatus = 0x01;
        gblSenseData.SenseKey = S_ILLEGAL_REQUEST;
        gblSenseData.ASC = ASC_LOGICAL_BLOCK_ADDRESS_OUT_OF_RANGE;
        gblSenseData.ASCQ = ASCQ_LOGICAL_BLOCK_ADDRESS_OUT_OF_RANGE;
```

```
} else {
    // Read blocks from the media and send the contents to the USB host
    // until TransferLength = 0.

    while (TransferLength._word > 0) {

        // Decrement the number of blocks remaining.

        TransferLength._word--;

        // Copy the specified block's data into msd_buffer.

        status = SectorRead(LBA._dword, (byte*)&msd_buffer[0]);

        // Increment the LBA.

        LBA._dword++;

        if (status == sdcValid) {

            // The sector-read operation succeeded.
            // Prepare to send 512 bytes to the USB host.
            // Set fields in the CSW.

            msd_csw.bCSWStatus = 0x00;
            msd_csw.dCSWDataResidue = 0x200; // 512 bytes

            // The next block to read begins where this one ended.

            ptrNextData = (byte *)&msd_buffer[0];

            while (msd_csw.dCSWDataResidue > 0)

                // The MSDDataIn function sends the data to the USB host.
                // dCSWDataResidue is decremented as the data is sent.
                // Continue until dCSWDataResidue = 0.

                MSDDataIn();

            // Reset dCSWDataResidue.

            msd_csw.dCSWDataResidue = 0x0;
```

```
        } else {

            // The command failed.
            // Store sense data to describe the error.

            msd_csw.bCSWStatus = 0x01;
            gblSenseData.SenseKey = S_MEDIUM_ERROR;
            gblSenseData.ASC = ASC_UNRECOVERED_READ_ERROR;
            gblSenseData.ASCQ = ASCQ_UNRECOEVERED_READ_ERROR;

            // Don't send any more data.

            msd_csw.dCSWDataResidue = 0x0;

            break;
            }
        } // End transfer length > 0
    } // End transfer length OK
}
```

READ CAPACITY

The host uses a READ CAPACITY command to learn how many bytes a device can store. In the data-transport phase, the device returns a structure that contains the LBA of the last block in the media and the number of bytes per block. Note that the command requests the LBA of the last block, not the number of blocks in the media. The first LBA is zero, so the LBA of the last block equals the number of blocks - 1.

There are two READ CAPACITY commands: READ CAPACITY(10) and READ CAPACITY(16). The commands differ in the length of the fields in the command block and response structure. SBC devices must support READ CAPACITY(10).

A MultiMediaCard host uses information in the card's CSD register to calculate the LBA of the final block. The MultiMediaCard specification shows how to do the calculations. The fields in the CSD register aren't all byte-aligned, so obtaining a value sometimes requires reading multiple bytes and selecting bits from each to obtain the value of interest.

```
DWORD gblNumBLKS=0x00;
DWORD gblBLKLen=0x00;
```

```
void MSDReadCapacityHandler()
{
    dword one = 0x1;
    dword C_size;
    dword C_mult;
    dword Mult;
    dword C_size_U;
    dword C_size_H;
    dword C_size_L;
    dword C_mult_H;
    dword C_mult_L;
    dword C_Read_Bl_Len;

    // The block length is in byte 5, bits 3..0 in the MultiMediaCard's CSD register.
    // Block length = 2^(C_Read_Bl_Len)
    // If block length = 512, C_Read_Bl_Len = 9 because 2^9 = 512.

    C_Read_Bl_Len = gblCSDReg._byte[5] & 0x0f;

    // Shift left C_Read_Bl_Len positions to get the block-length value.

    gblBLKLen._dword = one << C_Read_Bl_Len;

    // The C_size value is 12 bits.
    // The two MSbs are in byte 6, bits 1..0.
    // The next 8 bits are in byte 7.
    // The two LSbs are in byte 8, bits 7..6.

    C_size_U = gblCSDReg._byte[6] & 0x03;
    C_size_H = gblCSDReg._byte[7];
    C_size_L = (gblCSDReg._byte[8]&0xC0) >> 6;
    C_size = (C_size_U<<10) | (C_size_H<<2) | (C_size_L);

    // C_mult is a 3-bit value stored in two bytes.
    // The two MSbs are in byte 9, bits 1..0.
    // The LSb is in byte 10, bit 7.

    C_mult_H = gblCSDReg._byte[9] & 0x03;
    C_mult_L = (gblCSDReg._byte[10] & 0x80) >> 7;
    C_mult = (C_mult_H << 1 ) | C_mult_L;
```

```
// See the MultiMediaCard spec, section 5.3, for the calculations below.

Mult = one << (C_mult + 2);

// Return a value equal to the last LBA - 1.

gblNumBLKS._dword = Mult * (C_size + 1) - 1;

// Place gblNumBLKS and gblBLKLen in msd_buffer for sending to the host.

msd_buffer[0] = gblNumBLKS.v[3];
msd_buffer[1] = gblNumBLKS.v[2];
msd_buffer[2] = gblNumBLKS.v[1];
msd_buffer[3] = gblNumBLKS.v[0];
msd_buffer[4] = gblBLKLen.v[3];
msd_buffer[5] = gblBLKLen.v[2];
msd_buffer[6] = gblBLKLen.v[1];
msd_buffer[7] = gblBLKLen.v[0];

// Set fields in the CSW.

msd_csw.dCSWDataResidue = 0x08;    // Number of bytes in the response.
msd_csw.bCSWStatus = 0x00;         // Success.
}
```

START STOP UNIT

A host issues the START STOP UNIT command to request to change the device's power condition to active, idle, or standby and to request the device to load or eject its storage media. The command has no data-transport phase. SBC devices aren't required to support this command.

SYNCHRONIZE CACHE

A host sends a SYNCHRONIZE CACHE command to request the device to ensure that the specified sectors on the media and in any non-volatile cache contain the most recent data. The SYNCHRONIZE CACHE(10) and SYNCHRONIZE CACHE(16) commands vary in the size of the fields in the command block. This command has no data-transport phase. SBC devices aren't required to support this command.

VERIFY

The VERIFY command requests the device to test one or more sectors. If the BYTCHK bit in the command block equals zero, the device should attempt to read from the specified locations. If BYTCHK = 1, the host sends data in the data-transport phase, and the device should verify that the received data matches what is stored in the device. If the media uses error-checking protection information as specified in the response to an INQUIRY command, the verify operation checks this information as well.

There are four VERIFY commands: VERIFY(10), VERIFY(12), VER-IFY(16), and VERIFY(32). The commands vary in the size of the fields in the command block. The VERIFY(32) command block also contains additional fields. Support for this command is optional for SBC devices.

WRITE

The WRITE commands are the complements of the READ commands. The host issues a WRITE command to request to write a block of data to the device. In the command block, the LOGICAL BLOCK ADDRESS field specifies the LBA of the first block to write to, and the TRANSFER LENGTH field contains the number of blocks to write.

There are five WRITE commands: WRITE(6), WRITE(10), WRITE(12), WRITE(16), and WRITE(32). The commands vary in the sizes of the logi-cal-block-address and transfer-length fields and in the quantity and type of status and control information included in the command block. WRITE(6) and WRITE(10) are mandatory for SBC devices (except of course for read-only media). The specification recommends migrating all code from WRITE(6) to WRITE(10), but a host might still attempt to use WRITE(6). The Windows USB mass-storage driver uses WRITE(10).

After receiving a WRITE(10) command block, a device should receive the data to write in the data-transport phase and should write the received data to the specified locations in the storage media. The device doesn't have to know or care what is in the received blocks. All the device needs is a block number and data to write to the block.

The MSDWriteHandler function gets the LBA and number of blocks to write from the CBW in a WRITE(10) command. The function then calls the MSDDataOut function from Chapter 3 to write the received data to the storage media.

```
void MSDWriteHandler()
{
    byte        * adr;
    byte          Flags;
    word          i;
    DWORD         LBA;
    dword         sectorNumber;
    SDC_Error  status = sdcValid;
    WORD          TransferLength;

    // The command block stores MSB first. Device firmware stores LSB first.
    // The starting LBA to write to is in bytes 2-5 in the command block.

    LBA.v[3] = gblCBW.CBWCB[2];
    LBA.v[2] = gblCBW.CBWCB[3];
    LBA.v[1] = gblCBW.CBWCB[4];
    LBA.v[0] = gblCBW.CBWCB[5];

    // The number of blocks being written is in bytes 7-8 of the CBW.

    TransferLength.v[1] = gblCBW.CBWCB[7];
    TransferLength.v[0] = gblCBW.CBWCB[8];

    // Set bCSWStatus to a default value.

    msd_csw.bCSWStatus = 0x0; // Success.
```

```
while (TransferLength._word > 0) {

    // Read data received from the USB host and write the contents to the media
    // until TransferLength = 0.

    // Set dCSWDataResidue to the media's block size.

    msd_csw.dCSWDataResidue = 512;

    while (msd_csw.dCSWDataResidue > 0)

        // The MSDDataOut function reads data from the USB host.
        // dCSWDataResidue is decremented as the data is read.
        // Continue until dCSWDataResidue = 0.

        MSDDataOut();

    if (IsWriteProtected()) {

        // If the media is write protected, set the sense data
        // and bCSWStatus in the CSW.

        gblSenseData.SenseKey = S_NOT_READY;
        gblSenseData.ASC = ASC_WRITE_PROTECTED;
        gblSenseData.ASCQ = ASCQ_WRITE_PROTECTED;
        msd_csw.bCSWStatus = 0x01; // Command failed.

    } else {

        // The received data is in msd_buffer.
        // Write the data to the media beginning at the LBA specified in the CBW.

        status = SectorWrite((LBA._dword), (byte*)&msd_buffer[0]);
    }
```

```
        if (status) {

            // The sector write failed.

            msd_csw.bCSWStatus = 0x01;

            // Store sense data to describe the error.

            gblSenseData.SenseKey = S_MEDIUM_ERROR;
            gblSenseData.ASC = ASC_PERIPHERAL_DEVICE_WRITE_FAULT;
            gblSenseData.ASCQ = ASCQ_PERIPHERAL_DEVICE_WRITE_FAULT;
        }
        // Increment the LBA. Decrement the number of blocks remaining to write.

        LBA._dword++;
        TransferLength._word--;

        if (TransferLength._word > 0){

            // There is more data to receive.
            // Configure the endpoint's buffer descriptor to prepare for the data.

            MSD_BD_OUT.Cnt = MSD_OUT_EP_SIZE;
            MSD_BD_OUT.ADR = (byte*)&msd_buffer[0];

        } else {

            // All of the data has been received.
            // Configure the endpoint's buffer descriptor to prepare for the next command.

            MSD_BD_OUT.Cnt = sizeof(msd_cbw);
            MSD_BD_OUT.ADR = (byte*)&msd_cbw;
        }
    } // End: while (TransferLength._word > 0)

    return;
}
```

Multimedia Commands

Each of the commands below is documented in the Multimedia Commands (MMC) specification.

READ FORMAT CAPACITIES

The READ FORMAT CAPACITIES command requests a structure containing one or more descriptors that specify a number of blocks and a block length that the media can be formatted for. The device returns the structure in the data-transport phase. If the media is currently formatted, the first descriptor in the structure contains the values in use. If the media is unformatted, the first descriptor in the structure contains the values that will result in the maximum storage capacity. One or more alternate descriptors with different values can follow. This command is optional for SBC devices.

READ TOC/PMA/ATIP

Devices with CD or DVD media use the READ TOC/PMA/ATIP command to provide data from a table of contents (TOC), data from the program memory area (PMA), and absolute time in Pre-Grove (ATIP) data. The format of the response varies with the response type. The ATIP data contains information required by CD burners. The ATIP format is defined in "orange books" that Philips Electronics provides to companies with whom Philips has a CD-information or license agreement. SBC devices aren't likely to need this command and aren't required to support it.

Handling Commands and Events

On receiving a command, firmware must decode the command and prepare an appropriate response.

Decoding Commands

The SCSI command codes can have assigned friendly names:

```
#define INQUIRY                 0x12
#define READ_FORMAT_CAPACITY    0x23
#define READ_CAPACITY           0x25
#define READ_10                 0x28
#define WRITE_10                0x2a
#define REQUEST_SENSE           0x03
#define MODE_SENSE              0x1a
#define TEST_UNIT_READY         0x00
#define VERIFY                  0x2f
#define STOP_START              0x1b
```

The MSDCommandHandler function decodes a received command code and branches to one of the functions in this chapter to respond to the command. If the command isn't supported, the code sets the sense data and fields in bCSWStatus.

```
byte *ptrNextData;
void MSDCommandHandler(void)
{
   switch(gblCBW.CBWCB[0]) {
     case INQUIRY:
        MSDInquiryHandler();
     break;

     case READ_CAPACITY:
        MSDReadCapacityHandler();
     break;

     case READ_10:
        MSDReadHandler();
     break;

     case WRITE_10:
        MSDWriteHandler();
     break;
```

```
case REQUEST_SENSE:
  MSDRequestSenseHandler();
break;

case MODE_SENSE:
  MSDModeSenseHandler();
break;

case TEST_UNIT_READY:
  MSDTestUnitReadyHandler();
break;

case VERIFY:
  MSDVerifyHandler();
break;

case STOP_START:
  MSDStopStartHandler();
break;

default:

  // Use for all unsupported commands.

  ResetSenseData();
  gblSenseData.SenseKey=S_ILLEGAL_REQUEST;
  gblSenseData.ASC=ASC_INVALID_COMMAND_OPCODE;
  gblSenseData.ASCQ=ASCQ_INVALID_COMMAND_OPCODE;
  msd_csw.bCSWStatus=0x01;
  msd_csw.dCSWDataResidue=0x00;
break;
}
// Reset the data pointer to the beginning of the buffer.

ptrNextData=(byte*)&msd_buffer[0];
}
```

The UNIT ATTENTION Condition

When something changes that the host needs to know about before accessing the media, the device should generate a UNIT ATTENTION condition. Changes that require the UNIT ATTENTION condition include inserting removable media, a change in INQUIRY data, and a reset of the device or a logical unit.

A device in the UNIT ATTENTION condition should fail all commands except INQUIRY, REPORT LUNS, and REQUEST SENSE. On receiving a command other than these, a device should return 01h (command failed) in the bCSWStatus field of the CSW. The host then sends a REQUEST SENSE command to obtain status information.

In preparing a response to the REQUEST SENSE command, the device sets the SENSE KEY field to 06h (UNIT ATTENTION) and sets the ASC and ASCQ fields of the sense data to describe the reason for the condition. After returning the sense data, the device is no longer in the UNIT ATTEN-TION condition.

Informing the Host about Media Changes

A device that interfaces to a MultiMediaCard or other removable media should inform the USB host when a card is inserted. A device must also inform the host if the host attempts to access the device when the media has been removed or the device isn't ready to perform read, write, or verify oper-ations for another reason.

To inform the host that media has been inserted, a device can generate a UNIT ATTENTION condition and set ASC = 28h and ASCQ = 00h, which the SPC specification defines as NOT READY TO READY CHANGE, MEDIUM MAY HAVE CHANGED.

On receiving a media-access command when the media is removed, a device should set the SENSE KEY field to 02h (NOT READY) and set ASC = 3Ah and ASCQ = 00h, which the SPC specification defines as MEDIUM NOT PRESENT.

After a device reports that the media isn't present, a host may send periodic TEST UNIT READY commands to find out if media has been inserted. After a device reports that the media has changed, the host can send com-mands to learn about the new media.

In a similar way, a device that accesses files on its own (not via the USB host) should inform the USB host when firmware has written to a file or made other changes to a volume's contents. A device can do so via the UNIT ATTENTION condition as described above. Another option is to allow device firmware to access files on its own only when the device isn't attached to and enumerated by a USB host. For example, a data logger can collect data in the field and store the data in files. When the device is brought in from the field and attached to a USB host, the firmware no longer collects and stores data on its own and instead responds to commands from the USB host. Device firmware can use the presence of VBUS or successful enumeration of an attached device to determine whether the firmware can access files.

Reset Behavior

A device generates a UNIT ATTENTION condition after experiencing a reset. The SCSI Architectural Model specification describes three conditions that correspond to different reset types. The conditions are power on, hard reset, and logical-unit reset. A device sets an ADDITIONAL SENSE CODE value to indicate which type of reset occurred.

A power-on condition exists after power is applied. The power-on condition causes a hard-reset condition. A transport protocol can define other events that cause a device to enter the hard-reset condition. A hard reset in turn causes the device to enter the logical-unit reset condition. Other logical-unit reset events can cause the device to enter the logical-unit reset condition. Unlike the power-on and hard reset, a logical-unit reset doesn't reset mode-page and other parameters to default values.

The USB specifications define two reset types for mass-storage devices: the USB port reset and the Bulk-Only Mass Storage Reset request. The USB specifications don't map these resets to SCSI reset types and thus don't specify SCSI behaviors on resetting. Devices typically map the USB port reset to the SCSI hard reset. Some devices map the bulk-only mass-storage reset to the hard reset, while others map the bulk-only reset to the logical-unit reset. Problems can result if a host's expectations don't match a device's behavior after a reset.

7

Media Structure

Flash drives and hard drives have different hardware but use many of the same logical structures for storing and managing data. To write firmware that formats the media or reads and writes files in formatted media, you need to understand these structures and how to use the information in them.

This chapter explains how information is organized in the storage media and what information is stored in the master boot record sector that is the first sector in most storage devices.

A Look Inside

The logical structures, addressing methods, and file systems described in this book have their origins in the IBM PC, its derivatives, and the Microsoft operating systems developed for use on these computers. Over the years, the software components have evolved to support media with larger capacities and new capabilities. Some of the developments, such as the logical block addressing method, simplify the job of the mass-storage host and make it easier for embedded systems to support storage media. Other developments

```
+-------------------------------------------+
|           MASTER BOOT RECORD              |
+-------------------------------------------+
|                                           |
|         FIRST PRIMARY PARTITION           |
|                                           |
+-------------------------------------------+
|                                           |
|        SECOND PRIMARY PARTITION           |
|              (OPTIONAL)                   |
+-------------------------------------------+
|                                           |
|         THIRD PRIMARY PARTITION           |
|              (OPTIONAL)                   |
+-------------------------------------------+
|                                           |
|        FOURTH PRIMARY PARTITION           |
|              (OPTIONAL)                   |
+-------------------------------------------+
```

Figure 7-1: Storage media can be formatted with a master boot record and up to four primary partitions.

add support for capacities and abilities that embedded systems are unlikely to need. Windows and other operating systems support a variety of file systems, including options suitable for small embedded systems, so PCs and embedded systems can access the same media without problems.

Components of Formatted Media

As explained in Chapter 1, bytes in storage media are grouped in blocks called sectors. All of the sectors in the media have the same capacity, typically 512. Some file-system drivers support sector sizes that are multiples of 512.

Low-level formatting code allocates most of the sectors to one or more logical partitions, or volumes. (Figure 7-1) Formatting can be done by a PC, an embedded system, or another computer that interfaces to the media.

In most storage devices, the first sector in the media (sector zero) is the master boot record (MBR) sector. The sector contains an MBR structure, which in turn contains a partition table that defines the locations of up to four partitions. Under Windows, each partition appears as a separate volume, or logical drive with its own drive letter. The MBR sector also has an area that can contain executable code. A computer that boots from the storage device runs the executable code on boot up. In Windows systems, the Fdisk tool can perform the low-level formatting that stores the MBR structure in the first sector. Fdisk deletes all programs and data previously stored in the media.

Each volume begins with a boot sector that contains information specific to the volume's file system. (Don't confuse this boot sector with the master-boot-record sector.) File-system drivers in embedded systems often use a FAT file system. The term FAT refers to a family of file systems as well as the file allocation tables that every FAT system contains. The two most common FAT file systems are FAT16 and FAT32. A third FAT system, FAT12, is suitable only for smaller-capacity media and is uncommon these days even in embedded systems. (Floppy drives use FAT12.)

Every FAT volume contains the following elements: a reserved region that includes a boot sector, a FAT region that stores the FATs, and a file and directory data region that contains data clusters for storing files and directories. FAT12 and FAT16 volumes store the root directory in a dedicated root-directory region that precedes the data clusters, while FAT32 volumes store the root directory in any available data clusters.

A word about licensing: due to patent protections, manufacturers of some types of devices that implement FAT file systems may need to obtain a license from Microsoft. The devices include removable solid-state media and some consumer electronics devices. Microsoft provides source code and test specifications to licensees. For more information, see www.microsoft.com/mscorp/ip/tech/fat.asp.

Microsoft's NTFS is an alternative to FAT file systems for PCs. Because Microsoft hasn't publicly released a specification for NTFS, the file system isn't practical for use in embedded systems that don't use an operating system with NTFS support.

FAT file systems store files and directories in data clusters. Each cluster consists of one or more sectors. All clusters in a volume are the same size. Data clusters can provide larger-capacity units for program code to work with when storing and retrieving files.

The boot sector specifies what sectors are available for storing files and directories, what sectors contain the file allocation tables, and how many sectors are in a data cluster. The boot sector can also contain program code used in booting the computer. The FATs hold a record of the data clusters used by files.

The document that defines all three FAT file systems is a hardware white paper titled *FAT32 File System Specification* from Microsoft. Chapter 8 has more about FAT file systems.

Drives without an MBR Sector

Some storage devices don't have an MBR sector. Media that requires only a single volume might not want to waste 512 bytes on an MBR sector. Media without an MBR sector begins with the volume's boot sector.

For maximum compatibility with hosts, however, a device should include the MBR sector. A host can find it challenging to determine whether a device's media contains an MBR. One approach is to read the locations that would contain a partition table and attempt to determine if the contents describe a valid partition. The first bytes in the media can also offer a clue. In bootable FAT16 media without an MBR, the first three bytes are typically EBh 3Ch 90h. In bootable FAT32 media without an MBR, the first three bytes are typically EBh 58h 90h. A MultiMediaCard or SD Card straight from the package is formatted with an MBR sector.

Byte Order

The FAT file systems were developed for use on the x86 architecture in IBM PCs and their derivatives. The architecture of x86 CPUs is little endian, which means that multi-byte values are stored with the least significant byte at the lowest address. For example, in the MBR sector, addresses 510 and 511 must contain the signature AA55h. Because the storage is little endian, location 510 contains 55h (the least significant byte) and location 511 contains AAh (the most significant byte).

The Master Boot Record Sector

Sector zero, the Master Boot Record (MBR) sector, contains three items: an area for executable code, a partition table, and a boot signature (Figure 7-2).

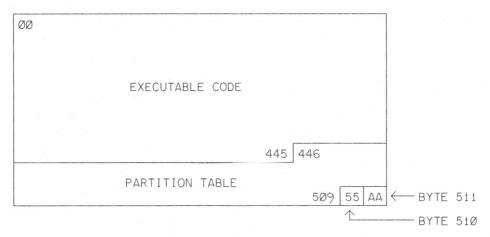

Figure 7-2: The MBR sector contains a partition table that specifies the location(s) of one or more primary partitions.

Executable Code

Bytes zero through 445 can contain executable code. When a PC boots, the system BIOS jumps to the executable code in the MBR sector of a storage device. The code searches the partition table for an active, or bootable, partition, and on finding one, boots the computer by running code stored in that partition's first sector. Like any low-level program code, the code stored in the MBR is specific to a CPU family. Executable code for a PC is useless if the system's CPU is a microcontroller with a different instruction set.

Embedded systems typically boot from a specific location in dedicated program memory rather than from storage media such as a flash-memory card or hard drive. An embedded-system host can ignore any executable code in the MBR sector. Because the partition table is in the same location in the MBR sector in all devices, firmware can read the information directly from the table.

The Partition Table

The partition table enables defining one or more partitions, or logical volumes, in the storage media. Many devices have just one volume. The partition table in the MBR sector has room for four 16-byte entries that each

169

specify the sectors that belong to a partition. The table is in bytes 446 through 509. An entry can begin at byte 446, 462, 478, or 494. Table 7-1 shows the contents of an entry.

Each partition entry has fields that define the partition's starting location when addressing via the CHS and LBA methods. The LBA field at byte 8 specifies the starting sector of the partition expressed as an offset from the beginning of the media (the MBR sector). The CHS values are ignored when using LBA. If a partition is bootable, executable code in the MBR may use CHS addresses to locate boot code in the partition.

The partition-type field at byte 4 specifies a file system and also indicates something about the partition's size (Table 7-2). Over the years, Microsoft's operating systems have expanded their support for file systems and for partition sizes and addressing methods within the file systems. For example, partition type 04h was added in MS-DOS 3.0 for FAT16 partitions of less than 32 MB. MS-DOS 4.0 added partition type 06h for FAT16 partitions between 32 MB and 2 GB. Partition types 0Ch and 0Eh must support LBA to enable PCs to use BIOS interrupt 13h to access the media. If the partition type is 00h, the entry is unused and the partition doesn't exist.

The final item in a partition-table entry, byte 12, is the total number of sectors in the partition. Most program code ignores this value and instead uses an equivalent value stored by the file system.

Extended Partitions

Devices with multiple partitions can use extended partitioning, where one of the partition-table entries is for an additional, extended, partition whose first sector contains an extended boot record (EBR) structure with its own partition table (Figure 7-3).

The partition table in the MBR contains information about the media's primary partition(s). The partition table in an extended partition's EBR can store at most one entry for a secondary partition and one entry for an additional extended partition. The additional extended partition, if present, contains its own EBR and partition table. The EBR sectors in extended partitions contain a partition table and signature but not executable code.

Any device with more than four partitions must use extended partitioning. Large-capacity FAT16 devices use extended partitioning when the available media is larger than the maximum allowed size for a FAT16 partition. (Many implementations limit FAT16 partitions to 2 GB. Another solution for large-capacity media is to use FAT32.) MS-DOS allows only one primary partition but supports extended partitions. Possibly because of this limitation, some formatting routines use extended partitioning for a second or third partition even though one partition table could hold all of the infor-

```
+----------------------------------------+
|          MASTER BOOT RECORD            |
+----------------------------------------+
|                                        |
|        FIRST PRIMARY PARTITION         |
|                                        |
+----------------------------------------+
|                                        |
|       SECOND PRIMARY PARTITION         |
|             (OPTIONAL)                 |
|                                        |
+----------------------------------------+
|                                        |
|        THIRD PRIMARY PARTITION         |
|             (OPTIONAL)                 |
|                                        |
+----------------------------------------+
|        EXTENDED BOOT RECORD 1          |
+----------------------------------------+
|                                        |
|         EXTENDED PARTITION 1           |
|                                        |
|  +----------------------------------+  |
|  |     EXTENDED BOOT RECORD 2       |  |
|  +----------------------------------+  |
|  |                                  |  |
|  |      EXTENDED PARTITION 2        |  |
|  |                                  |  |
|  |  +----------------------------+  |  |
|  |  |   EXTENDED BOOT RECORD N   |  |  |
|  |  +----------------------------+  |  |
|  |  |                            |  |  |
|  |  |    EXTENDED PARTITION N    |  |  |
|  |  |                            |  |  |
|  |  +----------------------------+  |  |
|  +----------------------------------+  |
+----------------------------------------+
```

Figure 7-3: With extended partitions, a device can have more than four partitions.

Table 7-1: A partition table entry contains information that enables the master computer to access locations in the storage media.

Byte in the Partition-table Entry	Size (bytes)	Description
0	1	Boot indicator 00h = do not boot from this partition 80h = boot from this partition
1	1	CHS addressing: starting head number
2	2	CHS addressing: bits 5..0: starting sector number bits 7..6: starting cylinder number, bits 9...8 bits 15..8: starting cylinder number, bits 7..0
4	1	Partition type
5	1	CHS addressing: ending head number
6	2	CHS addressing: bits 5..0: ending sector number bits 7..6: ending cylinder number, bits 9...8 bits 15..8: ending cylinder number, bits 7..0
8	4	LBA: the sector number of the partition's first sector, expressed as an offset from the MBR sector (sector zero)
12	4	Total number of sectors in the partition

mation. There is no defined limit to the number of extended partitions a device can contain.

The Boot Signature

The boot signature is the final item in the MBR sector. Byte 510 (1FEh) must equal 55h and byte 511 (1FFh) must equal AAh.

Table 7-2: The partition-type item in the partition table indicates the file system the partition uses.

Value (hex)	File System	Recommended Partition Size for Compatibility
00	–	Unused entry
01	FAT12	<= 16 MB
04	FAT16	>= 16 MB and < 32 MB
05	extended partition	0 to 2 GB
06	FAT16	32 MB to 2 GB
0B	FAT32	512 MB to 2 terabytes
0C	FAT32	512 MB to 2 terabytes, must support LBA
0E	FAT16	32 MB to 2 GB, must support LBA
0F	extended partition	0 to 2 GB, must support LBA

8

FAT File Systems

This chapter describes the FAT16 and FAT32 file systems and shows how to obtain information about a file from the file allocation tables.

Inside a FAT16 Volume

Media with capacities from 16 MB to 2 GB can use the FAT16 file system. Every FAT16 volume has these components:

- Reserved region, which contains the boot sector.
- FAT region, which contains two copies of the file allocation tables (FATs).
- Root-directory region.
- File and directory data region, which can hold files and subdirectories.

These components are stored in sequence in the volume.

To format a volume, or logical drive, under Windows XP, right-click the drive in Windows Explorer and click Format. The Window that appears

Figure 8-1: Windows Explorer enables formatting logical drives.

(Figure 8-1) shows the media's capacity and a combo box that enables selecting FAT (for FAT16) or FAT32. File systems that aren't suitable for the media don't display in the combo box. The default allocation size (cluster size) is likely to be the only option presented. You can also enter a Volume label for the media. Click Start to format the volume. Another option is to use the *format* command at a command prompt. The */a* parameter enables setting a cluster size. Type *help format* at the command prompt for a list of supported parameters. Remember that formatting destroys all data in the volume.

Reserved Region

The first region in a FAT16 volume is the reserved region, which consists of a single sector called the boot sector. The boot sector begins at the LBA value stored in the MBR sector's partition table, in byte 8 of the volume's entry in the table. In media that doesn't have a master boot record, the boot sector is the first sector. The sector contains a BIOS Parameter Block (BPB), an area reserved for boot code, and a boot signature.

BIOS Parameter Block

Table 8-1 shows the first 62 bytes in a FAT16 boot sector. Technically, the BIOS parameter block (BPB) consists of the data in bytes 11–35, while the remaining bytes are included in every boot sector but are not part of the BPB. A computer that is formatting a volume for FAT16 fills these locations with appropriate values. The information in the BPB enables a computer to locate the volume's FATs, the root directory, and the file-and-directory data region, also called the data area.

Byte 13 in the BPB specifies how many sectors are in a data cluster. Each cluster holds data that belongs to a single file. Large files can use multiple clusters. Any extra space at the end of a file's final cluster is unavailable for other uses. The choice of cluster size is a compromise between efficient access and efficient use of the storage media. A large cluster size is more efficient when accessing large files because the file-system software needs to locate and access fewer clusters. A small cluster size wastes less space, especially if there are many very small files.

The number of data clusters determines what file system to use, as described later in this chapter.

For maximum compatibility with mass-storage host software, several items in a FAT16 boot sector have required or recommended values, shown in Table 8-2. In theory all of the values except the number of reserved sectors can vary, but straying from the recommended values may cause problems with some hosts.

The location of the value that specifies the total number of sectors in the volume varies depending on the volume's capacity. If less than 32 KB, the value is in the two bytes beginning at byte 19 in the BPB. If equal to or greater than 32 KB, the value is in the four bytes beginning at byte 32. Program code generally uses these values rather than the equivalent value stored in the partition-table entry.

Offset zero can contain a jump instruction to boot code. For PCs, the instruction is 80x86 machine code. FAT16 volumes typically contain EBh 3Ch 90h, which means jump ahead 60 bytes to the boot code, which begins at byte 3Eh in the BPB. EBh is the jump instruction, 3Ch (60) is the number of bytes to jump, and 90h is a NOP (no operation).

Table 8-1: The boot sector contains low-level information about the media's formatting. These are the fields for a FAT16 volume (Sheet 1 of 2).

Byte	Description	Size (bytes)	Comments
0	Jump instruction to boot code.	3	For bootable media, byte zero contains EBh or E9h for an x86 unconditional jump. Set to 00h for non-bootable media.
3	String that identifies the operating system that formatted the media	8	Use "MSWIN4.1" for maximum compatibility.
11	Number of bytes per sector	2	Use 512 for maximum compatibility. Other allowed values are 1K, 2K, 4K, 8K, 16K, 32K, and 64K.
13	Number of sectors per cluster	1	Allowed values are 1, 2, 4, 8, 16, 32, 64, and 128. For maximum compatibility, cluster size must be 32K or less.
14	Number of reserved sectors	2	Must be 1.
16	Number of FATs (identical copies)	1	Use 2 for maximum compatibility.
17	Maximum number of entries in the root directory	2	Use 512 for maximum compatibility.
19	Total number of sectors if less than 32K	2	The total number of sectors in the media if less than 32K. The count begins with the boot sector and includes all regions. Otherwise zero.
21	Media descriptor	1	Use F8h for non-removable media and F0h for removable media. This value is also stored in the first byte of cluster zero but is generally unused in both locations.
22	Number of sectors per FAT	2	The number of sectors in one FAT.
24	Number of sectors per track	2	Not used in LBA.
26	Number of heads	2	Not used in LBA.
28	Number of hidden sectors	4	The number of hidden sectors that precede the partition that contains this FAT volume. Operating-system specific. Zero if the media doesn't have an MBR sector.
32	Total number of sectors	4	The total number of sectors in the volume if 32K or greater. The count begins with the boot sector and includes all regions. Otherwise zero.
36	Logical drive number of the partition	1	Operating-system specific.

Table 8-1: The boot sector contains low-level information about the media's formatting. These are the fields for a FAT16 volume (Sheet 2 of 2).

Byte	Description	Size (bytes)	Comments
37	Reserved	1	00h.
38	Extended boot signature	1	Set to 29h if the three fields below are present.
39	Volume serial number	4	Typically created using the date and time of formatting.
43	Volume label	11	Text that identifies the volume. Most software ignores this and instead uses the volume label in the partition's root directory. The two labels should be identical.
54	File system type	8	"FAT16"or "FAT". Not used to determine the file system type.

The bytes beginning at offset 54 can store text that identifies the file system, but program code shouldn't rely on this text to identify the file system. As I'll explain later in this chapter, the choice of file system depends entirely on the number of data clusters in the volume.

Boot Code

Locations 62 through 509 hold the boot code (448 bytes). As Chapter 7 explained, if the partition table indicates that a volume is bootable, on boot up, the executable code in the MBR jumps to the boot code in the volume's boot sector. The boot code loads the operating system. Embedded systems typically don't boot from storage devices and can ignore this code.

Boot Signature

In a valid boot sector, byte 510 contains 55h and byte 511 contains AAh. For media with sectors larger than 512 bytes, these locations remain the same even though they aren't the last bytes in the sector.

File Allocation Table Region

Following the reserved sector are two identical copies of the file allocation table (FAT). A FAT16 table has a 16-bit entry for each data cluster in the

Table 8-2: Recommended and required values for fields in a FAT16 boot sector.

Byte	Description	Recommended Value
3	Identifying string	"MSWin4.1"
11	Bytes per sector	512
14	Number of reserved sectors	1 (required)
16	FAT copies	2
17	Maximum root directory entries	512

volume. Files that require multiple clusters use the FAT to maintain a record of the clusters used by each file. Later in this chapter, I explain how program code can use the FAT to locate the clusters used by a file. The second FAT is a backup for use in repairing a damaged first copy.

Root Directory Region

In a FAT16 volume, the sectors following the FATs contain the root directory. The root directory typically can store up to 512 entries of 32 bytes each. If the sector size is 512, the root directory requires 32 sectors. The root directory contains information about the files and subfolders in the device's top-level directory. Note that the size of the root directory region limits the number of entries a FAT16 root directory can store. As Chapter 9 explains, files with long file names reduce the number of file entries the directory can store.

File and Directory Data Region

The sectors after the root directory are grouped into data clusters. A data cluster can consist of one or more sectors. Because the FAT has an entry for each cluster and reserves the first two entries for other purposes, the first data cluster is called cluster 2, with the rest following in sequence. Files and subdirectories are stored in the clusters.

Each subdirectory is a directory much like the root directory and can contain entries for files and additional subdirectories immediately below the subdirectory. An embedded-system host might support only the root directory, ignoring any entries for subdirectories.

Inside a FAT32 Volume

FAT32 is an option for larger media that can't use FAT16. A FAT32 system has other advantages as well, such as no limit on root-directory size and the availability of additional information for use in repairing damaged media and finding free clusters quickly. Compared to FAT16, a FAT32 system requires more storage space for the FATs because the entries are twice as long.

Every FAT32 volume has these components:

- Reserved region, which contains the boot sector.
- FAT region, which contains two copies of the file allocation tables (FATs).
- File and directory data region, which can hold the root directory, files, and subdirectories.

These components are stored in sequence in the volume.

The sections that follow focus on the differences between FAT32 and FAT16 and assume you're familiar with the preceding information about FAT16.

Reserved Region

The first region in a FAT32 volume is the reserved region, which consists of the boot sector, an FSInfo structure containing information to help in finding free clusters, and a backup copy of the boot sector.

The Boot Sector

As with FAT16, the boot sector begins at the LBA value stored in the volume's entry in the partition table. Table 8-3 shows the first 90 bytes in a FAT32 boot sector. Technically, the BIOS parameter block (BPB) consists of the data in bytes 11–63, while the remaining bytes are part of the boot sector but not in the BPB.

Compared to FAT16, a FAT32 BPB has these differences:

- The number of reserved sectors in byte 14 is typically 32 rather than 1.
- The maximum number of entries in the root directory in byte 17 is unused because FAT32 has no limit.

Table 8-3: A volume's boot sector contains low-level information about the media's formatting. These values are for a FAT32 volume (Sheet 1 of 2).

Byte	Description	Size (bytes)	Comments
0	Jump instruction to boot code.	3	For bootable media, byte zero contains EBh or E9h for an x86 unconditional jump. Set to 00h for non-bootable media.
3	String that identifies the operating system that formatted the media	8	Use "MSWIN4.1" for maximum compatibility.
11	Number of bytes per sector	2	Use 512 for maximum compatibility. Other allowed values are 1K, 2K, 4K, 8K, 16K, 32K, and 64K.
13	Number of sectors per cluster	1	Allowed values are 1, 2, 4, 8, 16, 32, 64, and 128. For maximum compatibility, cluster size must be 32K or less.
14	Number of reserved sectors	2	Includes all sectors that precede the FATs. Typically 32.
16	Number of FATs (identical copies)	1	Use 2 for maximum compatibility.
17	Unused	2	0000h.
19	Unused	2	0000h.
21	Media descriptor	1	Use F8h for non-removable media and F0h for removable media. This value is also stored in the first byte of cluster 0 and is generally unused in both locations.
22	Unused	2	0000h.
24	Number of sectors per track	2	Not used in LBA.
26	Number of heads	2	Not used in LBA.
28	Number of hidden sectors	4	The number of hidden sectors that precede the partition that contains this FAT volume. Operating-system specific.
32	Total number of sectors	4	The total number of sectors in the volume. The count begins with the boot sector and includes all regions.
36	Number of sectors per FAT	4	The number of sectors in one FAT.
40	Flags	2	Bits 3..0: zero-based number of the active FAT. Valid only if mirroring is disabled. Bits 6..4: reserved. Bit 7: 0 if the FAT is mirrored at runtime into all FATs; 1 if mirroring is disabled.

Table 8-3: A volume's boot sector contains low-level information about the media's formatting. These values are for a FAT32 volume (Sheet 2 of 2).

Byte	Description	Size (bytes)	Comments
42	Version number of the FAT32 volume	2	The high byte is the major revision number and the low byte is the minor revision number. Use 0000h.
44	Cluster number of the first cluster of the root directory.	4	Use 2 for maximum compatibility.
48	Sector number of the FSINFO structure within the reserved region	2	Usually 1.
50	The sector number of a backup copy of the boot record within the reserved area	2	Set to 6 for maximum compatibility. Set to zero if no backup copy is available.
52	Reserved	12	Set all bytes to 00h.
64	Logical drive number of the partition	1	Operating-system specific.
65	Reserved	1	00h.
66	Extended boot signature	1	Set to 29h to indicate that the three fields that follow are present.
67	Volume serial number	4	Typically created using the date and time of formatting.
71	Volume label	11	Text that identifies the volume.
82	File system type	8	"FAT32". Not used to determine the file system type,

- The total number of sectors is always at offset 32 because a FAT32 volume is always at least 32 KB.
- The number of sectors per FAT is in bytes 24h–27h.
- The cluster number of the root directory is at offset 44 because FAT32 has no dedicated location for the root directory.
- Byte 48 holds the location of the FSInfo structure and byte 50 holds the location of the backup boot sector. FAT16 doesn't have these components.
- A Flags field at byte 40 indicates whether the file system maintains identical FATs or whether only one FAT should be considered valid. If only

one FAT is considered valid, the Flags specify which one. A FAT16 BPB has no Flags field.

- Some fields that have identical functions are stored in different locations in FAT16 and FAT32 BPBs.
- The boot code, if present, begins at byte 90.

For maximum compatibility with mass-storage host software, several items in a FAT32 boot sector have recommended values, as shown in Table 8-4. In theory all of the values shown can vary, but straying from the recommended values can cause problems with some hosts.

As in a FAT16 BPB, byte 13 stores the number of sectors per cluster.

A FAT32 boot sector can contain boot code in bytes 90–509 and the sector must have a boot signature of AA55h in bytes 510–511. The jump instruction at offset 00h is typically EBh 58h 90h, which means jump ahead 88 bytes to the beginning of the boot code at 5Ah.

The FSInfo Structure

The FSInfo structure can contain information to help the master computer find free clusters quickly. The structure is in the location specified in byte 48 in the BPB. The location is typically in reserved sector 1, immediately following the boot sector. Table 8-5 shows the contents of the FSInfo structure.

The Backup Boot Sector

Sectors 6–8 in the reserved region can store a backup copy of the three sectors beginning with the volume's boot sector. The backup is for use in media repair if the original copy is damaged.

File Allocation Table Region

As with FAT16, following the reserved region are two copies of the file allocation tables (FATs). A FAT32 table has a 32-bit entry for each data cluster in the volume. The highest four bits are reserved, however. During formatting, all 32 bits of each entry are set to zero. After formatting, software that reads and writes to the FAT should preserve the contents of the four high bits.

The Flags field in the BPB specifies whether or not the FATs are mirrored. If mirroring is enabled, the file-system driver maintains two identical copies of

Table 8-4: Recommended values for fields in a FAT32 boot sector.

Byte	Description	Recommended Value
3	Identifying string	"MSWin4.1"
11	Bytes per sector	512
14	Number of reserved sectors	32
16	FAT copies	2
44	First cluster of the root directory	2
48	FSInfo sector	1
50	Location of backup copy of boot record	6

the FAT. If any portion of the area reserved for one of the FATs becomes damaged, the value in the Flags field can disable mirroring and specify which FAT the file system should use.

File and Directory Data Region

As with FAT16, the file-and-directory data region consists of data clusters that can store files and subdirectories. In a FAT32 system, this region stores the root directory. The first data cluster is cluster 2.

Selecting a File System

Which FAT file system a volume is formatted for depends entirely on the number of data clusters in the volume. The data clusters include all of the clusters beginning with cluster 2 in the file-and-directory data region. They don't include the MBR sector, reserved region, FAT region, or FAT16 root-directory sectors.

Cluster Sizes

The FAT32 specification says that a volume with fewer than 4085 data clusters is formatted as FAT12, and a volume with 4085 to 65524 data clusters is formatted as FAT16. Valid FAT12 cluster numbers are 2 to FEFh, so the maximum number of FAT12 clusters is actually 4078. Valid FAT16 cluster numbers are 2 to FFEFh, so the maximum number of FAT16 clusters is actually 65518. A volume with 65527 or more data clusters is formatted as FAT32.

Table 8-5: The FSInfo structure contains information that can help the file-system driver find free clusters quickly.

Byte	Size (bytes)	Description
0	4	FSI_LeadSig signature. Must equal 41615252h.
4	480	Reserved. Set all bytes to 00h.
484	4	FSI_StrucSig signature. Must equal 61417272h.
488	4	The number of the last known free cluster. Set to FFFFFFFh if unknown.
492	4	The cluster number where the file-system driver should start looking for free clusters. Set to FFFFFFFFh if unknown
496	12	Reserved. Set all bytes to 00h.
508	4	FSI_TrailSig signature. Must equal AA550000h.

Formatting software can select a file system by setting the cluster size so the number of clusters is in the desired range. Because some existing FAT implementations don't calculate the number of clusters correctly, Microsoft recommends formatting all volumes to have at least 16 clusters more than the specified minimum and 16 clusters less than the specified maximum for the file system. Also note that a few values are outside the recommended ranges for any FAT file system.

Table 8-6 shows the cluster sizes Windows XP Professional uses for FAT16 and FAT32 volumes of different capacities. For maximum compatibility, volumes smaller than 16 MB should use FAT12. Windows can't format volumes greater than 32 GB using FAT32 but can read volumes of this size if formatted in another operating system.

The FAT32 specification describes a method for calculating the number of data clusters in a volume. (It's not as straightforward as you might think.) Embedded systems that format storage media can do the calculations, or they can just use the same cluster size as Windows for their volume size.

A Hardware Solution

Device firmware typically implements support for FAT file systems. Another option is to interface to a chip that supports FAT communications. The uALFAT™ chip from GHI Electronics can access media formatted for the FAT12, FAT16, and FAT32 file systems. A microcontroller can communi-

Table 8-6: The data-cluster size varies with the file system and storage capacity. (Source: Windows XP Professional Resource Kit)

Volume Size	FAT16 Cluster Size	FAT32 Cluster Size
16 MB–32 MB	512 bytes	Not supported
33 MB–64 MB	1 KB	512 bytes
65 MB–128 MB	2 KB	1 KB
129 MB–256 MB	4 KB	2 KB
257 MB–512 MB	8 KB	4 KB
513 MB–1024 MB	16 KB	4 KB
1025 MB–2 GB	32 KB	4 KB
2 GB–4 GB	64 KB[1]	4 KB
4 GB–8 GB	Not supported	4 KB
8 GB–16 GB	Not supported	8 KB
16 GB–32 GB	Not supported	16 KB
[1]Not supported by all FAT16 file systems.		

cate with the chip using an asynchronous serial interface, SPI, or an I^2C bus. The chip also supports MultiMediaCard and SD-Card communications.

The chip responds to text commands. File commands enable opening, closing, reading, writing to, and deleting a file. Directory commands enable creating, changing, listing, and erasing a directory. Also supported are commands for reading and writing directly to sectors in the storage media. The chip requires +3.3V and +1.8V power supplies.

The uALFAT-SD development board includes a MultiMediaCard/SD-Card connector and a regulator to convert 3.3V to 1.8V. A quick way to experiment with the board is to insert a a MultiMediaCard or SD Card, connect the board to a PC, and use a terminal program such as Windows' Hyperterminal to send commands and receive responses.

To connect to a PC, connect the board's asynchronous serial pins to the corresponding pins on a Maxim MAX3232 or similar RS-232 transceiver. If your PC doesn't have an RS-232 port, connect the transceiver's RS-232 pins to corresponding signals on an RS-232/USB converter. Or use an FTDI Chip USB UART to interface the uAFLAT with a PC's USB port.

The File Allocation Table

The file allocation table contains an entry for each data cluster in a volume. In a FAT16 volume, each entry is 16 bits. In a FAT32 volume, each entry is 32 bits, with the lower 28 bits used to store a cluster number.

The First Two Entries

The first two entries in the FAT don't store cluster information. In entry zero, the lowest byte should match the media-type byte in byte 21 in the BPB. (The media-type byte is generally unused. To find out whether a device has removable media, a host can send an INQUIRY command and check the RMB bit in the response, as described in Chapter 6.) All other bits are set to 1.

Formatting a volume sets entry 1 in a FAT16 table to a value from FFF8h to FFFFh. The mass-storage host can set the two highest bits of the entry to indicate error conditions. Bit 15 may be set to zero to indicate a dirty volume, which means that the system shut down or the device was removed before all pending writes completed. Bit 14 may be set to zero to indicate that the file system's driver had an I/O error the last time the media was made available.

For entry 1 in a FAT32 table, bits 15..0 are the same as for FAT16, and bits 27..16 are 1s.

Data Clusters

Entry 2 in a FAT is the first entry for a data cluster. The first data cluster in the volume is thus called cluster 2. There is no data cluster 0 or data cluster 1. The other clusters follow cluster 2 in sequence, to a maximum of FFEFh (FAT16) or FFFFFEFh (FAT32). Table 8-7 shows the meanings of values in FAT entries.

The series of clusters used by a file is called a cluster chain (Figure 8-2). A file's directory entry contains the number of the file's first cluster. If a file in a FAT16 volume requires only one cluster, the FAT entry for that cluster contains a value from FFF8h to FFFFh. These values, called end-of-clus-

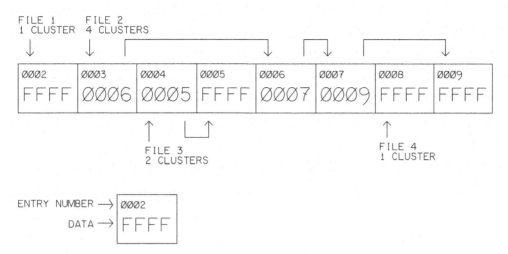

Figure 8-2: The FAT keeps a record of the clusters used by a file. FAT16 entries are 2 bytes.

ter-chain (EOC) markers, indicate that the cluster is the last cluster used by a file or directory. For example, if the file's only cluster is 0008h, entry 0008h in the FAT contains an EOC marker.

If a file requires two clusters, the FAT entry for the file's first cluster contains the number of the file's next cluster and the entry for the second cluster contains an EOC marker. For example, if a file uses clusters 0004h and 0005h in sequence, entry 0004h contains 0005h, and entry 0005h contains an EOC marker.

In a similar way, if a file requires more than two clusters, the FAT entry for each cluster except the last contains the number of the file's next cluster, and the entry for the last cluster contains an EOC marker. For example, if a file uses clusters 0003h, 0006h, 0007h, and 0009h in sequence, entry 0003h contains 0006h, entry 0006h contains 0007h, entry 0007h contains 0009h, and entry 0009h contains an EOC marker. A file whose clusters aren't contiguous is called a fragmented file.

A FAT32 table works the same way except the entries are 32 bits with the highest four bits ignored.

Using the FAT is essential for large files, but an embedded system that doesn't need large files could choose to support files that fit in single clusters only.

Table 8-7: A FAT entry tells whether a cluster is available, bad, or in use and if in use, the number of the next cluster in a file or directory, if any.

FAT16 Range (hex)	FAT32 Range (hex) (ignore bits 28--31)	Description
0000	0000000	available cluster
0001	0000001	reserved cluster
0002--FFEF	0000002--FFFFFEF	the number of the next cluster in the file
FFF0--FFF6	FFFFFF0--FFFFFF6	reserved (not currently defined)
FFF7	FFFFFF7	bad cluster
FFF8--FFFF	FFFFFF8--FFFFFFF	the file's last cluster (EOC marker)

Accessing the FAT

The PIC18F4550 FAT16 firmware that follows shows how to convert a data-cluster number to a logical block address, how to read and write to the FAT, how to find a file's next cluster, and how to find an empty cluster.

Volume Information

A DISK structure can hold in information about a volume and its FAT:

```
#define FAT16    2
#define FAT32    3

typedef struct
{
    byte*   buffer;      // pointer to a buffer equal to one sector
    dword   firsts;      // LBA of the volume's first sector
    dword   fat;         // LBA of the volume's FAT
    dword   root;        // LBA of the volume's root directory
    dword   data;        // LBA of the volume's data area
    word    maxroot;     // maximum number of entries in the root directory
    dword   maxcls;      // maximum number of data clusters in the volume
    word    fatsize;     // number of sectors in the FAT
    byte    fatcopy;     // number of copies of the FAT
    byte    SecPerClus;  // number of sectors per cluster
    byte    type;        // type of FAT (FAT16, FAT32)
    byte    mount;       // TRUE if the media is mounted, FALSE if not mounted)
} DISK;
```

File Information

A FILE structure can store information about a file, including its location in a volume and a location currently being accessed in the file. (Chapter 9 has more about directories, and Chapter 10 has more about accessing files.)

```
// A short file name has 11 or fewer characters, not counting the dot.

#define FILE_NAME_SIZE   11

typedef struct
{
    unsigned   write :1;          // Set if the file was opened for writing.
    unsigned   FileWriteEOF :1;   // Set if writing and have reached the end of the file.
}FileFlags;

typedef struct
{
    DISK       *dsk;              // a DISK structure for the volume containing the file
    word       cluster;          // number of the first file's cluster
    word       ccls;             // current cluster
    word       sec;              // current sector in the current cluster
    word       pos;              // current byte location in the current sector
    dword      seek;             // current byte location in the file
    dword      size;             // file size
    FileFlags  Flags;            // write mode and end-of-file indicators
    word       time;             // last update time
    word       date;             // last update date
    char       name[FILE_NAME_SIZE];   // file name
    word       entry;            // position of the file's entry in its directory
    word       chk;              // FILE structure checksum = ~( entry + name[0])
    word       attributes;       // file's attributes
    word       dirclus;          // first cluster of the file's directory
    word       dirccls;          // current cluster of the file's directory
} FILE;
```

A FILEOBJ is a pointer to a FILE structure:

```
typedef FILE     * FILEOBJ;
```

Functions in this chapter use these defines:

```
#define CLUSTER_FAIL        0xffff
#define LAST_CLUSTER        0xfff8
#define LAST_CLUSTER_FAT16  0xfff8
```

Obtaining a Cluster's Logical Block Address

A file's directory entry and FAT entries store cluster numbers. To read data from the storage media, firmware must specify a logical block address. The Cluster2Sector function accepts a pointer to a DISK structure and a cluster number and returns the LBA of the cluster's first sector.

```
dword Cluster2Sector(DISK *dsk, word cluster)
{
    dword sector;

    // Data clusters 0 and 1 don't exist.
    // If cluster = 0 or 1, assume it's the root directory.

    if (cluster == 0 || cluster == 1)

        sector = dsk -> root + cluster;

    else

        // The data area begins with cluster 2.
        // Subtract 2 from the cluster number to get the cluster number within the data area.
        // Multiply the result by the number of sectors per cluster to get the sector number
        // within the data area.
        // Add the number of the first sector in the data area to get the absolute sector
        //  number for the cluster.

        sector = (u32)((u32)((u32)cluster-2) * (u32)disk->SecPerClus) + (u32)disk->data;

    return(sector);
}
```

Reading from the FAT

The FATread function accepts a pointer to a DISK structure (dsk) and a cluster number (ccls), reads the FAT entry for that cluster, and returns the value read, which is the number of the next cluster in the file or directory or an EOC marker. The function calls the SectorRead function from Chapter 5.

The function uses the RAMreadW macro to read a word at the address specified by a base address (a) plus an offset(f):

```
#define RAMreadW(a, f) *(word *)(a + f)
```

```
word FATread(DISK *dsk, word ccls)
{
    word    c;
    word    d;
    dword   l;
    word    p;
    byte    q;

    // Get the address of the file's current cluster.
    // The address is two bytes, LSB first.

    p = ccls;

    // The LBA of the FAT sector containing the cluster's data is the FAT's starting address
    // plus the high byte of the current cluster.
    // (Each sector contains 256 two-byte entries.)

    l = dsk -> fat + (p >> 8);

    // Read the sector.

    if ( SectorRead( l, dsk -> buffer) != sdcValid)

        return CLUSTER_FAIL;

    // To get the value stored in the cluster's entry,
    // read 2 bytes in the buffer of retrieved data
    // beginning at offset = low byte of current cluster's address << 1.
    // Shift left 1 (multiply by 2) because each entry is 2 bytes.

    c = RAMreadW(dsk -> buffer, ((p & 0xFF) << 1));

    if (c >= LAST_CLUSTER_FAT16)

        // The entry is an EOC marker.

        c = LAST_CLUSTER;

    return c;
}
```

Writing to the FAT

The FATwrite function accepts a pointer to a DISK structure (dsk), a cluster number (cls), and a value to write to the FAT entry for the cluster (v). The function gets the LBA of the sector containing the entry to write to, reads the sector into a buffer, writes the value to the entry, and writes the sector back to the storage media. The function calls the SectorRead and Sector-Write functions from Chapter 5.

The function uses the RAMwrite macro to write a value (d) to the address specified by a base address (a) plus an offset(f):

```
#define RAMwrite(a, f, d) *(a + f) = d

word FATwrite(DISK *dsk, word cls, word v)
{
    byte    c;
    byte    i;
    dword   l
    dword   li;
    word    p;
    byte    q;

    // Each entry is 2 bytes.
    // To get the offset of the entry in the FAT, multiply the cluster number by 2.

    p = cls * 2;

    // To get the sector containing the entry, divide the entry's offset by 512 .

    l = dsk -> fat + (p >> 9 );

    // To get the offset within the sector, set bits 9-16 of the entry's offset to zero.

    p &= 0x1ff;

    // Read the sector into a buffer.

    if ( SectorRead( l, dsk->buffer) != sdcValid)
        return FAIL;
```

```
// Copy the passed value (v) into the FAT entry for the passed cluster number (cls)
// in the buffer. The LSB is at the lower offset.

RAMwrite(dsk -> buffer, p, v);
RAMwrite(dsk -> buffer, p+1, (v >> 8));

// Write the edited buffer to both FAT copies

for ( i = 0, li = l; i < dsk -> fatcopy; i++, li += dsk -> fatsize)

    if ( SectorWrite(l, dsk -> buffer) != sdcValid)
        return FAIL;

if (c >= LAST_CLUSTER_FAT16)

    // The entry is an EOC marker.

    c = LAST_CLUSTER;

return c;

}
```

Finding a File's Next Cluster

The FILEget_next_cluster function can find the next cluster in a file. The function accepts a FILEOBJ pointer to a FILE structure (fo) and a number (n) that specifies how many clusters beyond the current cluster to look. The function sets the FILE structure's ccls member to the requested cluster number. If n = 1, the function sets ccls to point to the cluster following the current cluster value in the passed file structure.

```
#define CE_GOOD                 0  // No error.
#define CE_BAD_SECTOR_READ      7  // Error in reading a sector.
#define CE_FAT_EOF              60 // Attempt to read beyond the FAT's EOF.
#define CE_INVALID_CLUSTER      9  // The cluster number > maxcls.

byte FILEget_next_cluster(FILEOBJ fo, word n)
{
    word    c;
    word    c2;
    DISK    *disk;
    byte    error = CE_GOOD;
```

```
    // Save the FILE structure's dsk member.

    disk = fo -> dsk;

    do {

        // Save the file's current cluster number.
        c2 = fo -> ccls;

        // Read the next cluster number from the FAT entry for the current cluster.

        if ( (c = FATread(disk, c2)) == FAIL)

            error = CE_BAD_SECTOR_READ;

        else
        {
            if ( c >= disk -> maxcls)
            {
                // The cluster number is greater than the volume's last cluster's number.
                // Set a return value but then check to see if the entry is an EOC marker.

                error = CE_INVALID_CLUSTER;
            }
            c2 = LAST_CLUSTER;

            if ( c >= c2)
            {
                // The entry is an EOC marker, so the current cluster is the file's last one.

                error = CE_FAT_EOF;
            }
        }
    // The cluster number is valid. Store the new current cluster number.

    fo -> ccls = c;

    // Quit on finding the desired cluster or on error.

    } while (--n > 0 && error == CE_GOOD);

    return(error);
}
```

Performing Sequential Reads

The FATReadQueued function is identical to the FATread function above except that it's optimized for doing multiple, sequential reads of the FAT. The function reads a sector from the media only if the entry to read is the first one in a sector. Otherwise, the function assumes that the passed DISK structure's buffer member contains the sector with the entry to read.

```
word FATReadQueued( DISK *dsk, word ccls)
{
    word    c;
    word    d;
    dword   l;
    word    p;
    byte    q;

        // Save the passed cluster number.

        p = ccls;

        // Each sector holds 256 two-byte entries.
        // If the LSB of the cluster number = 0, the FAT entry is in a new sector.

        if ((ccls & 0xFF) == 0x00)
        {
            // Get the sector number.
            // The LBA of the FAT sector containing the cluster's data is the FAT's starting
            // address plus the high byte of the current cluster's address.
            // (Each sector contains 256 two-byte entries.)

            l = dsk -> fat + (p >> 8 );

            // Read the sector containing the entry.

            if (SectorRead( l, dsk -> buffer) != sdcValid)
                return CLUSTER_FAIL;
        }
        // To find the number of the next cluster,
        // read 2 bytes in the buffer of retrieved data
        // beginning at offset = low byte of current cluster's address << 1.
        // Shift left 1 (multiply by 2) because each entry is 2 bytes.

        c = RAMreadW( dsk -> buffer, ((p & 0xFF) << 1));
```

```
    if (c >= LAST_CLUSTER_FAT16)

        // The entry is an EOC marker.

        c = LAST_CLUSTER;
    return c;
}
```

Finding an Empty Cluster

To find an empty cluster in the FAT, firmware reads entries until finding an entry that contains 0000h.

The FATfindEmptyCluster function accepts a FILEOBJ pointer to a FILE structure and returns the number of an available cluster. The function starts looking at the cluster immediately following the file structure's current cluster number (ccls). If ccls is the file's final cluster and the function is looking for a cluster to append to the file, the new cluster will be the one following the current cluster if possible. The firmware thus avoids creating fragmented files when not required.

```
#define CLUSTER_EMPTY    0x0000
#define END_CLUSTER      0xFFFE

word FATfindEmptyCluster(FILEOBJ fo)
{
    word    c;
    word    curcls;
    DISK    *disk;
    word    value = 0x0;

    // Save the DISK structure and current cluster number.

    disk = fo -> dsk;
    c = fo -> ccls;

    // Cluster 2 is the first cluster.

    if (c < 2)
        c = 2;

    curcls = c;
```

```
// Read the FAT entry for the current cluster.

FATread(disk, c);

// Starting at the cluster immediately following the current cluster number,
// scan through the FAT looking for an empty cluster.

while (c)
{
   c++;

   // If we get to the end of the FAT, start from the beginning.

   if (value == END_CLUSTER || c >= disk -> maxcls)

      c = 2;

   // If we get to the current cluster, there are no empty entries.

   if ( c == curcls)
   {
      c = 0;
      break;
   }
   // Read an entry.

   if ( (value = FATReadQueued(disk, c)) == CLUSTER_FAIL)
   {
      c = 0;
      break;
   }

   // Quit the loop on finding an empty cluster.

   if (value == CLUSTER_EMPTY)
      break;

}
return(c);
```

9

Directories

This chapter explains how directories store information and shows how to access and store information in directories and subdirectories. The code in this chapter uses the FILE and DISK structures from Chapter 8.

The Contents of an Entry

The root directory contains a 32-byte entry for each file in the root directory and each subdirectory directly under the root directory. These entries are sometimes called DOS 8.3 entries or just 8.3 entries because each can store a file name no longer than eight characters before the dot and three characters after the dot (for example, MYFILE01.TXT). The limitation dates to the MS-DOS operating system.

If the file-system driver supports long file names, any name that doesn't fit in an 8.3 entry is stored in one or more additional 32-byte entries that precede the 8.3 entry, and the 8.3 entry stores a short version of the file name. An 8.3 entry uses upper-case text only, so another use for long-file-name entries is to support lower-case text.

Every file and subdirectory has a directory entry. The root directory doesn't have an entry.

File Entries

Table 9-1 shows the contents of a directory entry. The essential fields are the DOS 8.3 fields. The additional fields are optional for many applications.

The File Name

The file-name field at byte zero contains the characters before the dot. The file-extension field at byte 8 contains the characters after the dot. (The dot isn't stored in the directory.) All text is upper case.

In an entry that contains a file name, any unused locations in the file-name and extension fields should contain the code for a space (20h).

In an unused entry, the first byte in the file-name field is 00h or E5h. The value 00h means that all of the entries that follow in the directory are also available.

An 8.3 name has several limitations:

- Each character code in the file name and extension is eight bits. Original 8.3 entries in PCs use character codes from the system's OEM code page, which defines character codes for a geographical region.
- All text characters are stored as upper case.
- An 8.3 file name must begin with a letter or a number. In addition to upper-case letters and numbers, a name can contain spaces and any of these characters:

  $ % ' - _ @ ~ ' ! ( )

- Windows doesn't allow any of these as file names: CON, AUX, COM1–COM4, LPT1–LPT3, PRN, NUL.

Attributes

The Attributes field at byte 11 contains six bits that provide information about the entry. Table 9-2 lists the bits and their meanings. If bits 0–3 are all 1s, the entry is a long-file-name entry.

Table 9-1: The main directory entry for a file has 32 bytes.

Byte	Length (bytes)	Description	DOS 8.3 (original)
0	8	Short file name. The file name before the dot using the system's OEM code page. Eight characters maximum, upper case only.	yes
8	3	File extension. The file name after the dot using the OEM code page. Three characters maximum, upper case only.	yes
11	1	Attributes.	yes
12	1	Reserved for Windows NT. Set to zero on formatting.	no
13	1	File creation time, hundredths of a second portion. Valid values are 0–199.	no
14	2	File creation time, hour, minute, seconds portion: bits 15..11 hours, valid range 0–23; bits 10..5 minutes, valid range 0–59; bits 4..0 seconds / 2, valid range 0–29	no
16	2	File creation date: bits 15..9 years since 1980, valid range 0–127; bits 8..5 month, valid range 1–12; bits 4..0 day, valid range 1–31	no
18	2	Last accessed date: bits 15..9 years since 1980, valid range 0–127; bits 8..5 month, valid range 1–12; bits 4..0 day, valid range 1–31	no
20	2	For FAT16, zero. For FAT32, the high word of the file or directory's first cluster.	no
22	2	Last modified time: bits 15..11 hours, valid range 0–23; bits 10..5 minutes, valid range 0–59; bits 4..0 seconds / 2, valid range 0–29	yes
24	2	Last modified date: bits 15..9 years since 1980, valid range 0–127; bits 8..5 month, valid range 1–12; bits 4..0 day, valid range 1–31	yes
26	2	For FAT16, the number of the file or directory's first cluster. For FAT32, the low word of the file or directory's first cluster.	yes
28	4	File size in bytes.	yes

Table 9-2: The attribute bits in a directory entry provide additional information about a file.

Bit	Name	Meaning When Set to 1
0^1	R: read only	The file can't be written to. (Some hosts allow writing after prompting "Are you sure?")
1^1	H: hidden	Hide the file's directory listing from view unless the user has requested to view hidden files.
2^1	S: system	The file is a critical system file. Hide the file's directory listing from view unless the user has requested to view system files.
3^1	V: volume	The entry is for the volume label. A volume can have only one entry with this attribute. The entry must be in the root directory. The cluster number for this entry is zero.
4	D: directory	The entry is for a directory rather than for a file.
5	A: archive	The file hasn't been backed up since the last write operation to the file. The file-system driver should set this bit to 1 on creating, renaming, or writing to a file. Backup utilities can set the bit to zero to indicate that the file has been backed up.
6	–	Always zero.
7	–	Always zero.
[1]If bits 0–3 are all set to 1, the entry is a long-file-name entry.		

Date and Time Fields

Three sets of data-and-time fields can store when a file was created, when the file was last modified, and when the file was last accessed.

On file creation, the file-modified date and time fields (bytes 22–25) store the current date and time. Every time the file's contents are modified, the file-system driver should update the values to the current date and time. The time is specified in units of two seconds. These fields were in the original 8.3 entries, and every system that has a real-time clock should store values in these fields on creating or modifying a file. When copying or moving a file, this date and time should remain unchanged.

The file-creation date and time fields (bytes 13–17) store the date and time when a file was created. As with the file-modified time, one field stores the time with a resolution of two seconds. An additional time field stores hundredths of a second (0–199). The two values added together give the time. These fields weren't part of the original 8.3 entries. When copying a file, the copy's entry should have the current date and time. When moving a file, the creation date and time should remain unchanged. If unused, these fields should contain zeros.

The file-last-accessed date (bytes 18–19) stores the date when the file was last accessed. Many applications don't update this value or do so in inconsistent ways, so the stored information is of little use. If unused, these fields should contain zeros.

The FAT32 specification says that the file-modified date and time are required. The other dates and times are optional. An embedded system should support the file-modified fields if possible.

First Cluster

The first-cluster entry at offset 26 is the number of the file's first data cluster (FAT16) or the low word of the file's first data cluster (FAT32). For FAT32 volumes, offset 20 contains the high word of the file's first data cluster. The first data cluster in the data area is cluster 2, so the first-cluster number must be 2 or greater.

File Size

The file size field at offset 28 stores the size of the file in bytes.

Directory Entries

A directory entry is the same as a file entry with these exceptions:

Bit 4 in the Attributes field is set to 1 to indicate that the entry is for a directory.
The file-size field is zero.

In a FAT16 partition, the root directory follows the FATs. In a FAT32 partition, the root directory typically begins in cluster 2 in the data area. Offset 44 in a FAT32 volume's boot sector contains the cluster number where the root directory begins.

The first two entries in a subdirectory are the *dot* and *dotdot* entries:

.
..

```
00000000h: 2E 20 20 20 20 20 20 20 20 20 20 10 00 43 B0 A1 ; .        ..C°¡
00000010h: 3C 34 3C 34 00 00 B1 A1 3C 34 10 01 00 00 00 00 ; <4<4..±¡<4......
00000020h: 2E 2E 20 20 20 20 20 20 20 20 20 10 00 43 B0 A1 ; ..       ..C°¡
00000030h: 3C 34 3C 34 00 00 B1 A1 3C 34 00 00 00 00 00 00 ; <4<4..±¡<4......
00000040h: 46 49 4C 45 32 20 20 20 54 58 54 20 00 C6 C1 A1 ; FILE2   TXT .ÆÁ¡
00000050h: 3C 34 3C 34 00 00 2A 9D 3C 34 13 01 12 00 00 00 ; <4<4..*□<4......
00000060h: 49 4D 41 47 45 31 20 20 54 49 46 20 00 12 C2 A1 ; IMAGE1  TIF .Â¡
00000070h: 3C 34 3C 34 00 00 87 72 3C 34 14 01 70 35 04 00 ; <4<4..‡r<4..p5..
00000080h: 46 49 4C 45 31 20 20 20 54 58 54 20 00 44 C2 A1 ; FILE1   TXT .DÂ¡
00000090h: 3C 34 3C 34 00 00 22 9D 3C 34 22 02 0A 00 00 00 ; <4<4.."□<4".....
000000a0h: 53 55 42 32 20 20 20 20 20 20 20 10 00 9C DC A1 ; SUB2       ..œÜ¡
000000b0h: 3C 34 3C 34 00 00 DD A1 3C 34 23 02 00 00 00 00 ; <4<4..Ý¡<4#.....
000000c0h: 00 00 00 00 00 00 00 00 00 00 00 00 00 00 00 00 ; ................
000000d0h: 00 00 00 00 00 00 00 00 00 00 00 00 00 00 00 00 ; ................
```

Figure 9-1: Directory entries for a subdirectory with three files and one subdirectory. The first two entries are the dot and dotdot entries.

To help in understanding these entries, assume that a volume has a directory called sub1, and that sub1 has a subdirectory called sub2. Figure 9-1 shows the directory entries.

The *dot* entry points to the current subdirectory, sub2. The entry's file name is a dot followed by seven spaces (". "). The file size is zero. The contents of the date and time fields and the directory's high and low cluster numbers match the values in sub1's directory entry for sub2.

The *dotdot* entry points one level up, to the sub1 subdirectory in the example. The entry's file name is two dots followed by six spaces (".. "). The file size is zero. The contents of the date and time fields are the same as in the *dot* entry. The high and low cluster numbers match the values for the directory one level up. These values are the cluster number in sub1's dot entry. If sub1 is the root directory, the cluster number is zero.

The Volume Label Entry

A volume's root directory contains the one and only volume-label entry. The entry's fields have the same meanings as they do for files with two exceptions: bit 3 in the Attributes field is set to 1 to indicate that the entry is for a volume label, and for names longer than 8 characters, the file-system software doesn't insert a dot between the file-name and file-extension fields. (Long-file-name entries also set the volume bit but are not volume entries.)

Most software uses this volume label rather than the label stored in the partition's boot sector. The volume-label entry doesn't display in the root directory's directory listing.

Subdirectory Entries

A directory entry with the directory attribute equal to 1 and the volume attribute equal to zero defines a subdirectory under the directory. A subdirectory can use any available data clusters.

A small embedded system might support only the root directory, ignoring any subdirectory entries in the root directory and any files stored in subdirectories. Firmware that doesn't support subdirectories can avoid overwriting any inaccessible files and directories created by another host because the FATs identify the clusters as in use.

Handling Long File Names

In a file system that supports long file names, a file or directory name can be as long as 255 characters including one or more dots and extensions. A file's complete path has a maximum of 260 characters, however, so volumes with many levels of directories must use shorter names.

Each entry for an item with a long file name (LFN) has an 8.3 entry preceded by one or more 32-byte LFN entries. Systems that don't support long file names use the 8.3 entry and ignore the LFN entries. Under Windows, typing *dir /x* at a command prompt shows both the short and long file names.

A small embedded system might choose to support 8.3 file names only. Because every file with a long file name also has an 8.3 file name, a system can access any file using 8.3 file names. If a system that supports only 8.3 file names renames a file that had a long file name, the checksums in the LFN entries will almost always be invalid so the 8.3 file name will be the only valid name.

LFN Entries

Table 9-3 shows the fields in an LFN entry. Each entry stores up to 13 Unicode characters. Each character code is two bytes.

Table 9-3: Each long-file-name entry can store up to 13 characters.

Byte	Size (bytes)	Description
0	1	Ordinal field: the order of this entry in the series of LFN entries
1	2	Unicode character 1
3	2	Unicode character 2
5	2	Unicode character 3
7	2	Unicode character 4
9	2	Unicode character 5
11	1	Attributes. Must have bits 0–3 set.
12	1	Type. Set to zero to indicate a LFN entry.
13	1	Checksum
14	2	Unicode character 6
16	2	Unicode character 7
18	2	Unicode character 8
20	2	Unicode character 9
22	2	Unicode character 10
24	2	Unicode character 11
26	2	Cluster. Must equal zero. Included for compatibility with disk utilities.
28	2	Unicode character 12
30	2	Unicode character 13

A long file name can have lower-case characters, a leading dot (.myfile.txt), multiple dots (myfile.v1.txt), and spaces (my file.txt). Trailing dots (myfile.) and trailing spaces (myfile) are ignored. Any character that is valid in an 8.3 entry is valid in a long file name. Long file names allow a few additional character codes as well.

Unused character locations should contain FFFFh. The name should end in a null (0000h) if there is room in the final long-file-name entry.

The first byte in an LFN entry is the Ordinal field. In the LFN entry that immediately precedes the file's 8.3 entry, the Ordinal field contains 1. In the next LFN entry above, the Ordinal field contains 2, and so on up to a maximum of 20. In the Ordinal field with the highest number, bit 6 is set to 1 to indicate that the entry is the last one for the item.

```
00000060h: 43 78 00 74 00 00 00 FF FF FF FF 0F 00 43 FF FF ; Cx.t...ÿÿÿÿ..Cÿÿ
00000070h: FF FF FF FF FF FF FF FF FF FF 00 00 FF FF FF FF ; ÿÿÿÿÿÿÿÿÿÿ..ÿÿÿÿ
00000080h: 02 67 00 20 00 66 00 69 00 6C 00 0F 00 43 65 00 ; .g. .f.i.l...Ce.
00000090h: 20 00 6E 00 61 00 6D 00 65 00 00 00 2E 00 74 00 ;  .n.a.m.e....t.
000000a0h: 01 54 00 68 00 69 00 73 00 20 00 0F 00 43 69 00 ; .T.h.i.s. ...Ci.
000000b0h: 73 00 20 00 61 00 20 00 6C 00 00 00 6F 00 6E 00 ; s. .a. .l...o.n.
000000c0h: 54 48 49 53 49 53 7E 31 54 58 54 20 00 54 2F A3 ; THISIS~1TXT .T/£
000000d0h: 3C 34 3C 34 00 00 22 9D 3C 34 24 02 0A 00 00 00 ; <4<4.."□<4$.....
```

Figure 9-2: A file with the name "This is a long file name.txt" requires four 32-byte entries. The 8.3 file name is THISIS~1.TXT.

Figure 9-2 shows a directory entry for a file named "This is a long file name.txt". The entry at 00C0h contains the 8.3 file name and extension ("THISIS~1" and "TXT"). The entry at 00A0h contains the first 13 characters in the long file name: "This ", "is a l", "on". The entry at 0080h contains the next 13 characters: "g fil", "e name", and ".t". The entry at 0060h contains the final two characters: "xt", with the remaining character locations set to FFFFh.

The characters in the LFN entry with the highest ordinal number appear first in the file name, with the rest following in sequence. The entry that follows the LFN entry with an ordinal number of 1 is the 8.3 entry.

In the attributes field, bits 0–3 are all set to 1 to indicate that the entry is a long-file-name entry. The cluster field is maintained for compatibility with the 8.3 entries and should equal zero.

The Checksum

A checksum field matches an LFN entry with its 8.3 entry. The LFNChecksum function shows how to compute the checksum. The function accepts an 11-character 8.3 file name (without the dot) and returns the checksum.

```
int LFNChecksum(char * ShortFileName){

    int Bit7;
    int Character;
    int Checksum = 0;
```

```
// Step through the 11 characters in the short file name.

for (Character = 0; Character < 11; ++Character){

    // Save bit 0's value in Bit7.

    if (1 & Checksum) {

        Bit7 = 0x80; }

    else {

        Bit7 = 0x0; }

    // Shift the checksum right.

    Checksum = Checksum >> 1;

    // Add bit 7 to the result.

    Checksum = Checksum | Bit7;

    // Add the next character in the file name.

    Checksum += ShortFileName[Character];

    // Truncate the result to 8 bits.

    Checksum = Checksum & 0xFF;
    }
// The result after stepping through all 11 characters is the checksum.

    return(Checksum);
}
```

Creating a Short File Name

To convert a long file name to a short file name to store in an 8.3 entry, follow these steps:

1. Delete any spaces.

2. Delete any dots except the last dot before the extension, if present.

3. Truncate the name portion (before the dot) to six characters.

4. If there is an extension, truncate it to three characters.

5. Convert all characters from Unicode to ANSI or another 8-bit character set.

6. Convert all characters to upper case.

7. Convert any illegal 8.3 characters to underscores (_).

8. The seventh character is a tilde (~).

9. Set the eighth character to the lowest number that results in a unique file name, beginning with 1.

For example, the long file name johnsmith.txt becomes JOHNSM~1.TXT, and the long file name johnsmythe.txt in the same directory becomes JOHNSM~2.TXT. If the number following the ~ is greater than 9, the name preceding the ~ must be truncated further to enable creating a unique short file name. When five or more names have the same initial characters and extensions, Windows XP Professional uses a slightly different method to create the short file names.

Using Directories

Device firmware that supports a file system must be able to read information from directory entries and create and update directory entries when a file is created or written to. The code that follows performs these functions.

Storing an Entry

A DIRENTRY structure can store a directory entry's 32 bytes:

```
#define DIR_NAMESIZE    8
#define DIR_EXTENSION   3
#define NULL            0
#define FALSE           0
#define TRUE            !FALSE
```

```
typedef struct __DIRENTRY
{
    char    DIR_Name[DIR_NAMESIZE];          // name
    char    DIR_Extension[DIR_EXTENSION];    // extension
    byte    DIR_Attr;                        // attributes
    byte    DIR_NTRes;                       // reserved by NT
    byte    DIR_CrtTimeTenth;                // time created, tenths of second portion
    word    DIR_CrtTime;                     // time created
    word    DIR_CrtDate;                     // date created
    word    DIR_LstAccDate;                  // last access date
    word    DIR_FstClusHI;                   // high word of entry's first cluster number
    word    DIR_WrtTime;                     // last update time
    word    DIR_WrtDate;                     // last update date
    word    DIR_FstClusLO;                   // low word of entry's first cluster number
    dword   DIR_FileSize;                    // file size
}_DIRENTRY;

typedef _DIRENTRY * DIRENTRY;
```

Reading an Entry

The Cache_File_Entry function returns a DIRENTRY structure containing the 32 bytes of a directory entry. The function accepts a pointer to a FILE structure (fo), a pointer to the number of the entry within its directory (curEntry), and a value (ForceRead) that helps the code decide whether to read a sector from the media or use the data in the passed FILE structure's dsk -> buffer member.

If ForceRead is true, the function retrieves a sector from the storage media. If ForceRead is false, the function reads a sector from the storage media only if an entry is the first one in a sector. Otherwise the function uses the data in the passed buffer. Firmware can thus call the function repeatedly to retrieve a directory's entries in sequence while reading from the media only when beginning a new sector. The FindEmptyEntries function in Chapter 10 uses the ForceRead parameter in this way.

In the passed file structure, the dirclus member must contain the number of the first cluster of the entry's directory. If ForceRead is false, the dirccls member must contain a directory-cluster number where the code should begin looking for the entry. To begin looking at the beginning of the directory, dirccls should equal dirclus.

This function is the most complicated one in this book. Examine the comments carefully to understand it.

```
// A 512-byte sector can hold sixteen 32-byte directory entries.

#define DIRENTRIES_PER_SECTOR  0x10

DIRENTRY Cache_File_Entry( FILEOBJ fo, word * curEntry, byte ForceRead)
{
    word        ccls;
    word        cluster;
    DIRENTRY dir;
    DISK        *dsk;
    byte        numofclus;
    byte        offset2;
    dword       sector;

    // Save the file structure's DISK member.

    dsk = fo -> dsk;

    // Save the number of the first cluster of the file's directory.

    cluster = fo -> dirclus;

    // Save the number of the directory cluster to begin looking for the file in.
    // This value is unused if ForceRead is true.

    ccls = fo -> dirccls;

    // Get the number of the entry's sector within the directory.
    // A sector can hold 16 directory entries. Shift right 4 times to get the entry number.
    //  For example, if curEntry < 10h, it's the directory's first sector and offset2 = 0.
    // If curEntry >= 10h and < 20h, it's the directory's second sector and offset2 = 1.

    offset2  = (*curEntry >> 4);
    offset2 = offset2; // emulator issue

    if (cluster != 0)

        // It's not the root directory.
        // To get the number of the entry's sector within its cluster,
        // divide the sector number obtained above by the number of sectors per cluster.
        // The remainder (offset2) is the sector's number within its cluster.
```

```
    // (The first sector is sector 0.)

    offset2  = offset2 % (dsk -> SecPerClus);

if (ForceRead || (*curEntry & 0xf) == 0)
{
    // ForceRead is true OR the entry is the first one in a sector ((*curEntry & 0xf) == 0).
    // If either Condition 1 or Condition 2 below is true,
    // don't assume that ccls is the cluster to begin looking in for the entry to read.
    // Instead, read the entry's cluster number from the FAT:

    // Condition 1: ForceRead is true.
    // Condition 2: the entry IS in a cluster's first sector (offset2 = 0)
    // AND the entry ISN'T in the directory's first cluster (*curEntry > 16).

    if ((offset2 == 0 && (*curEntry) > DIRENTRIES_PER_SECTOR) || ForceRead)
    {
        if (cluster == 0)
        {
            // It's the root directory. The current cluster = 0.

            ccls = 0;
        }
        else
        {
            // It's not the root directory.

            if (ForceRead)

                // Get the number of curEntry's cluster within its directory:
                //    (curEntry / directory entries per cluster)

                // directory entries per cluster =
                // ((directory entries / sector) * (sectors / cluster))

                numofclus =
                    ((word)(*curEntry) /
                    (word)(((word)DIRENTRIES_PER_SECTOR)
                    * (word)dsk -> SecPerClus));
```

```
            else

                // The entry is in a cluster's first sector
                // AND the entry's cluster isn't the first one in the directory
                // AND it's not the root directory.
                // Get the next cluster number.

                numofclus = 1;

            // To find the cluster containing curEntry,
            // get the directory's cluster numbers from the FAT until reaching the
            // cluster specified by numofclus or the directory's last cluster.
            // On entering the loop, ccls = the passed dsk -> dircclus member.

            while (numofclus)
            {
                // Read the next cluster number from the current cluster's FAT entry.

                ccls = FATread(dsk, ccls);

                if (ccls >= LAST_CLUSTER)

                    // There is no next cluster.
                    break;
                else
                    numofclus--;
            }
        }
} // End: read a cluster number from the FAT.

// We have a cluster number for the entry, either retrieved from the FAT
// or obtained from the passed FILE structure.
// If ccls is an EOC marker (LAST_CLUSTER code),
// the directory doesn't have as many clusters as we thought. We can't get the entry.

if (ccls < LAST_CLUSTER)
{
    // The current cluster isn't the last one in the file.
    // We need to read a sector from the media.
    // Store the cluster number in the FILE structure.

    fo -> dirccls = ccls;
```

```
// Get the LBA of the cluster's first sector.

sector = Cluster2Sector (dsk, ccls);

// If it's the root directory (cluster 0), be sure that curEntry's sector isn't
// at or beyond the start of the volume's data area.
// (curEntry's sector = the cluster's initial sector (sector) +
// the number of the sector in the cluster containing curEntry (offset2))

if (ccls == 0 && (sector + offset2) >= dsk->data)
{
   dir = ((DIRENTRY)NULL);
}
else
{
    // The sector is in a valid location
    // (either the root-directory area or the volume's data area).
    // Read the data in the sector containing curEntry.
    // sector = the cluster's first sector.
    // offset2 = the number of the sector within the cluster.

    if ( SectorRead( sector + offset2, dsk->buffer) != sdcValid)

       dir = ((DIRENTRY)NULL);

    else
    {
       // The sector read was successful.
       // Get the requested entry.

       if (ForceRead)

           // The directory entry is in the DISK structure's buffer member.
           // ((*curEntry) % DIRENTRIES_PER_SECTOR) =
           // the number of the entry within the sector.

           dir = (DIRENTRY)((DIRENTRY)dsk -> buffer)
              + ((*curEntry) % DIRENTRIES_PER_SECTOR);
```

```
                else

                    // ForceRead is false, so the entry is the first one in the DISK
                    // structure's buffer member.
                    // (from the if (ForceRead | (*curEntry & 0xf) == 0 ) test above)

                        dir = (DIRENTRY)dsk -> buffer;
                    }
                } // End: read an entry from the media
            } // End: a valid cluster was found

            else
                // The cluster number wasn't valid.

                dir = ((DIRENTRY)NULL);
        }
        else
            // ForceRead is false AND curEntry isn't the first entry in the sector.
            // OK to read the directory entry directly from the passed DISK structure's buffer.
            // (No need to read a sector from the storage media.)

            // ((*curEntry) % DIRENTRIES_PER_SECTOR) =
            //    the number of the entry within the sector.

            dir =
                (DIRENTRY)((DIRENTRY)dsk -> buffer) +
                    ((*curEntry) % DIRENTRIES_PER_SECTOR);
        return(dir);
    }
```

Getting the Main Entry

The LoadDirAttrib function returns a file's 8.3 entry in DIRENTRY structure. The function accepts a FILEOBJ pointer to a FILE structure (fo) and a pointer to the number of the file's entry in its directory (fHandle). The function ignores any long-file-name entries.

The function calls the Cache_File_Entry function in this chapter. In the passed file structure, the dirclus member must contain the number of the first cluster of the file's directory.

```
#define ATTR_LONG_NAME  0x0f
#define DIR_DEL              0xE5   // deleted entry
#define DIR_EMPTY            0      // all entries that follow are empty
#define NULL                 0

DIRENTRY LoadDirAttrib(FILEOBJ fo, word *fHandle)
{
    DIRENTRY   dir;
    byte       a;

    // Get the directory entry and store the sector with the entry
    // in the FILE structure's dsk -> buffer member.

    dir = Cache_File_Entry( fo, fHandle, TRUE);

    // Read the first character of the file name.

    a = dir -> DIR_Name[0];

    if (a == DIR_EMPTY)
        dir = (DIRENTRY)NULL;  // The entry is empty.

    if (dir != (DIRENTRY)NULL)
    {
        if ( a == DIR_DEL)
            dir = (DIRENTRY)NULL;  // The entry is deleted.
        else
        {
            // The entry exists. Get the directory's attributes.

            a = dir -> DIR_Attr;
```

```
      // Get the first entry that isn't a long-file-name entry.

      while (a == ATTR_LONG_NAME)
      {
         (*fHandle)++;

         // Retrieve a directory entry and get the attributes.
         // The ForceRead parameter is false
         // to prevent unnecessary sector reads.

         dir = Cache_File_Entry( fo, fHandle, FALSE);
         a = dir -> DIR_Attr;
      }
   }
}
return(dir);
}
```

Updating an Entry

The Write_File_Entry function accepts a FILEOBJ pointer to a FILE structure and a pointer to the number of the file's entry in its directory (curEntry). The FILE structure's dsk -> buffer member must contain the contents of the sector to be written, and the dirccls member must contain the number of the entry's directory cluster. The function calculates the sector to write to and writes the contents of the buffer to the storage media.

The function calls the SectorWrite function from Chapter 5 and the Cluster2Sector function from Chapter 8.

```
byte Write_File_Entry( FILEOBJ fo, word *curEntry)
{
   word    ccls;
   DISK    *dsk;
   byte    offset2;
   dword   sector;
   byte    status;

   // Save the FILE structure's dsk member and directory cluster.

   dsk = fo -> dsk;
   ccls = fo -> dirccls;
```

```
// A sector can hold 16 directory entries.
// Shift right 4 times to get the number of the sector within the directory.
// If curEntry < 10h, it's the directory's first sector and offset2 = 0.
// If curEntry >= 10h and < 20h, it's the directory's second sector and offset2 = 1.

offset2  = (*curEntry >> 4);

// If it's not the root directory,
// divide the sector number obtained above by the number of sectors per cluster.
// The remainder (offset2) is the sector number within the cluster.

if (ccls != 0)
    offset2 = offset2 % (dsk -> SecPerClus);

// Get the sector number of the passed directory cluster.

sector = Cluster2Sector(dsk, ccls);

// Write the data in dsk -> buffer to the entry's sector in the media.

if (SectorWrite(sector + offset2, dsk -> buffer) != sdcValid)
    status = FALSE;
else
    status = TRUE;

return(status);
}
```

Updating the Time and Date

The IncrementTimeStamp function accepts a DIRENTRY structure (dir) and writes time and date information in the fields that hold the file's last-modified time and date.

The function emulates a real-time clock for systems that don't have one. The function increments the time in units of two seconds on each write. A system with a real-time clock should of course obtain the current values from the clock and store these in the DIRENTRY structure.

```
void IncrementTimeStamp(DIRENTRY dir)
{
    byte        seconds;
    byte        minutes;
    byte        hours;
    byte        day;
    byte        month;
    byte        year;

    // Get the time and date information from the passed DIRENTRY structure.

    seconds =   (dir -> DIR_WrtTime & 0x1f);
    minutes =   ((dir -> DIR_WrtTime & 0x07E0) >> 5);
    hours =     ((dir -> DIR_WrtTime & 0xF800) >> 11);

    day =       (dir -> DIR_WrtDate & 0x1f);
    month =     ((dir -> DIR_WrtDate & 0x01E0) >> 5);
    year =      ((dir -> DIR_WrtDate & 0xFE00) >> 9);

    // Increment the time.
    // Seconds is in units of 2 seconds (0-29).

    if (seconds < 29)
        seconds++;
    else
    {
        seconds = 0x00; // It's a new minute.
        if (minutes < 59)
        {
            minutes++;
        }
        else
        {
            minutes = 0; // It's a new hour.
            if (hours < 23)
            {
                hours++;
            }
```

```
        else
        {
            hours = 0; // It's a new day.
            if (day < 28)
            {
                day++;
            }
            else
            {
                day = 1;  // It's a new month. (Assumes 28 days/month.)
                if (month < 12)
                {
                    month++;
                }
                else
                {
                    month = 1; // It's a new year.
                    year++;
                }
            }
        }
    }
}

dir->DIR_WrtTime = (word)(seconds);
dir->DIR_WrtTime |= ((word)(minutes) << 5);
dir->DIR_WrtTime |= ((word)(hours) << 11);

dir->DIR_WrtDate = (word)(day);
dir->DIR_WrtDate |= ((word)(month) << 5);
dir->DIR_WrtDate |= ((word)(year) << 9);
}
```

10

File Operations

After the storage media has been formatted with a file system, firmware can create, read, modify, and delete files. This chapter presents firmware that performs these operations.

The code in this chapter uses the FILE and DISK structures introduced in Chapter 8 and the DIRENTRY structure introduced in Chapter 9.

The functions that access files use return values of type CETYPE:

typedef byte CETYPE;

```
#define CE_GOOD                0    // No error
#define CE_NOT_INIT            6    // Card isn't initialized due to an error
#define CE_BAD_SECTOR_READ     7    // Error in reading a sector
#define CE_WRITE_ERROR         8    // Couldn't write to the sector
#define CE_FILE_NOT_FOUND      10   // Couldn't find the file
#define CE_DIR_FULL            17   // All of the entries are in use
#define CE_DISK_FULL           18   // All of the clusters are full
#define CE_WRITE_PROTECTED     22   // The card is write protected
#define CE_BADCACHEREAD        28   // Sector read failed
#define CE_EOF                 61   // End of file reached
```

Cluster Operations

In creating and writing to files, a mass-storage host must be able to allocate clusters to files. A host might also want to erase the contents of a cluster. The following functions show how to perform these operations.

Erasing a Cluster

Deleting a file typically just removes the directory entry and marks the file's cluster(s) as available. The clusters may still contain data from the deleted file. When allocating an available cluster to a new file, the host may want to erase the cluster's contents by writing zero to each of the cluster's bytes.

The EraseCluster function accepts pointer to a DISK structure (disk) and a cluster number to erase (cluster) and returns a status code. The function calls the SectorWrite function from Chapter 5 and the Cluster2Sector function from Chapter 8.

```
byte EraseCluster(DISK *disk, word cluster)
{
    CETYPE      error;
    byte        index;
    byte        NumofSectors;
    dword       SectorAddress;

    // Get the LBA of the passed cluster number.

    SectorAddress = Cluster2Sector(disk, cluster);

    // Set the buffer's data to zeroes.

    memset(disk -> buffer, 0x00, SDC_SECTOR_SIZE);

    // Write the buffer's contents to the sector in the storage media.

    for (index = 0; index < disk -> SecPerClus && error == CE_GOOD; index++)
    {
        if (SectorWrite(SectorAddress++, disk -> buffer) != sdcValid)
            error = CE_WRITE_ERROR;
    }
    return(error);
}
```

Reserving an Available Cluster

The FILECreateHeadCluster function reserves an available cluster, which the host can then allocate to a file. The function accepts a pointer to a FILE structure (fo) and a pointer to a variable that will contain the number of a reserved, empty cluster (cluster). The function returns a status code.

The function calls the FATfindEmptyCluster and FATwrite functions from Chapter 8, the LoadDirAttrib function from Chapter 9, and the EraseCluster function above.

```
CETYPE FILECreateHeadCluster(FILEOBJ fo, word *cluster)
{
    word    curcls;
    DISK    *disk;

    // Save the FILE structure's dsk member.

    disk = fo -> dsk;

    // Use the FAT to find an available cluster.

    *cluster = FATfindEmptyCluster(fo);

    if (*cluster == 0)
        error = CE_DISK_FULL;
    else
    {
        // Mark the cluster as in use and the last one in the chain.

        if (FATwrite(disk, *cluster, LAST_CLUSTER_FAT16) == FAIL)
            error = CE_WRITE_ERROR;

        // Erase the cluster's contents.

        if (error == CE_GOOD)
        {
            error = EraseCluster(disk,*cluster);
        }
    }
    return(error);
}
```

Allocating a File's First Cluster

The CreateFirstCluster function stores a cluster number in a file's directory entry. The function accepts a pointer to a FILE structure (fo) and returns a status code. The function calls the LoadDirAttrib and Write_File_Entry functions from Chapter 9 and the FILECreateHeadCluster function above.

```
CETYPE CreateFirstCluster(FILEOBJ fo)
{
    word        cluster;
    DIRENTRY    dir;
    CETYPE      error;
    word        fHandle;

    // Save the number of the file's entry in the directory.

    fHandle = fo -> entry;

    // Allocate a cluster for the file.

    if ((error = FILECreateHeadCluster(fo, &cluster)) == CE_GOOD)
    {
        // Get the file's directory entry.

        dir = LoadDirAttrib(fo, &fHandle);

        // Store the file's cluster number in the directory entry.

        dir -> DIR_FstClusLO = cluster;

        // Write the entry to the directory.

        if (Write_File_Entry(fo, &fHandle) != TRUE)
            error = CE_WRITE_ERROR;
    }
    return(error);
}
```

Allocating Additional Clusters

If a write operation needs additional storage beyond the clusters allocated to a file, the host must find a new available cluster and allocate it to the file. Another situation where the host needs to allocate an additional cluster is when adding an entry to a subdirectory whose cluster(s) are full. The FILEallocate_new_cluster function can perform these tasks.

The function accepts a FILEOBJ pointer to a FILE structure, finds an available cluster, adds the cluster to the file's cluster chain in the FAT, sets the FILE structure's ccls member to the new cluster's number, and returns a status code. The function calls the FATfindEmptyCluster and FATwrite functions from Chapter 8.

```c
byte FILEallocate_new_cluster( FILEOBJ fo)
{
    word  c;
    word  curcls;
    DISK  *dsk;

    // Save the FILE structure's dsk and ccls members.

    dsk = fo -> dsk;
    c = fo -> ccls;

    // Find an empty cluster.

    c = FATfindEmptyCluster(fo);

    if (c == 0)
        return CE_DISK_FULL;

    // Mark the cluster as used and as the last one in the chain.

    FATwrite( dsk, c, LAST_CLUSTER_FAT16);

    // Write the cluster's number in the FAT entry for the FILE structure's ccls member.

    curcls = fo -> ccls;
    FATwrite( dsk, curcls, c);

    // Set the FILE structure's ccls member to the new, empty cluster's number.

    fo -> ccls = c;

    return CE_GOOD;
}
```

Managing Files

To prepare to read or write to a file, a host must obtain information about the file from the file's directory entry. A host might also need to create or delete a file. The functions that follow show how to perform these operations.

Obtaining File Information

The Fill_File_Object function reads information from a file's directory entry and stores the information in a FILE structure. The function accepts a pointer to a FILE structure (fo) and a pointer to the number of the file's entry in its directory (fHandle). The function returns a status code. The FILEfind function later in this chapter shows how to find the number of a file's directory entry.

The function calls the Cache_File_Entry function from Chapter 9. Cache_File_Entry is called with ForceRead false, so in the FILE structure passed to the function, the dsk -> buffer member must contain the sector with the file's directory entry (unless it's the first entry in a sector), the dirclus member must contain the number of the first cluster in the file's directory, and the dirccls member must contain the dirclus value or another directory-cluster number where the code should begin looking for the entry.

Defines

```
#define DIR_DEL        0xe5  // deleted entry
#define DIR_EMPTY      0     // last entry in a directory

#define FOUND          0     // directory entry match
#define NOT_FOUND      1     // directory entry not found
#define NO_MORE        2     // no more files found
```

The Function

```
byte Fill_File_Object(FILEOBJ fo, word *fHandle)
{
    byte        a;
    byte        character;
    DIRENTRY dir;
    byte        index;
    byte        status;
    dword       temp;
    byte        test = 0;

    // Get the file's directory entry.
    // Assumes that fo -> dsk -> buffer contains the sector containing the entry to read
    // (unless it's the first entry in a sector).

    dir = Cache_File_Entry(fo, fHandle, FALSE);

    // Read the first character of the file name from the entry.

    a = dir -> DIR_Name[0];

    if (dir == (DIRENTRY)NULL || a == DIR_EMPTY)
    {
        status = NO_MORE;  // The entry doesn't exist or is empty.
    }
    else
    {
        if ( a == DIR_DEL)

            status = NOT_FOUND; // The entry is deleted.

        else
        {
            status = FOUND;
```

```
// An entry exists. Store the entry's name in the file structure's name member.

for (index=0; index < DIR_NAMESIZE; index++)
{
   character = dir -> DIR_Name[index];

   fo -> name[test++] = character;
}
// If the entry has an extension, store it in the file's structure's name member.

character = dir -> DIR_Extension[0];

if (character != ' ')
{
   for (index = 0; index < DIR_EXTENSION; index++)
   {
      character = dir->DIR_Extension[index];

      fo -> name[test++] = character;
   }
}
// Store the passed entry number.

fo -> entry = *fHandle;

// Store the entry's file size.

fo -> size = (dir -> DIR_FileSize);

// Store the entry's initial cluster number.

temp = (dir -> DIR_FstClusHI << 16);
temp |= dir -> DIR_FstClusLO;
fo -> cluster = temp;

// Store the entry's date and time.

fo -> time = (dir -> DIR_WrtTime);
fo -> date = (dir -> DIR_WrtDate);
```

```
// Store the entry's attributes.

a = dir->DIR_Attr;
fo -> attributes = a;

}  // End: the entry isn't deleted
} // End: an entry exists

return(status);
}
```

Finding a File

The FILEfind function searches for a specific file in a directory or for an empty entry. The function accepts two FILEOBJ pointers to FILE structures. One structure (foCompareTo) contains a file name to search for and the other (fodest) will hold information about a file or empty entry if found. The third parameter (cmd) indicates whether to search for an entry that matches the file name in foCompareTo (1) or an empty entry (2). The function returns a status code.

The function calls the Cache_File_Entry function from Chapter 9 and the Fill_File_Object function above. In the passed file structure, the dirclus member must contain the number of the first cluster in the directory to search.

```
#define ATTR_MASK        0x3f
#define ATTR_HIDDEN      0x02
#define ATTR_VOLUME      0x08
#define FOUND            0      // directory entry match

CETYPE FILEfind(FILEOBJ foDest, FILEOBJ foCompareTo, byte cmd)
{
    word        attrib;
    byte        character;
    word        fHandle = 0;
    byte        index;
    byte        state;
    CETYPE      statusB = CE_FILE_NOT_FOUND;
    byte        test;
```

```
// Set the destination FILE structure's current cluster to the directory's cluster.

foDest -> dirccls = foDest -> dirclus;

// Read a directory entry.

if ( Cache_File_Entry(foDest, &fHandle, TRUE) == NULL)
{
    statusB = CE_BADCACHEREAD;
}
else
{
    // Read entries until finding the file or the end of the directory.

    while (1)
    {
        if (statusB!=CE_GOOD)
        {
            // Store information about the file.

            state = Fill_File_Object(foDest, &fHandle);

            if (state == NO_MORE)
            {
                // The entry doesn't exist or is empty.

                break;
            }
        }
        else
        {
            // There was a problem in reading the file information.

            break;
        }

        if (state == FOUND)
        {
            // An entry was found. Read the attributes.

            attrib = foDest -> attributes;

            attrib &= ATTR_MASK;
```

```
        // If the entry is for a volume ID or hidden file, skip it.

        if ((attrib != ATTR_VOLUME) && (attrib & ATTR_HIDDEN) != ATTR_HIDDEN)
        {
           statusB = CE_GOOD;
           character = (byte)'m'; // random value

           // Look for a name match.

           for (index = 0; (statusB == CE_GOOD) && index < DIR_NAMECOMP; index++)
           {
              // Get a character from the found file's name.

              character = foDest -> name[index];

              // Get the corresponding character from the file name we're searching for.

              test = foCompareTo -> name[index];
              if (tolower(character) != tolower(test))

                 // Quit the loop if a character doesn't match.

                 statusB = CE_FILE_NOT_FOUND;
           }
        }
     } // End: An entry was found.

     else
     {
        // An empty or deleted entry was found.

        if ( cmd == 2)
           statusB = CE_GOOD;
     }
     // Increment the number of the entry in the directory.

     fHandle++;

   } // End: loop until found or end of directory.
} // End: Cache_File_Entry was successful.

   return(statusB);
}
```

Creating a Directory Entry

After finding an empty entry, a host can store information about a new file or subdirectory. The PopulateEntries function accepts pointers to a FILE structure (fo), a file name (name), and the number of the file's entry in its directory (fHandle). The function stores the file name and other information in the entry and returns a status code.

The function calls the Cache_File_Entry and Write_File_Entry functions from Chapter 9. In the passed file structure, the dirclus member must contain the number of the first cluster in the entry's directory.

```
#define ATTR_ARCHIVE       0x20
#define DIR_NAMECOMP     (DIR_NAMESIZE + DIR_EXTENSION)   // 11

byte PopulateEntries(FILEOBJ fo, char *name , word *fHandle)
{
    byte        csum;
    DIRENTRY dir;
    byte        error = CE_GOOD;
    byte        index;
    byte        nameptr;
    byte        temp;

    // Get the file's directory entry.
    // The FILE structure's dirclus member is the first cluster
    // of the directory containing the entry to read.

    dir = Cache_File_Entry( fo, fHandle, TRUE);

    // Copy information into the entry.

    strncpy(dir -> DIR_Name, name, DIR_NAMECOMP);

    dir -> DIR_Attr = ATTR_ARCHIVE;
    dir -> DIR_NTRes = 0x00;
```

// A system with a real-time clock would retrieve these values from the clock
// instead of using these fixed values.

```
dir -> DIR_CrtTimeTenth =0x64;        // creation time, hundredths of a second (1 sec.)
dir -> DIR_CrtTime =       0x43C5;    // creation time (8:30:10)
dir -> DIR_CrtDate =       0x34B0;    // creation date (5/16/2006)
dir -> DIR_LstAccDate =    0x34B0;    // last access date
dir -> DIR_FstClusHI =     0x0000;    // high word of this enty's first cluster number
dir -> DIR_WrtTime =       0x43C6;    // last modified time (8:30:12)
dir -> DIR_WrtDate =       0x34B0;    // last modifled date
dir->DIR_FstClusLO =       0x0000;    // low word of this entry's first cluster number
dir->DIR_FileSize =        0x0;       // file size
```

// Save information in the file structure.

```
fo -> size =         dir -> DIR_FileSize;
fo -> time =         dir -> DIR_CrtTime;
fo -> date =         dir -> DIR_CrtDate;
fo -> attributes =   dir -> DIR_Attr;
fo -> entry =        *fHandle;
```

// Write the entry to the directory.

```
Write_File_Entry(fo,fHandle);

return(error);
}
```

Finding an Available Entry

To create a file, the host must find an available entry in the directory the file will reside in. The FindEmpyEntries function performs this task. The function accepts a pointer to a FILE structure (fo) that contains the number of a directory's first cluster and a pointer to a variable that will hold the number of the found entry within the directory (fHandle). To start at the beginning of the directory, fHandle should equal zero. In the passed file structure, the dirclus member must contain the number of the first cluster in the directory to search. The function returns a status code. The function calls the Cache_File_Entry function from Chapter 9 and the FILEAllocate_New_Cluster function above. (The FILEfind function in this chapter can also find an available directory entry.)

```
byte FindEmptyEntries(FILEOBJ fo, word *fHandle)
{
    byte        a;
    byte        amountfound;
    word        bHandle;
    DIRENTRY dir;
    byte        status = NOT_FOUND;

    // Call Cache_File_Entry with the ForceRead parameter = TRUE
    // to read the directory's sector from the media into fo -> dsk -> buffer.
    // fHandle contains the number of the entry to read in the directory.

    if ((dir = Cache_File_Entry(fo, fHandle, TRUE)) == NULL)
    {
        status = CE_BADCACHEREAD;
    }
    else
    {
        while (status == NOT_FOUND)
        {
            amountfound = 0;
            bHandle = *fHandle;

            // Look for a deleted or empty entry.

            do
            {
                // Get an entry.
                // Set the ForceRead parameter FALSE so the function reads from the media
                // only when necessary (when starting a new sector).

                dir = Cache_File_Entry(fo, fHandle, FALSE);

                // Read the first character of the file name.

                a = dir -> DIR_Name[0];

                // Increment the entry number.

                (*fHandle)++;
```

```
// Stop looking on finding a deleted or empty entry
// or on reaching the end of the cluster.

} while ((a == DIR_DEL || a == DIR_EMPTY) && (dir != (DIRENTRY)NULL)
    && (++amountfound < 1));

if (dir == NULL)
{
    // It was the cluster's last entry.
    // Get the cluster number of the directory.

    a = fo -> dirccls;

    if (a == 0)

        // It's the root directory.
        // The root directory is full and can't be expanded in FAT16.

        status = NO_MORE;
    else
    {
        // It's not the root directory. Save the current cluster number.

        fo -> ccls = a;

        // Allocate a new cluster to the directory.

        if (FILEallocate_new_cluster(fo) == CE_DISK_FULL)
            status = NO_MORE;
        else
        {
            // The first entry (and all entries) in a new cluster are empty.

            status = FOUND;
        }
    }
} // End: It's the cluster's last entry.
```

```
        else
        {
          if (amountfound == 1)
          {
            // An empty cluster was found.

            status = FOUND;
          }
        }
      } // End: while (status == NOT_FOUND)

      // Save the number of the found entry.

      *fHandle = bHandle;

    } // End: search for an entry.

    if (status == FOUND)
      return(TRUE);
    else
      return(FALSE);
}
```

Creating a File

The CreateFileEntry function creates a new entry for a file in a directory. The function accepts pointers to a FILE structure (fo) and a variable that will hold the number of the file's entry in its directory (fHandle). The function also allocates a cluster for the file. The function returns a status code.

The function calls the FindEmptyEntries, PopulateEntries, and CreateFirstCluster functions from this chapter. The FILE structure's name member holds the name of the file to create.

```
CETYPE CreateFileEntry(FILEOBJ fo, word *fHandle)
{
    CETYPE    error = CE_GOOD;
    byte      index;
    char      name[11];
    byte      size;
```

```
// Save the file's name from the FILE structure.

for (index = 0; index < FILE_NAME_SIZE; index ++)
{
    name[index] = fo -> name[index];
}
if (error == CE_GOOD)
{
    *fHandle = 0;

    // Find an empty entry in the directory.

    if (FindEmptyEntries(fo, fHandle))
    {
        // Store the file's data in the entry.

        if ((error = PopulateEntries(fo, name ,fHandle)) == CE_GOOD)
        {
            // Allocate a cluster to the file.

            error = CreateFirstCluster(fo);
        }
    }
    else
    {
        error = CE_DIR_FULL;
    }
}
return(error);
}
```

Deleting a File

To delete an existing file in the FAT16 file system, the storage media's host must do the following:

1. Search the file's directory for the entry containing the name of the file to delete.

2. Save the cluster number from the file's directory entry.

3. Mark the directory entry as deleted by storing E5h in the entry's first byte.

4. Examine the FAT entry for the saved cluster number. If the entry isn't an EOC marker, save the cluster number and store 0000h in the entry to mark it as available.

5. Repeat step 4 until finding an EOC marker. Replace the EOC marker with 0000h.

The FAT_erase_cluster_chain function accepts a cluster number (cluster) and a pointer to a DISK structure (dsk) and stores 0000h in all FAT entries in the chain beginning with the passed cluster number. The function calls the FATread and FATwrite functions from Chapter 8.

```
byte FAT_erase_cluster_chain (word cluster, DISK *dsk)
{
    word    c;
    word    c2;

    enum    _status {
        Good,
        Fail,
        Exit
    } status;

    status = Good;

    // Valid cluster numbers start at 2.

    if (cluster == 0 || cluster == 1)
    {
        status = Exit;
    }
    else
    {
        while (status == Good)
        {
            // Get the FAT entry for the passed cluster number.

            if (c = FATread(dsk, cluster)) == FAIL)
                status = Fail;
```

```
        else
        {
            // Valid cluster numbers start at 2.

            if (c == 0 || c == 1)
            {
                status = Exit;
            }
            else
            {
                c2 = LAST_CLUSTER;

                if ( c >= c2)

                    // The cluster is the last one in the chain.

                    status = Exit;

                // Erase the fat entry by storing an empty-cluster code in the entry.

                if (FATwrite(dsk, cluster, CLUSTER_EMPTY) == FAIL)
                    status = Fail;

                // Set the current cluster to the value read from the FAT entry.

                cluster = c;
            }
        }
    } // End: while not the end of the chain and no error.
}
    if (status == Exit)

    // All of the FAT entries in the chain have been erased.

    return (TRUE);

else
    return(FALSE);

}
```

The FILEerase function erases a file's directory entry and if requested, the FAT entries for all of the file's clusters. The function accepts a FILEOBJ pointer to a file structure (fo), a pointer to a directory entry (fHandle), and a value (EraseClusters) that indicates whether the function should erase the FAT entries for all of the file's clusters.

In the passed file structure, the dirclus member must contain the number of the first cluster in the directory with the file entry. The function calls the Cache_File_Entry from Chapter 9 and the FAT_erase_cluster_chain function above. The function returns a status code.

```
CETYPE FILEerase(FILEOBJ fo, word *fHandle, byte EraseClusters)
{
    byte      a;
    word      clus;
    DIRENTRY  dir;
    DISK      *disk;
    CETYPE    status = CE_GOOD;

    // Save the DISK structure.

    disk = fo -> dsk;

    // Set the directory's current cluster number to the directory's first cluster.

    clus = fo -> dirclus;
    fo -> dirccls = clus;

    // Read the sector containing the entry to erase.

    dir = Cache_File_Entry(fo, fHandle, TRUE);

    // Was a non-empty, non-deleted entry returned?

    a = dir->DIR_Name[0];

    if (dir == (DIRENTRY)NULL || a == DIR_EMPTY)
    {
        status = CE_FILE_NOT_FOUND;
    }
    else
    {
        if ( a == DIR_DEL)
            status = CE_FILE_NOT_FOUND;
```

```
    else
    {
      a = dir->DIR_Attr;

      // Mark the entry as deleted.

      dir->DIR_Name[0] = DIR_DEL;

      // Save the number of the entry's first cluster.

      clus = dir->DIR_FstClusLO;

      // Write the revised directory entry to delete the file.

      if (status != CE_GOOD || !(Write_File_Entry( fo, fHandle)))
        status = CE_ERASE_FAIL;
      else
      {
        if (EraseClusters)
        {
          // Erase the FAT entries for the file's clusters.

          status =
            ((FAT_erase_cluster_chain(clus, disk)) ? CE_GOOD : CE_ERASE_FAIL);
        }
      }
    } // End: a not empty, not deleted entry was returned
  } // End: a not empty entry was returned

  return (status);
}
```

Opening a File

The FILEopen function performs several actions to prepare a file for reading or writing. The function retrieves a file's directory entry, copies information from the entry into a FILE structure, initializes other members of the FILE structure, reads the file's first sector into the file structure's dsk -> buffer member, and sets the file structure's FLAGS.write member to indicate whether the file is open for reading or writing.

The function accepts a pointer to a file structure (fo), a pointer to the number of the file's entry in its directory (fHandle), and a character that specifies whether to open the file for append (a), read (r), or write (w). In the passed file structure, the dirclus member must contain the number of the first cluster in the file's directory.

The function calls the SectorRead function from Chapter 5, the Cluster2Sector function from Chapter 8, the Cache_File_Entry function from Chapter 9, and the Fill_File_Object function from this chapter.

After calling the function, firmware can use the information in the FILE structure to perform operations on the file's contents.

```c
CETYPE FILEopen (FILEOBJ fo, word *fHandle, char type)
{
    DISK        *dsk;
    CETYPE      error = CE_GOOD;
    dword       l;
    byte        r;

    // Save the FILE structure's dsk member.

    dsk = (DISK *)(fo -> dsk);

    if (dsk -> mount == FALSE)

        error = CE_NOT_INIT;  // The media isn't available.

    else
    {
        // Get the file's directory entry and store the directory's sector
        // in the dsk -> buffer member of the file structure (fo).

        Cache_File_Entry(fo, fHandle, TRUE);

        // Fill the file structure with information from the directory entry.

        r = Fill_File_Object(fo, fHandle);

        if (r != FOUND)

            error = CE_FILE_NOT_FOUND;
```

```
        else
        {
            // A file was found.
            // Initialize FILE structure members.

            fo -> seek = 0;            // Byte offset in the file.
            fo -> ccls = fo -> cluster;  // The current cluster = the file's first cluster.
            fo -> sec = 0;             // The sector in the cluster.
            fo -> pos = 0;             // The byte in the sector.

            // Determine the LBA of the file's current cluster.

            l = Cluster2Sector(dsk, fo -> ccls);

            // Read the cluster's first sector into the DISK structure's buffer member.

            if ( SectorRead( l, dsk -> buffer) != sdcValid)

                error = CE_BAD_SECTOR_READ;

            // Set the FILE structure's flags.

            fo -> Flags.FileWriteEOF = FALSE;

            if (type == 'w' || type == 'a')
            {
                // Open the file for writing or appending.

                fo -> Flags.write = 1;
            }
            else
            {
                // Open the file for reading.

                fo -> Flags.write = 0;
            }
        } // End: a file was found.
    } // End: the media is available.

    return (error);
}
```

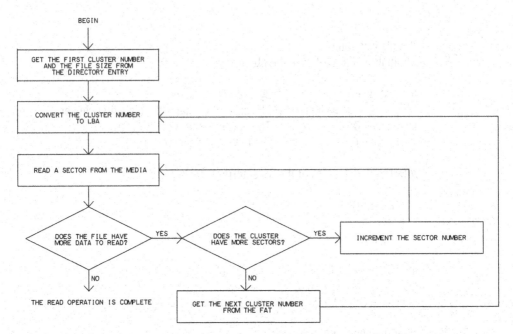

Figure 10-1: A mass-storage master performs these actions to read the contents of a file.

Reading from a File

The FILEopen function above can prepare to read from a file. Because storage media typically requires reading complete sectors, each read from the media reads a sector's worth of data even if the firmware requires just one or a few bytes.

Tasks

To read a file's contents, firmware must perform the following actions (shown in Figure 10-1):

1. Get the file's size and the number of the file's first cluster from the directory entry and convert the cluster number to an LBA sector number.

2. Read data from the cluster's sector(s).

3. To read more data, get the next cluster number from the current cluster's FAT entry, convert the cluster number to an LBA sector number, and read the data in the cluster's sector(s).

4. Repeat step 3 as needed until a FAT entry indicates that the entry's cluster is the last cluster in the file.

Performing a Read Operation

The fread function reads data from a file into a buffer. The function accepts a FILEOBJ pointer to a FILE structure (fo), a pointer to a buffer to store the data to be read (dest), and the number of bytes to read (count). The function returns a status code. In the FILE structure, pos is the offset to begin reading from within the sector, seek is the offset to begin reading from within the file, ccls is the number of the cluster to read from, and sec is the number of the sector to read within the cluster. The function returns a status code.

The RAMread macro reads a byte at an address (a) plus an offset (f) in RAM:

```
#define RAMread(a, f)  *(a + f)
```

The fread function calls the SectorRead function from Chapter 5 and the Cluster2Sector and FILEget_next_cluster functions from Chapter 8.

```
CETYPE fread (FILEOBJ fo, void *dest, word count)
{
    DISK        *dsk;
    CETYPE      error = CE_GOOD;
    dword       l;
    word        pos;
    dword       seek;
    dword       size;
    dword       temp;

    dsk = (DISK *)fo -> dsk;
    temp = count;
```

```
// Save the offset to begin reading from within the current sector,
// the offset to read from within the file, and the file's size.

pos = fo -> pos;
seek = fo -> seek;
size = fo -> size;

// Get the sector number of the file's current cluster.

l = Cluster2Sector(dsk, fo -> ccls);

// Add the number of the current sector within the cluster.

l += (word)fo -> sec;

// Read the sector's data.

if ( SectorRead( l, dsk->buffer) != sdcValid)

    error = CE_BAD_SECTOR_READ;

// Read from the file until finished or an error.

while (error == CE_GOOD && temp > 0)
{
    if (seek == size)

        // It's the end of the file.

        error = CE_EOF;

    else
    {
        // If we've reached the end of a sector, load another sector.

        if (pos == SDC_SECTOR_SIZE)
        {
            // Reset the offset within the sector.

            pos = 0;
```

```
    // Increment the sector number.

    fo -> sec++;

    // The sector number (sec) should be a value between 0 and SecPerClus - 1.
    // If sec = SecPerClus, the sector is the first sector in a new cluster.

    if (fo -> sec == dsk -> SecPerClus)
    {
        // Get the next cluster in the file and start in the cluster's first sector.

        fo -> sec = 0;
        error = FILEget_next_cluster( fo, 1);
    }
    if (error == CE_GOOD)
    {
        // Get the sector number of the current cluster, which may have changed.

        l = Cluster2Sector(dsk,fo -> ccls);

        // Add the number of the current sector within the cluster.

        l += (word)fo -> sec;

        // Read the sector's data.

        if (SectorRead( l, dsk -> buffer) != sdcValid)

            error = CE_BAD_SECTOR_READ;
    }
} // End: load new sector

if (error == CE_GOOD)
{
    // A sector's data is in the DISK structure's buffer member.
    // Copy a byte from the specified offset (pos) in the DISK structure's buffer
    // to the dest buffer.

    *(char *)dest = RAMread(dsk -> buffer, pos++);
```

```
        dest = dest + 1;  // Increment the dest buffer offset.
        seek++;           // Increment the number of the byte to copy.
        (temp)--;         // Decrement the number of bytes remaining to copy.
      }
   } // End: if not end of file
} // while no error and more bytes to copy

// Save the offset within the sector.

fo->pos = pos;

// Save the offset within the file.

fo->seek = seek;

return(error);
}
```

Writing to a File

The FILEopen function in this chapter can prepare to write to a file. Because storage media typically requires writing complete sectors, each write to the media writes a sector's worth of data. To write to a portion of a sector, firmware reads the sector's contents into a buffer, changes the data in the desired location(s), and writes the entire buffer back to the storage media. As Chapter 1 explained, to write to the media, a MultiMediaCard's controller may need to erase an entire erase block that contains multiple sectors and write the data back to the erased sectors, including the new data.

Tasks

To write to an empty file, firmware must perform the following actions (shown in Figure 10-2):

1. Allocate a cluster in the FAT, store the cluster number in the file's directory entry, and convert the cluster number to an LBA sector number.

2. Write data to the cluster's sector(s).

3. To write more data, search the FAT for an available cluster, store the cluster number in the FAT entry for the file's current cluster, store an EOC

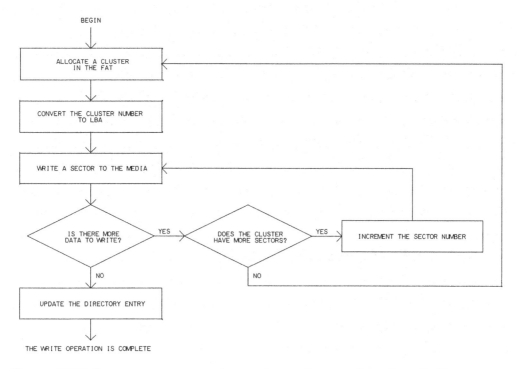

Figure 10-2: A mass-storage master performs these actions to write to an empty file.

marker in the new cluster's FAT entry, convert the cluster number to an LBA sector number, and store the additional data in the cluster's sector(s).

4. Repeat step 3 as needed until all of the file's data has been written.

5. Update the file's directory entry.

To append data to an existing file, before writing to the file, firmware can get the file's size from the directory entry and use the value to calculate the sector and offset to begin writing to the file. To overwrite a file that uses multiple clusters, firmware can use the FAT to find the clusters already allocated to the file.

Performing a Write Operation

The fwrite function writes a specified number of bytes beginning at a specified location in a file. The function accepts a FILEOBJ pointer to a FILE structure (fo), a pointer to a buffer containing the data to write (src), and the number of bytes to write (count). In the FILE structure, pos is the offset to begin writing to within the sector, seek is the offset to begin writing to within the file, ccls is the number of the cluster to write to, and sec is the number of the sector to write to within the cluster. The function returns a status code.

The function calls the IsWriteProtected, SectorRead, and SectorWrite functions from Chapter 5, the FILEget_next_cluster and Cluster2Sector functions and RAMWrite macro from Chapter 8, and the FILEallocate_new_cluster function from this chapter. To enable writing to the file, Flags.write must be true. The File_Open function in this chapter sets this value.

```
CETYPE fwrite( FILEOBJ fo, void * src, word count)
{
    DISK *      dsk;
    CETYPE      error = CE_GOOD;
    dword       l;
    word        pos;
    byte        sectorloaded = FALSE;
    dword       seek;
    dword       size;
    word        tempo;

    // To enable writing, Flags.write must be true and IsWriteProtected must return false.

    if (fo->Flags.write)
    {
        if (!IsWriteProtected())
        {
            // It's OK to write to the media.

            tempo = count;

            // Save the file structure's dsk structure, the offset within the current sector,
            // and the absolute offset in the file.

            dsk = fo -> dsk;
            pos = fo -> pos;
            seek = fo -> seek;
```

```
// Get the sector number of the file's current cluster.

l = Cluster2Sector(dsk,fo -> ccls);

// Add the number of the current sector within the cluster.

l += (word)fo -> sec;

// Read the sector.

if (SectorRead(l, dsk->buffer) != sdcValid)

    error = CE_BAD_SECTOR_READ;

sectorloaded = TRUE;

// Save the file's size.

size = fo -> size;

// Write to the file until finished or an error.

while (error == CE_GOOD && tempo > 0)
{
   if (seek == size)
   {
      // It's the end of the file. Set the flag.

      fo -> Flags.FileWriteEOF = TRUE;
   }
```

```
// If we've reached the end of a sector, write the data to the media and
// load another sector.

if (pos == SDC_SECTOR_SIZE)
{
    if (sectorloaded)
    {
        // The DISK structure's buffer member contains data to be written.
        // Copy the data to the storage media.

        if (SectorWrite( I, dsk -> buffer) != sdcValid)

            error = CE_WRITE_ERROR;
    }
    // Reset the offset within the sector.

    pos = 0;

    // Increment the sector number.

    fo -> sec++;

    // The sector number (sec) must be a value between 0 and SecPerClus - 1.
    // If sec = SecPerClus, the sector is the first sector in a new cluster.

    if (fo -> sec == dsk -> SecPerClus)
    {
        // Reset the sector number for the new cluster.

        fo -> sec = 0;

        if (fo -> Flags.FileWriteEOF)

            // It's the end of the file. Allocate a new cluster for additional data.

            error = FILEallocate_new_cluster(fo);

        else

            // Not the end of the file. Get the next cluster allocated to the file.

            error = FILEget_next_cluster( fo, 1);
    }
```

```
                if (error == CE_DISK_FULL)
                {
                    return error;
                }
                if (error == CE_GOOD)
                {
                    // Read the next sector from the media.
                    // Get the sector number of the file's current cluster.

                    l = Cluster2Sector(dsk, fo -> ccls);

                    // Add the number of the current sector within the cluster.

                    l += (word)fo -> sec;

                    // Read the new sector's data.

                    if (SectorRead( l, dsk -> buffer) != sdcValid)

                        error = CE_BAD_SECTOR_READ;

                    sectorloaded = TRUE;
                }
            } // End: write a sector to the media and read the next sector.

        if (error == CE_GOOD)
        {
            // A sector's data is in the DISK structure's buffer member.
            // Copy a byte from the passed buffer (src) to the
            // specified offset (pos) in the DISK structure's buffer.

            RAMwrite (dsk -> buffer, pos++, *(char *)src);

            // Increment the offset of the byte to write.

            src = src + 1;

            // Increment the offset of the byte within the file.

            seek++;
```

```
        // Decrement the number of bytes remaining to write.

        tempo--;
    }
    if (fo -> Flags.FileWriteEOF)

        // The data was appended to the file, so increment the file size.

        size++;

} // End: write to the file (except for the last sector).

// If no error, write the final sector's data to the media.

if (error == CE_GOOD)
{
    // Get the sector number of the current cluster.

    l = Cluster2Sector(dsk, fo -> ccls);

    // Add the number of the current sector within the cluster.

    l += (word)fo -> sec;

    // Copy data from the DISK structure's buffer item to the storage media.

    if (SectorWrite(l, dsk->buffer) != sdcValid)

        error = CE_WRITE_ERROR;
    }
    // Save the position within the current sector, the byte number within the file,
    // and the file size.

    fo->pos = pos;
    fo->seek = seek;
    fo->size = size;
}
else
    error = CE_WRITE_PROTECTED;
}
```

```
    else
        error = CE_WRITE_ERROR;

    return(error);
}
```

Closing a File

When finished writing to a file, firmware must update the file's directory entry. The fclose function handles this task. The function accepts a FILE-OBJ pointer to a FILE structure for the file and returns a status code.

The function calls the LoadDirAttrib, IncrementTimeStamp, and Write_File_Entry functions from Chapter 9.

```
CETYPE fclose(FILEOBJ fo)
{
    CETYPE      error = CE_GOOD;
    DIRENTRY dir;
    word        fHandle;

    // Set fHandle to the number of the file's entry in its directory.

    fHandle = fo -> entry;

    // Nothing to do if the file wasn't opened for writing.

    if (fo -> Flags.write)
    {
        // Get the file's attributes.

        dir = LoadDirAttrib(fo, &fHandle);

        // Update the time and date.

        IncrementTimeStamp(dir);

        // Set the DIRENTRY structure's DIR_FileSize member to the file's size.

        dir -> DIR_FileSize = fo -> size;
```

```
        // Write the file's entry in its directory.

        if (Write_File_Entry(fo, &fHandle))
            error = CE_GOOD;
        else
            error = CE_WRITE_ERROR;

        // The file is no longer open for writing.

        fo -> Flags.write = FALSE;
    }
    return(error);
}
```

11

Embedded Hosts

With support for mass storage, just about any USB host can communicate with off-the-shelf mass-storage devices, including hard drives and flash drives. This chapter looks at what's involved in designing and programming an embedded system that functions as a USB host. Much of this information can be helpful to device designers as well, especially the information about common device problems that hosts experience.

Inside an Embedded Host

As Chapter 1 explained, a host's function is in many ways a mirror image of a device's function. All USB hosts must detect device attachment and removal and manage power and bus traffic. Chip vendors typically provide example firmware for performing these tasks.

On detecting a device with an interface descriptor that specifies the mass-storage class, a host that supports mass storage should examine the interface descriptor and the device's response to a SCSI INQUIRY command to learn which SCSI command set the device claims to support. The host can then proceed with other mass-storage communications. A host that supports a file system can also create, read, write to, and delete files on its own.

OTG Devices and Conventional Hosts

A USB host in an embedded system can be a conventional USB host or an On-The-Go device. A system that never functions as a USB device must function as a conventional host. If the system must function as a USB host and device at the same time, the system must contain separate SIEs for the USB host and device functions. The SIEs can be on a single chip or different chips. If the system functions as both a USB host and device but not both at the same time, the system can be an OTG device.

Conventional hosts and OTG hosts have different requirements in some areas. Support for external hubs is required in a conventional host and optional in an OTG device. A conventional host must provide 500 mA per port (or 100 mA if battery powered), while an OTG device needs to provide just 8 mA per port unless a supported peripheral requires more. A conventional host must provide bus power at all times, while an OTG device can switch off bus power when unneeded.

General Host Functions

The host enumerates each device to learn about its capabilities. To enumerate a device, a host typically issues the following standard USB requests:

Set Address. To set the device's address on the bus.

Get Descriptor (device). To read the device descriptor.

Get Descriptor (configuration). To read the configuration descriptor and subordinate descriptors, including the interface and endpoint descriptors.

Set Configuration. To configure the device and enable communications.

The host can also request any string descriptors the device supports, including the descriptor containing the serial number.

Figure 11-1 shows bus events and host requests directed to a newly attached USB flash drive on a Windows XP host. The host requests some descriptors multiple times and resets the bus after the first Get Descriptor request. This

Item	Comment
Enter text here	*Enter text here*
SEQ Reset (10.1 ms)	
CHIRP High speed Detection Handshake	
⊞ GetDescriptor (Device)	18 bytes (12 01 00 02 00 00 00 40 7D 0D 00 19 00 01 01 02 03 01)
SEQ Reset (7.1 ms)	
CHIRP High speed Detection Handshake	
⊞ SetAddress (3)	No data
⊞ GetDescriptor (Device)	18 bytes (12 01 00 02 00 00 00 40 7D 0D 00 19 00 01 01 02 03 01)
⊞ GetDescriptor (Configuration)	9 bytes (09 02 27 00 01 01 00 80 64)
⊞ GetDescriptor (String lang IDs)	4 bytes (04 03 09 04)
⊞ GetDescriptor (String iSerialNumber)	26 bytes (1A 03 30 00 37 00 35 00 36 00 30 00 44 00 33 00 41 00...
⊞ GetDescriptor (Configuration)	39 bytes (09 02 27 00 01 01 00 80 64 09 04 00 00 03 08 06 50 00...
⊞ GetDescriptor (String lang IDs)	4 bytes (04 03 09 04)
⊞ GetDescriptor (String iProduct)	34 bytes (22 03 55 00 53 00 42 00 20 00 44 00 49 00 53 00 4B 00...
⊞ GetDescriptor (String lang IDs)	4 bytes (04 03 09 04)
⊞ GetDescriptor (String iProduct)	34 bytes (22 03 55 00 53 00 42 00 20 00 44 00 49 00 53 00 4B 00...
⊞ GetDescriptor (Device)	18 bytes (12 01 00 02 00 00 00 40 7D 0D 00 19 00 01 01 02 03 01)
⊞ GetDescriptor (Configuration)	9 bytes (09 02 27 00 01 01 00 80 64)
⊞ GetDescriptor (Configuration)	39 bytes (09 02 27 00 01 01 00 80 64 09 04 00 00 03 08 06 50 00...
⊞ GetDescriptor (String lang IDs)	2 bytes (04 03)
⊞ GetDescriptor (String lang IDs)	4 bytes (04 03 09 04)
⊞ GetDescriptor (String iSerialNumber)	2 bytes (1A 03)
⊞ GetDescriptor (String iSerialNumber)	26 bytes (1A 03 30 00 37 00 35 00 36 00 30 00 44 00 33 00 41 00...
⊞ SetConfiguration (1)	No data

Figure 11-1: Requests sent by a Windows host to enumerate a mass-storage device. (Screen capture from Ellisys USB Explorer.)

is one example of host communications. Hosts aren't required to use this exact sequence of requests. The device doesn't need to know or care why the host is sending a request or resetting the bus and shouldn't assume anything about what a host will do next. The device just needs to respond appropriately when something happens.

Mass Storage Functions

After enumeration, a host can use USB requests and SCSI commands to learn more about a device and to prepare to read and write to the storage media. Figure 11-2 shows communications from a Windows host after com-

⊞ 📎 GetMaxLun	1 byte (00)
⊞ 📎 Inquiry (Page 0)	36 bytes (00 80 00 01 1F 00 00 00 20 20 20 20 20 20 20 20 55 53...
⊞ 📎 Read Format Capacities	No data
⊞ 📎 Request Sense	18 bytes (70 00 06 00 00 00 00 0A 00 00 00 00 28 00 00 00 00 00)
⊞ 📎 Read Format Capacities	12 bytes (00 00 00 08 00 03 D8 00 02 00 02 00)
⊞ 📎 Read Capacity (Lba 0)	8 bytes (00 03 D7 FF 00 00 02 00)
⊞ 📎 Read (Lba 0)	512 bytes (FA BE 00 7C BF 00 7A B9 00 01 FC 0E 1F 0E 07 F3 A5 ...
⊞ 📎 Mode Sense	4 bytes (03 00 00 00)
⊞ 📎 Mode Sense	36 bytes (23 00 00 00 05 1E F0 00 10 20 02 00 01 EC 00 00 00 00...
⊞ 📎 Read Capacity (Lba 0)	8 bytes (00 03 D7 FF 00 00 02 00)
⊞ 📎 Read Capacity (Lba 0)	8 bytes (00 03 D7 FF 00 00 02 00)
⊞ 📎 Read (Lba 0)	512 bytes (FA BE 00 7C BF 00 7A B9 00 01 FC 0E 1F 0E 07 F3 A5 ...
⊞ 📎 Read (Lba 0)	512 bytes (FA BE 00 7C BF 00 7A B9 00 01 FC 0E 1F 0E 07 F3 A5 ...
⊞ 📎 Read Capacity (Lba 0)	8 bytes (00 03 D7 FF 00 00 02 00)
⊞ 📎 Read Capacity (Lba 0)	8 bytes (00 03 D7 FF 00 00 02 00)
⊞ 📎 Read (Lba 0)	512 bytes (FA BE 00 7C BF 00 7A B9 00 01 FC 0E 1F 0E 07 F3 A5 ...
⊞ 📎 Test Unit Ready	No data

Figure 11-2: Commands used by a Windows host after enumerating a flash drive. (Screen capture from Ellisys USB Explorer.)

pleting enumeration. These requests and commands are typical for Windows XP, but hosts aren't required to use this exact sequence:

Get Max LUN. This USB class-specific request asks for the highest LUN number supported by the device. Devices with single LUNs are the only ones allowed to stall this request. The host can use the commands below to initialize communications with each logical unit from zero up to the value returned.

INQUIRY. The host requests 36 bytes of data about a logical unit.

READ FORMAT CAPACITIES. The host requests a structure containing one or more descriptors that specify a number of blocks and a block length that the media can be formatted for.

READ CAPACITY(10). The host requests the highest LBA supported by the logical unit and the number of bytes in that logical block (typically 512).

READ(10). The host reads sector zero, which should be either an MBR sector with a partition table or a FAT boot sector (assuming the volume is formatted for a FAT file system).

MODE SENSE(6) with PAGE CODE = 1Ch and SUBPAGE CODE = 00h. The host requests the Informational Exceptions Control Mode page in page_0 format.

MODE SENSE(6) with PAGE CODE = 3Fh and SUBPAGE CODE = 00h. The host requests all mode pages with subpage = 00h in page_0 format.

TEST UNIT READY. The host requests a CSW and checks the value in bCSWStatus to determine if the logical unit is ready for use. If bCSWStatus = 00h, the logical unit is ready. If the value isn't zero, the host can issue a REQUEST SENSE command to learn more.

READ(10). The host can use additional READ commands to read the boot sector, root directory, and other information in a volume.

Handling Non-compliant Devices

Not every mass-storage device complies perfectly with the mass-storage specifications. The mass-storage drivers in Windows and Linux include many work-arounds to enable communicating with non-compliant devices. An embedded host that wants to communicate with a variety of off-the-shelf devices will need to implement many of these work-arounds. If you're writing device firmware, you'll want to avoid these errors.

In Linux, the source file unusual_devs.h in the USB mass-storage driver lists non-compliant devices and shows what the operating system does to enable communicating.

Below are some behaviors found in non-compliant devices.

Descriptor Problems

The device's bInterfaceSubClass is FFh instead of 06h or another value defined by the USB mass-storage specifications.

The device's bInterfaceProtocol is invalid (should be 50h for bulk-only transport).

The device has no serial number or the serial number has invalid characters as defined in the bulk-only transport specification.

Multiple devices with the same Vendor ID and Product ID have the same serial number.

Different device or firmware revisions have the same bcdDevice value.

Control Transfer Problems

A device with multiple LUNs doesn't implement the Get Max LUN request.

When the endpoint isn't halted, receiving a Clear Feature (ENDPOINT_HALT) request for the endpoint causes the device to crash.

On receiving a Clear Feature (ENDPOINT_HALT) request followed by a Get Status (ENDPOINT) request, the device crashes.

The device doesn't implement the Bulk-only Mass Storage Reset request properly. To work around this failure, a host might need to issue a Set Port Feature (PORT_RESET) request to the device's hub port.

On receiving a Set Interface request, the device doesn't reset the data toggles for the bulk endpoints.

General Problems with Commands

The device has a single LUN but responds to commands for any LUN.

The signature in the CSW is incorrect.

The device returns no data or incorrect data in the dCSWDataResidue field.

The data-transport phase fails unless there is a delay of up to 120 μsecs. between the end of the command-transport phase and the beginning of the data-transport phase.

After completing enumeration, the device requires a few seconds before it responds properly to received CBWs.

In commands where the device may return variable-length data in the data-transport phase, after returning all available data but less than the requested amount of data, the device returns 01h (failed) in the bCSWStatus field of the CSW.

The device can only do transfers of 32 KB, or can only do transfers of 32 KB or less, or returns invalid dCSWDataResidue data in the CSW for transfers greater than 32 KB.

Problems with Specific SCSI Commands

Specific commands challenge some devices:

INQUIRY

The device crashes if the ALLOCATION LENGTH parameter doesn't equal 36.

The device returns an incorrect value in the VERSION field (byte 2). See the SPC specification or other relevant command-set documents for the correct values for your device.

The device returns 05h (SPC-3) in the VERSION field but the device doesn't support the REPORT LUNS command (mandatory for SPC-3).

The device returns an incorrect value in the ADDITIONAL LENGTH parameter.

When a UNIT ATTENTION condition exists, the device fails the command and returns a sense key of UNIT ATTENTION. (The device should perform the command and should not report or clear the UNIT ATTENTION condition.)

MODE SENSE

The device crashes if the ALLOCATION LENGTH parameter doesn't equal 192.

When the PAGE CODE parameter equals 3Fh (Return all subpage 00h mode pages in page_0 format), the device crashes.

The device doesn't implement all mode pages required by relevant specifications.

The device doesn't implement all mandatory versions of the command. Read/write devices that are bootable and that don't have a PDT of 05h (CD/DVD drive) must support MODE SENSE(10).

PREVENT ALLOW MEDIUM REMOVAL

On receiving the command, the device stops functioning or behaves as if the storage media is removed even if it isn't.

READ

The device doesn't implement all mandatory versions of the command. Devices that comply with SBC-2 or SBC-3 should implement both READ(6) and READ(10).

READ CAPACITY

The LOGICAL BLOCK ADDRESS field contains an incorrect value (the correct value + 1) because the device is reporting the number of sectors rather than the LBA of the highest sector.

REQUEST SENSE

In devices with removable media, when the media changes, the device doesn't set the SENSE KEY to 06h (UNIT ATTENTION) to indicate the change (required by SBC-2 and SBC-3).

START STOP UNIT

On receiving the command, the device crashes.

WRITE

The device doesn't implement all mandatory versions of the command. Writable devices that comply with SBC-2 or SBC-3 should implement both WRITE(6) and WRITE(10).

Host Options

PCs and other desktop computers are USB hosts that have drivers for communicating with mass-storage devices. Several vendors offer USB host-controller chips for use in embedded systems. Just about any of these chips is suitable for use in a mass-storage host. Many can function as a conventional host or as an OTG device. To speed up project developing, look for a development kit with mass-storage support or use an embedded operating system that has a mass-storage driver included or available from a third party.

Cypress EZ-HOST

Cypress Semiconductor offers the CY4640 Mass Storage Reference Design Kit for the CY7C67300 EZ-Host microcontroller.

The chip has two host/device SIEs and four USB transceivers that allow the device to have any of these configurations:

1 to 4 hosts
1 or 2 devices
1 host and 1 device
1 OTG device and one device-only function
1 OTG device and up to two additional hosts

In a mass-storage host application, the chip can be configured to function as a mass-storage host, as an OTG device that can function as a mass-storage host and device, or as a mass-storage host and device at the same time.

The development board also has an IDE interface that connects to a daughter board that can hold a small hard drive. With a drive attached, the development board can function as a USB drive.

The kit includes a GNU C compiler, assembler, linker, debugger, a development environment, and utilities. Example firmware supports FAT file systems and USB host communications with mass-storage devices.

Host Software

Several sources offer software for use in embedded systems functioning as mass-storage hosts. Windows CE 5.0 includes a USB host mass-storage driver. Linux includes mass-storage drivers and is suitable for some embedded applications. Other sources offer USB host stacks for use with a variety of embedded-system operating systems, host controllers, and CPU architectures. Sources for host stacks with mass-storage support include Accelerated Technology, Intoto, Jungo Ltd., Micro Digital, On Time Software, and SoftConnex.

A Mass-storage Host Module

Another approach to designing an embedded host is the USBwiz™ chip from GHI Electronics. This is the same company that offers the uALFAT chip described in Chapter 8. The USBwiz is a Philips LPC2138 ARM processor programmed to support FAT file systems and several USB device classes, including mass storage. The chip interfaces to a Philips ISP1160 USB host controller chip.

Figure 11-3: The USBwiz-OEM board enables just about any microcontroller to access USB drives and flash-memory cards.

The USBwiz-OEM (Figure 11-3) is a circuit board that contains a USBwiz, an ISP1160, a MultiMediaCard/SD-card connector, and dual USB connectors for attaching devices. The USBwiz uses a +3.3V supply. The USBwiz-OEM board requires a +5V supply and has an on-board 3.3V regulator.

Microcontrollers can communicate with the USBwiz using an asynchronous serial interface, SPI, or an I²C bus. The USBwiz responds to commands sent in text mode, with commands and values sent as ANSI text, or in framed mode, with commands and values sent as binary values. In text mode, this command reads E8h bytes from a file opened with handle 0:

RF #0 E8

This command prepares the USBwiz to receive 10h bytes to be written to a file opened with handle 0Bh:

WF #B 10

On receiving the command above, the USBwiz returns a prompt character ("). The microcontroller writes the 16 bytes to the USBwiz, and the USBwiz returns a prompt character (") to indicate that the data was received. Framed mode also supports reading and writing to sectors in the storage media. File commands enable opening, closing, reading, writing to, and deleting a file. Directory commands enable creating, changing, listing, and erasing a directory.

The USBwiz can interface directly to MultiMediaCard/SD Cards, and the host controller can communicate with USB drives. The USBwiz assigns drive letter A: to a connected MultiMediaCard/SD Card and drive letters B: to K: in sequence to a USB drive's logical units.

A quick way to experiment with the USBwiz-OEM is to attach a flash drive, connect the board's serial port to a PC, and use a terminal program such as Windows' Hyperterminal to send commands and receive responses. To connect to a PC, connect the board's asynchronous serial-port pins to the corresponding pins on a Maxim MAX3232 or similar RS-232 transceiver. If your PC doesn't have an RS-232 port, connect the transceiver's RS-232 pins to corresponding pins on an RS-232/USB converter. Or use an FTDI Chip to interface the USBwiz to a PC's USB port.

Index

Index

Index